Black
Love
Is A
Revolutionary
Act

Black Love Is A Revolutionary Act

by Umoja
(formerly Anon)

TROJAN HORSE PRESS

First Edition - 1C
First Printing: May 2011

Library of Congress Control Number: 2010939683
ISBN: 978-0-9822061-1-9
ISBN: 0-9822061-1-9

Disclaimer for resemblance to real persons

This book includes political satire and works of fiction. Names, characters, places, and incidents are either the product of the authors' imaginations or used fictitiously. Any resemblance to actual persons, living or dead, business establishments, events, or locales is entirely coincidental. The publisher does not have any control over and does not assume any responsibility for any third-party websites or their content.

Printed and bound Manufactured in the United States of America

Trojan Horse Press
PO Box 245
Hazel Crest, IL 60429

email: info@trojanhorse1.com
website: www.trojanhorse1.com

Cover Design by P. Evans

Dedication

To our beautiful black sisters, our mothers, wives, lovers, and best friends.
To our strong, courageous black brothers, wherever you are, fighting for justice.

And a very special dedication to:

Dr. Frances Cress Welsing
Mr. Neely Fuller, Jr.
The Honorable Elijah Muhammad
Malcolm X
Muhammad Ali
Mr. Haki R. Madhubuti

Acknowledgements

This book could not have been written or completed without the ground-breaking works of Neely Fuller, Jr., Dr. Frances Cress Welsing, the Honorable Elijah Muhammad, Haki R. Madhubuti, Dr. Yosef Ben-Jochannan, John Henrik Clarke, Marcus Garvey, Dr. Mwalimu K. Bomani Baruti, Chancellor Williams, W.E.B. DuBois, Malcolm X, George Orwell, Tony Brown, Jawanza Kunjufu, Carter G. Woodson, James Baldwin, Willard Motley, and many others too numerous to mention. Naturally, we accept total responsibility for any misinterpretations of their works, and for any errors that appear in this book.

A very special thanks to Gus T. Renegade and Justice (C.O.W.S. at www.contextofwhitesupremacy.com), Ed Williams (www.counter-racism.com), Dr. Kamau Kambon, D.H., B. Harris, K. Richardson, D. Robinson, and of all our friends, family, and mentors who shared their special insights, wisdom, and patience with us.

We hope we have done some justice to all who inspired us to complete the second book in the Trojan Horse Trilogy, and hope that we will inspired others in the fight for universal justice for all the people on our Creator's planet.

About the Authors

Why the authors use a pseudonym

There is nothing original about the ideas presented here. Wiser minds have come before and will certainly come long after this book was written. The authors are not falsely modest; we are acknowledging we did not invent the wheel.

The authors are not seeking fame. This is not an attempt to be mysterious or provoke curiosity. This is not a gimmick or a perverse, reverse publicity ploy. In today's media-obsessed world, there is too much focus on "show" and not enough on "substance." The authors choose not to participate.

The authors reserve the right NOT to be a distraction to the message. We are the least important part of this book. You, the reader, are more important. Even more important, is what you do with this information.

Every word in this book was designed to inform, provoke discussion, decrease confusion, reduce hostility, minimize conflict, and to promote the kinds of constructive actions that are necessary to replace the system of Racism/White Supremacy with a system of universal justice for *** all the people on the planet. ***

You may not agree with everything or anything written here. We have presented *our* truths to the best of our ability. If this book inspires you to seek your own truths, the book has been a success.

(The pseudonym, Anon, used for our first book, "Trojan Horse: Death Of A Dark Nation" has been replaced by "Umoja" - the Swahili word for "UNITY.")

The Purpose of this Book

If you are looking for a book to show you how to put the romance back in your love life, ***this book is not for you.*** The kind of 'black love' this book promotes has nothing to do with bubble baths or candlelight dinners.

This book was written to encourage black males and black females to be on guard against the sinister forces that are destroying our relationships and the steps we can and must take to save the black family, our black children, and ourselves.

At the risk of offending some readers, we will not waste any time being politically correct. That being said, this book was not written to oppose the rights, dignity, and freedoms of any group of people. However, when a group of people is dedicated to destroying the God-given rights, dignity, and freedoms of another group, they must be EXPOSED and OPPOSED.

What This Book Is Not About

It is not about excusing blacks from all personal responsibility for the condition of blacks in America; anymore than detailing the horrors of the Jewish Holocaust is the same as excusing Jews from all personal responsibility; or acknowledging the genocide of Native Americans is the same as excusing them from all personal responsibility.

However, when a group is so severely traumatized that their deaths rise to the level of GENOCIDE, it is crucial that their story be told; and any "blame" that exists on their part SHRINKS in importance to the crimes committed against them. What is the MAIN responsibility of the SURVIVING victims of MASS INJUSTICE?

TO MAKE SURE IT NEVER HAPPENS AGAIN.

We hope you will read this book with an open, inquiring mind. Thank you for allowing us to share our insights (and solutions) with you.

"If you know the enemy and know yourself, you need not fear the result of a hundred battles.

If you know yourself but not your enemy, for every victory gained you will also suffer a defeat.

If you know neither the enemy nor yourself, you will succumb in every battle."

-- Sun Tzu,
'The Art of War' (544-496 BC)

Contents

Introduction

Do you remember the last time you saw...

a black couple holding hands in public?

a black man and woman making love on a TV or movie screen?

or a black stranger look you in the eye, smile, and say:

Hello, brother?

Hello, sister?

Where did our "Black Love" go?

What happened to the love between the black male and black female that sustained us for 500 years of slavery and racist oppression?

As the civil rights clock spins backwards and black poverty and unemployment skyrockets, the percentage of blacks dating and marrying interracially has never been higher, and the black male and black female have never been farther apart.

In a post-integration society has 'Black Love' gone out of style?

We sincerely hope this book will help to answer that question.

Prologue:

The End of a Marriage

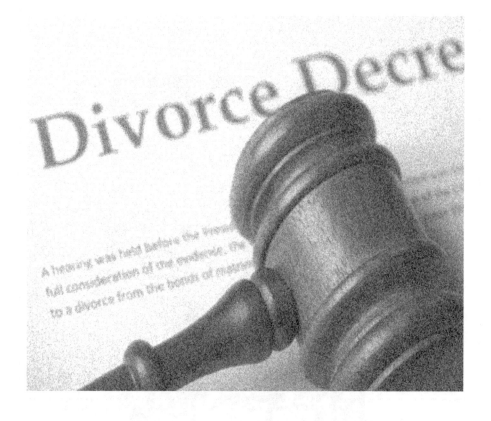

CHAPTER ONE

THE END OF A MARRIAGE

The "Perfect Couple"

They met in college through mutual friends. The moment he saw her, he knew she would be his wife. After twenty years of marriage and three children, they still laugh at each other's jokes and cuddle like teenagers in darkened movie theaters.

They laugh, too, whenever their friends and family call them "the perfect couple," because no marriage was perfect. Secretly, they are proud to wear the label because their union had survived the marital storms that sank much weaker vessels.

As a daily reminder, an engraved plaque hangs on the wall above their bed: *"What God has joined together, let no man put asunder."*

The Unthinkable Happens

On a cold, moonlit night in their quiet suburban neighborhood, a shadowy figure slips in through the partially open kitchen window. The peacefully sleeping couple is startled awake by a flashlight shining in their faces.

The armed intruder -- a powerfully built man in a white Halloween mask -- orders the couple to strip naked then pushes the wife to the floor, and rapes her at gunpoint. The husband watches helplessly, afraid they will both be killed if he resists.

The rapist leaves in the early dawn hours, taking their wallets, wedding rings, and peace of mind with him. The ordeal lasts less than an hour, but it feels like a lifetime to the terrified, traumatized couple.

The Husband

The husband is emotionally devastated because he could not protect his wife from the armed rapist. He tries to comfort her, but eventually, the weight of the ordeal consumes him. He begins to resent his wife for witnessing his lack of courage (manhood), and starts to project his feelings of rage and inadequacy onto her.

He wonders if his wife did something to provoke the attack. Did the rapist look familiar, he asks, then reminds her that she had been unfaithful (once) during their marriage.

Why was their house -- out of all the houses in the neighborhood – singled out? Didn't he warn her constantly to lock the windows before going to bed? His questions and barely disguised accusations initiate the first of many bitter arguments between them.

The husband decides there was only one reason he wasn't able to protect his wife: *she didn't deserve to be protected.* His "damaged" wife becomes the major obstacle to reclaiming his manhood and self-respect.

Lately, he finds himself flirting with strange women and taking their phone numbers. Sometimes, he calls them from his office; other times from the privacy of his car. He has never once cheated on his wife, but he has also never felt like less than a man.

The husband withdraws sexually because he is sure his wife despises him. The truth is, he cannot sustain an erection because he can't get the image of the man raping his wife out of his head.

The Wife

When the intruder rips off her nightgown, the wife cries out to her husband, even though she knows he can't save her without risking both their lives. She tearfully submits, praying they will survive the night.

After the ordeal ends, the wife is completely distraught. She knows what happened was not her husband's fault, but he is the man; *she is not.* Had he made the smallest attempt to rescue her, she would have more respect for him. When he implies that the rape was her fault -- her contempt and resentment mushrooms.

She is certain he sees her as "damaged goods" because he never touches her anymore. The truth is, she doesn't want to be touched because she cannot get the image of her naked and frightened husband out of her head.

He's a coward, she decides bitterly, and wonders why she never noticed it before. Thus, the deadly process of unraveling what was once a loving, successful marriage begins.

The End Of A Loving Marriage

The rapist is never caught or punished, and the couple never seeks counseling because they are too ashamed to admit they need it. The husband and wife are so busy blaming each other they have lost sight of who is really responsible.

Less than a year after the rape, their marriage has deteriorated to the point where a divorce is inevitable.

Try to Imagine...

Your son, daughter, mother, father, grandmother, grandfather, wife, or husband being beaten, tortured, stripped naked, fondled, raped, or murdered right in front of your eyes -- and there was nothing you could do to stop it from happening.

And if you can't imagine that, imagine this:

YOU are standing naked on a slave auction block, and there are dozens of slave traders randomly examining every part and every orifice (opening) of your precious body...*and there was nothing you could do to stop it from happening to YOU.*

To understand the GENDER WARS between the black male and female, we must start where it all began:

At the beginning...

Black Gender Wars

(After racism/white supremacy)

**The Biggest Problem
in Black America
is NOT crime, drugs,
poverty, or
inferior schools;**

**it's the BLACK GENDER WAR
between the Black Male
and Black Female**

CHAPTER TWO

WHAT ARE BLACK GENDER WARS?

The best place to start is by defining "Gender Wars"

Q: What are "Gender Wars?"
A: Gender Wars are the **by-product of a sexist culture**, where the male is pitted against the female, and the female is pitted against the male, usually by more powerful people behind the scenes.

Q: Why are "Black Gender Wars" a bigger problem than crime, drugs, poverty, or inferior schools?
A: Because crime, drugs, poverty, and inferior schools are the SYMPTOMS -- NOT the CAUSE of our relationship problems. The real problem is the WAR being waged against the black community by the white supremacy system.

The black male and female are like two feuding parents trapped in a burning house that was set on FIRE by a gang of serial arsonists. Even though their children are dying from burns and smoke inhalation, the mother and father are arguing and blaming each other for a fire they did not create INSTEAD of working TOGETHER to put the fire out. Our mutual enemy (the white supremacy system) is COMPLETELY RESPONSIBLE for the fire. However, once the FIRE is raging, OUR MAIN PRIORITY should be *to put the fire out -- or GET OUT of that burning house (the white supremacy system).*

Q: How do powerful people profit from "Gender Wars?"
A: Once the male and female are DIVIDED; they will soon be CONQUERED. The gender wars between males and females create demoralized adults, children, families, and communities. This "manufactured" conflict allows the powerful elite to take advantage AND take control of a divided population.

Q: How are Gender Wars "manufactured?"
A: By creating an economic and political system that ARTIFICIALLY makes one sex (typically male) superior to the other. A sexist society views the exploitation and degradation of females as normal and desirable. Like most victims of injustice, abused females eventually rebel against male oppression, creating a disastrous effect on the children, the family, and the society.

Q: Aren't Gender Wars normal for every culture?
A: No, Gender Wars occur ONLY when sexism is present. There have been African (and other non-white) cultures where gender conflicts are nonexistent because females have different but equally important roles BUT there has NEVER been a European culture that was free of sexism. Bottom line, any society that promotes gender wars is setting the stage for its own destruction.

Q: How are Black Gender Wars and White Gender Wars different?
A: White males and females will put their Gender Wars on hold to unite against their mutual (perceived) enemies OR to benefit their group (race) under the banner of white supremacy. The exact opposite is true for black males and females, who will blindly wage war against each other even while outside enemies are devastating their children, families, and communities.

Q: How did Black Gender Wars begin?
A: Black Gender Wars began during slavery when slave-owners pitted the male slave against the female; parent against child; house slave against field slave; and light-skinned slaves against dark-skinned slaves.

After our original AFRICAN CULTURE was destroyed during slavery, and blacks were forced to integrate into the white culture, we began to imitate the dysfunctional relationship between the white male and white female. To this day, the materialistic, sexist, and antagonistic white male/female relationship has become the STANDARD for most black relationships.

However, it is futile and self-defeating for black males to imitate white male sexism because black males LACK THE POWER to effectively practice it. In reality, black male sexism actually WEAKENS the black male's ability to overcome his racist oppression because it alienates the black female at a critical time when her FULL COOPERATION is desperately needed.

In other words, the black male NEEDS the SUPPORT and RESPECT of black females collectively to transform himself from slave negro to SELF-RESPECTING BLACK MAN.

Q: Where are Black Gender Wars most likely to occur?
A: Anywhere and everywhere black men and women interact: at home, school, work, sex, play; church; even between two strangers passing in the street.

Q: How many types of Black Gender Wars are there?
A: Three: (1) male VS female; (2) male VS male; and (3) female VS female.

Examples Of Black Male VS Black Female Gender Wars:

- Black fathers abandoning the black mothers of their children
- Black mothers using their children to hurt or financially exploit the father(s)
- Black males uplifting white females above black females
- Black females uplifting white males above black males
- The rising black divorce rate
- The falling black marriage rate
- The increase of interracial relationships for black males and females
- Domestic abuse and rape of black females and males
- ***BLACK NEIGHBORHOODS THAT RESEMBLE WAR ZONES***

Examples Of Black Male VS Black Male Gender Wars:

- Black fathers abusing, abandoning, or competing with their sons
- Black males who encourage destructive ways in younger males

- Black males who refuse to support or encourage other black males
- Black men who betray other black men for ego, jealousy, or profit
- Black men who pursue the wives of other black men and break up families
- Black neighborhoods that resemble war zones
- ***BLACK MEN KILLING OTHER BLACK MEN***

Examples Of Black Female VS Black Female Gender Wars:

- Black mothers abusing, abandoning, or competing with their daughters for male attention
- Black females who encourage destructive behavior in other black females
- Black females who condone "sexism" against other black females
- Black females who demonize younger black females instead of mentoring them
- Black females who attack or degrade other black females out of jealousy
- Black females who refuse to speak to or be cordial to other black females
- Black females who refer to other black females as 'bitches' and 'hos'
- Black females who refuse to support or encourage other black females
- ***BLACK FEMALES WHO PURSUE THE HUSBANDS OF OTHER BLACK FEMALES AND BREAK UP BLACK FAMILIES***

Black Gender Wars Are Anti-Family AND Anti-Survival

The FAMILY is the FOUNDATION of every society on earth, and MARRIAGE is the legal, moral, and spiritual COMMITMENT a man and woman make to raise their children within the ***protection of a stable, committed home***. Unfortunately, some blacks feel a lifetime commitment is too old-fashioned, too confining, and totally unnecessary for bringing children into the world.

This belief is illogical for three reasons:

1. If a black male and female cannot commit to staying together, it is unlikely they can or will commit to raising mentally sane black children. The end result is uncommitted, disconnected baby mommas and daddies, broken children, broken families, and a broken nation.
2. The traditional MARRIAGE model adopted by the MOST SUCCESSFUL ETHNIC GROUPS in America is being rejected by the LEAST SUCCESSFUL ETHNIC GROUP in America (blacks).
3. It is impossible to build strong business/economic bases without building strong communities. Strong communities require strong families. Strong families require strong men and women who are COMMITTED to raising their children UNDER ONE ROOF. We cannot build strong black families, communities, or strong business bases until we end Black Gender Wars.

We cannot end Black Gender Wars until we understand the 13 Recipes that created them; who benefits from Black Gender Wars; and what WE must do to END them.

13 Recipes for Black Gender Wars

13 RECIPES FOR BLACK GENDER WARS

1. Building The Perfect Slave
2. 500 Years of Justice Denied
3. Racial Memories
4. Slave Traditions
5. The Secret Shame of Slavery
6. The Post Traumatic Slavery Syndrome
7. Racism/White Supremacy
8. Integration
9. False Beauty Standards
10. Degrade the Black Female
11. Demonize the Black Male
12. Interracial Relationships
13. Pit The Black Male Against The Black Female

WHY DOES THE FIRST RECIPE FOR BLACK GENDER WARS START WITH SLAVERY?

"I already know about slavery but that was a long time ago, I got to protect my spirit from all that negative stuff, I got enough stress in my life." -- a comment made by a black female after hearing about this book.

The authors understand. **Completely.** Some blacks are reluctant (and afraid) to deal with the painful topic of slavery. Some are ashamed of the history of blacks in America. Some feel being knowledgeable about slavery will hamper them on their jobs because they work closely with whites.

Some are sexually involved with whites and feel it is too "disloyal" to think or talk about slavery. Some blacks resist the notion of blaming our past for our present condition, and do not want to be defined or limited by our tragic history. Others simply don't know how to deal with their pain and anger in a non-destructive manner and avoid the topic altogether.

That being said, the Authors **take no pleasure** in detailing the 500-plus years of terror, torture, rape, and murder of millions of African men, women, and children. However, it is absolutely necessary to dissect the genesis, the origins, and the BIRTHPLACE of Black Gender Wars to find real solutions.

It took 500 years for the black male/black female relationship to get into this condition. It is unreasonable and illogical to think it can be repaired WITHOUT examining the HISTORY that damaged it.

We cannot create real solutions if we do not understand the real problems. Anything else -- including wearing more eye makeup, shinier clothing, being better in bed, more passive, more aggressive, more muscular, thinner, taller, shorter, being more college-educated, making more money, driving a nicer car, joining a bigger church, etc. -- WILL NOT SOLVE THE PROBLEM BETWEEN BLACK MALES AND BLACK FEMALES.

Just like a man with a swollen toe who thinks the toe is the problem because he can SEE it is discolored, and he can FEEL it is painful to the touch, so he focuses on his toe when the real problem is an undiagnosed case of diabetes. Until he understands that his toe is a SYMPTOM, not the REAL PROBLEM, he will NOT find a REAL SOLUTION to his problem.

If we want to heal the black male/black female relationship, we must find the ORIGIN of our problems.

Some of what you are about to read will (and should) anger you. Injustice always angers the man or woman of conscience. However, aimless anger is wasted emotion; but **RIGHTEOUS ANGER** -- if channeled constructively and logically -- can transform an entire nation. It is our greatest hope that our book inspires the intellectual warrior inside you, who will FIGHT *for the revival and the survival of BLACK LOVE.*

Recipe #1

Building The Perfect Slave

DESCRIPTION OF A SLAVE SHIP.

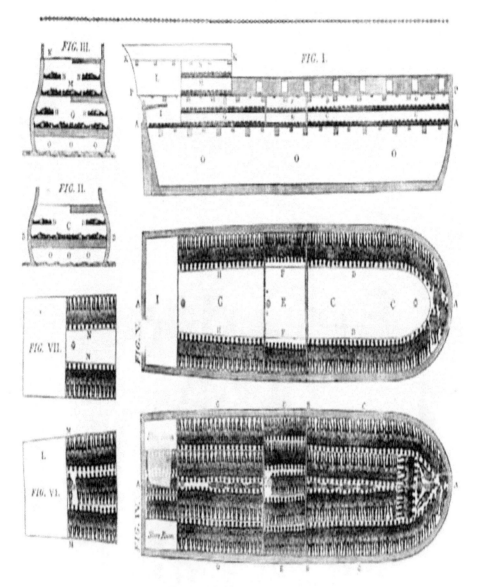

A detailed drawing of the slave ship, Brookes, showing how 482 people were to be packed onto the decks.

CHAPTER THREE

THE TRANSATLANTIC SLAVE VOYAGE

BLACK GENDER WARS began with the kidnapping, rape, and murder of millions of African men, women, and children.

Slaves were herded into the dark holds of slave ships, with their right foot shackled to the left foot of the person to their right. About 18 inches separated one layer of slaves from the next.

Trapped with no fresh air, light, and very little food, lying in their own feces for six weeks or longer, some captives suffocated to death from being so tightly packed, they were unable to move or breathe.

The ones who survived the journey were subject to rape, beatings, and starvation. They suffered from anemia, urinary infections, ulcers, scurvy, dysentery, and other diseases from filthy water, rancid food, inadequate sanitation, and exposure to rain, sun, and extreme temperatures.

An estimated *one out of every five captives died* before reaching America. In total, **over one million Africans died on the voyage to America** from injuries, illnesses, suicide, and murder. Some starved themselves to death, and others simply lost the will to live.

Mothers and fathers jumped overboard with their children to spare them from an unknown and terrifying fate. There were occasional victories when desperate captives killed the crews of the slave ships and escaped.

It is hard to imagine the sheer terror felt by those helpless African men, women, and children, who had no idea where they were going OR even why they had been kidnapped. Unfortunately, the worst was yet to come: *400 years of the most brutal system of slavery in known human history.*

The most accurate description of the Transatlantic Slave journey:

Hell On Earth

African Males Captured By Slave Traders

"Nothing that has happened to men in modern times has been more significant than the buying and selling of human beings out of Africa into America from 1441 to 1870." -- W.E.B. DuBois

CHAPTER FOUR

DID AFRICANS SELL BLACKS INTO SLAVERY?

In April, 2010, Harvard Professor Henry Louis Gates, Jr. wrote a New York Times op-ed piece called, "Ending the Slavery Blame-Game," where he lays a good part of the blame for American slavery at the feet of the African people:

> "...many elite Africans visited Europe in that era...it is difficult to claim that Africans were ignorant or innocent."

Gates quotes the works of several white scholars, some of who claim 90 percent of Africans shipped to the New World were captured by Africans and then sold to European traders.

It is true some Africans were involved in the TransAtlantic slave trade -- as were some Arabs and Jews, but it is illogical and anti-historical to place most or even half the blame for 400 years of American slavery on African people.

It is a FACT that America -- NOT Europe -- was the final destination for millions of African slaves during the Transatlantic Slave Trade. Even if some elite Africans *"visited Europe,"* Europe did NOT build an African slave plantation system on its own soil, therefore, Africans "visiting Europe" proves little other than some elite Africans ventured outside Africa on occasion.

The timing of this article – shortly after Professor Gates was "roughed up" and arrested for breaking into his own house by a white policeman -- may or may not be significant but is certainly worth mentioning.

Setting The Record Straight

FACT #1: When the Transatlantic Slave Trade began, there were many tribal wars on the continent of Africa. Europeans took advantage of the political instability in Africa by pitting one tribe against the other and giving guns to the side they thought most likely to win.

This "divide-and-conquer" strategy along with superior weapons (guns and gunpowder) allowed the Europeans to seize African labor, land, resources, and people.

FACT #2: Africans did NOT sell their "own people" to European slave-traders. Every African from the continent of Africa is NOT of the same NATIONALITY, just like every European on the European continent is NOT French, but in fact, may be German, Polish, or Italian.

A nationality represents membership in a particular nation or sovereign state where people share a common culture, ethnicity, traditions, land, language, and national identity.

An illustration from 1860 showing how slaves were transported on the upper deck of the ship Wildfire. (Source: Library of Congress)

132 slaves were thrown overboard from the ship Zong after disease broke out. Slaves lost through drowning were covered by insurance.

For example, Nigerians and Ugandans are Africans of different nationalities even though both are from the African continent. The Africans who sold people from OTHER African tribes (nationalities) into slavery were selling the "losers" of their tribal wars – NOT their own family members, kinsmen, or "people."

FACT #3: If Africans are guilty of selling their own "people," Europeans are guilty of the same crime. Slavery was so widespread in early medieval Europe that the Roman Catholic Church tried repeatedly to ban it. In fact, the word "slave" comes from the word "sklabos," which means "Slav" – a person of Eastern European descent.

> *"Enslavement was a very real possibility for anyone...who lived along the shores in places like Italy, France, Spain, and Portugal, and even as far north as England and Iceland." – Robert Davis, professor of history at Ohio State University, and author of "Christian Slaves, Muslim Masters: White Slavery in the Mediterranean, the Barbary Coast, and Italy, 1500-1800."*

Italian merchants bought and sold thousands of eastern Europeans during the 1400s, but were never accused of selling their "own people" into slavery because Italians and eastern Europeans are NOT members of the same (white) tribes.

When the Germans waged war against the French in World War II, they were NOT accused of killing their "own people" because the Germans are NOT French, and the French are not German.

It would easy (and accurate) to describe Hitler's invasion of France as his (failed) attempt to enslave France, yet he was never accused of trying to enslave his "own people." Why? Because the French and the Germans are *Europeans of different nationalities (tribes).*

FACT #4: African chiefs were NOT the CO-CONSPIRATORS of the European slave-traders during the Transatlantic Slave Trade. Africans did NOT "lure" Europeans to Africa to buy slaves. Europeans came to Africa seeking goods and spices and stumbled across an even more valuable resource: *African slave labor.*

The participation of (some) Africans in the TransAtlantic Slave Trade does NOT alter one fundamental fact: *Africans NEVER shipped a single African to America.* In fact, when word spread about the horrors of slavery abroad, some Africans tried to stop the kidnappings.

There is no denying that Africans participated in the slave trade. However, it is historically and morally incorrect to make Africans the scapegoats for the European crime of slavery.

The Arab, European, and Jewish slave-traders -- who made *the bulk of their wealth from slavery -- are the MOST ACCOUNTABLE.*

When the TransAtlantic Slave Trade began, the European mentality had already evolved into a white supremacist mindset, and the idea of treating Africans as equal trading partners was wholly unacceptable. Rather than barter on good faith, European slave-traders resorted to trickery, robbery, kidnapping, rape, and murder.

"Had the African needs and the European needs been considered on an equal basis, there could have been an honest exchange between the African and European and the European could still have had labor in large numbers without the slave trade and the massive murder that occurred in the slave trade." – John Henrik Clarke, black historian

FACT #5: 400 years of slavery did NOT make Africa one of the richest nations on earth. There are NO multi-national (black) African corporations that were enriched by the TransAtlantic Slave Trade.

However there are hundreds, perhaps thousands, of corporations in America and Europe -- AIG, Aetna, Lloyd's of London, JP Morgan Chase Manhattan Bank to name a few -- that built vast global empires on the backs of African slave labor and Africa's mineral wealth.

FACT #6: The Africans had NO ROLE WHATSOEVER in creating the American institutions that benefited from 400 years of slavery, or in the rape, torture, and murder of African slaves.

Africans did NOT rob African slaves of their language, culture, religion, history, or identity. They did NOT create or participate in Reconstruction, the Black Codes, the Ku Klux Klan, lynch mobs, chain gangs, or Jim Crow.

FACT #7: The Transatlantic Slave Trade Was Europe's first venture into globalization. The mass enslavement of Africans was a European global conspiracy that began in the early to mid 1400s *and made the bulk of its wealth by selling and enslaving other human beings.*

Contrary to most Western history books, Adam Smith (1723-1790) -- often called the "father of modern economics" -- did NOT oppose slavery on economic OR moral grounds, but used his "free market" economic theories to JUSTIFY SLAVERY.

Adam Smith's economic theories encouraged a "laissez faire" (lawless) environment, with few safeguards or oversights, so slavery could continue unhindered by the (nonexistent) morality of those who cruelly exploited African men, women, and children.

The FACT is, African slaves provided the FREE LABOR that built the coffee, cotton, cocoa and sugar plantations in North and South America; the gold and silver mines; and the field and domestic labor that allowed the French, English, Spanish, Dutch, and North American Europeans to build international empires and enjoy the immense wealth that still exists today.

FACT #8: The Transatlantic Slave Trade was UNLIKE any other form of slavery. Before the European enslavement of African people, slaves were still seen as HUMAN BEINGS, and were allowed to eat their native foods; speak their native languages; practice their native religions; keep their family names; even marry, buy their freedom, and become citizens.

The TransAtlantic Slave Trade was the FIRST TIME slave-traders DELIBERATELY and SYSTEMATICALLY destroyed the identity AND the sanity of their captives (victims) in order to create a permanent race of slaves.

The EVIDENCE of the greatest CRIME against humanity in known human history can still be seen among the psychologically devastated black population in America.

FACT #9: Placing the blame for the TransAtlantic Slave Trade on Africans is a crime SECOND ONLY TO THE SLAVE TRADE ITSELF.

The "African history" taught by the Western educational system is the whitewashed version that paints Africans as greedy savages who sold their own fathers, mothers, sisters, brothers, children, and neighbors to European traders for the price of a few trinkets. This was done to make Africans the scapegoats for European/American slavery -- *the most brutal slavery system that has ever existed in the known history of mankind.*

Why are the Western media and academic communities so DETERMINED (and so DESPERATE) to hide the truth about the Transatlantic Slave Trade?

Because every crime against humanity is linked to a criminal organization, and once the criminals are identified, MASSIVE REPARATIONS will be next.

FACT #10: If Jewish victims and their descendants received reparations for a 12-year Holocaust, and Japanese victims and their descendants received reparations for a three-year injustice, it is LOGICAL that the descendants of the 400-year African Holocaust are MORE entitled than the Jews and the Japanese combined --

26 TIMES OVER!

"It has been important to present the matters above to dispel the notion of an African slave trade that involved mutuality as a generalized dynamic on the part of Africans. If we can accept the documented facts of our history above and beyond propaganda, we can begin to heal. We can begin to love one another again and go on to regain our liberties on Earth."
-- Oscar L. Beard, Consultant in African Studies

SLAVERY A SYSTEM OF INHERENT CRUELTY.

FLOGGING A SLAVE FASTENED TO THE GROUND.

CHAPTER FIVE

TERROR, TORTURE, MURDER, AND MADNESS: "BREAKING-IN" AFRICAN SLAVES

African men, women, and children were whipped, beaten, buried alive under piles of insects, raped, dismembered, disfigured, blinded, branded, crippled, tortured, lynched, boiled in molasses, water-boarded, and burned alive. Some of this happened in the "breaking-in camps," that were designed to destroy the will of African men and women who refused to "submit" to slavery, rape, and degradation.

For striking a white person or for reading a book, a slave's hand might be cut off. Runaways slaves were subjected to a variety of punishments: severe whippings; a nose slit; an ear or a hand amputated; the tendons cut in one leg; the pulling out of teeth; branded with hot irons on the face; castrated; or sentenced to death.

Tales of Terror, Torture, Murder, And Madness

"In my father's time and all along my mother's time that's when they chained the colored people and cut them all to pieces with cat-o'nine-tails and sprinkled salt and pepper on them." – Mrs. Holmes, (first name unknown), former slave, Nashville, TN.

Incidents in the Life of a Slave Girl. Written by Herself: Jacobs, Harriet A. (Harriet Ann), 1813-1897

Mrs. Flint, like many (white) southern women, was totally deficient in energy. She had not strength to superintend her household affairs; but her nerves were so strong, that she could sit in her easy chair and see a woman whipped, till the blood trickled from every stroke of the lash.

She was a member of the church; but partaking of the Lord's supper did not seem to put her in a Christian frame of mind. If dinner was not served at the exact time on that particular Sunday, she would station herself in the kitchen, and wait till it was dished, and then spit in all the kettles and pans that had been used for cooking.

She did this to prevent the cook and her children from eking out their meager fare with the remains of the gravy and other scrapings. The slaves could get nothing to eat except what she chose to give them. Provisions were weighed out by the pound and ounce, three times a day.

Tools Of Torture

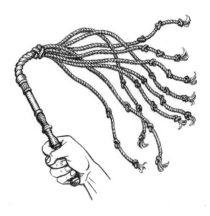

Cat-o'nine-tails

A commonly used whipping device during slavery was the "cat-o'nine-tails." The "Cat" was made up of nine knotted pieces of cotton cord, about two-and-a-half feet long, which lacerated (sliced) the skin open, causing agonizing pain.

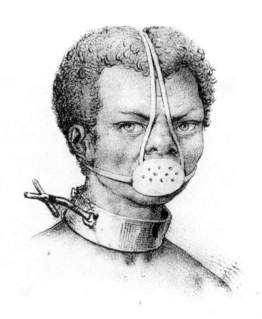

Slave wearing an IRON MUZZLE as a form of punishment.

Dr. Flint was an epicure. The cook never sent a dinner to his table without fear and trembling; for if there happened to be a dish not to his liking, he would either order her to be whipped, or compel her to eat every mouthful of it in his presence. The poor, hungry creature might not have objected to eating it; but she did object to having her master cram it down her throat till she choked.

When I had been in the family a few weeks, one of the plantation slaves was brought to town, by order of his master. It was near night when he arrived, and Dr. Flint ordered him to be taken to the work house, and tied up to the joist, so that his feet would just escape the ground. In that situation he was to wait till the doctor had taken his tea.

I shall never forget that night. Never before, in my life, had I heard hundreds of blows fall, in succession, on a human being. His piteous groans, and his "O, pray don't, massa," rang in my ear for months afterwards. There were many conjectures as to the cause of this terrible punishment. Some said master accused him of stealing corn; others said the slave had quarreled with his wife, in presence of the overseer, and had accused his master of being the father of her child. They were both black, and the child was very fair.

I went into the work house next morning, and saw the cowhide still wet with blood, and the boards all covered with gore. The poor man lived, and continued to quarrel with his wife. A few months afterwards, Dr. Flint handed them both over to a slave-trader.

There was a planter in the country, not far from us, whom I will call Mr. Litch. He was an ill-bred, uneducated man, but very wealthy. He had six hundred slaves, many of whom he did not know by sight. His extensive plantation was managed by well-paid overseers. There was a jail and a whipping post on his grounds; and whatever cruelties were perpetrated there, they passed without comment. He was so effectually screened by his great wealth that he was called to no account for his crimes, not even for murder.

Various were the punishments resorted to. A favorite one was to tie a rope round a man's body, and suspend him from the ground. A fire was kindled over him, from which was suspended a piece of fat pork. As this cooked, the scalding drops of fat continually fell on the bare flesh.

I could tell of more slaveholders as cruel as those I have described. They are not exceptions to the general rule. I do not say there are no humane slaveholders. Such characters do exist, notwithstanding the hardening influences around them. But they are "like angels' visits—few and far between."

***

Slave whip and chains

WILSON CHINN, a Branded Slave from Louisiana.
Also exhibiting Instruments of Torture
used to punish Slaves.

Photographed by KIMBALL, 477 Broadway, N.Y

Entered according to Act of Congress, in the year 1863, by
Geo. H. Hanks, in the Clerk's Office of the United States for
the Southern District of New-York.

Slave paddle

The paddle was made of a piece of hickory timber about one inch thick, three inches in width, and about eighteen inches in length, bored full of quarter-inch auger holes. The person being flogged was stripped naked, bent over double, with their hands tied together. When the paddle hit flesh, the blood gushed through the holes of the paddle, creating blisters.

Oh, yassuh, Marse John good 'nough to us an' we get plenty to eat, but he had a oberseer name Green Bush what sho' whup us iffen we don't do to suit him. Yassuh, he mighty rough wid us be he didn't do de whippin' hisse'f. He had a big black boy name Mose, mean as de debil an' strong as a ox, and de oberseer let him do all de whuppin'. An', man, he could sho' lay on dat rawhide lash. He whupped a nigger gal 'bout thirteen years old so hard she nearly die, an' allus atterwa'ds she hab spells of fits or somp'n. Dat make Marse John pow'ful mad, so he run dat oberseer off de place an' Mose didn' do no mo' whuppin'. -- Walter Calloway, former slave, Alabama

***

"Slavery was the worst days was ever seed in the world. They was things past tellin', but I got the scars on my old body to show to this day. I seed worse than what happened to me. I seed them put the men and women in the stock with they hands screwed down through holes in the board and they feets tied together and they naked behinds to the world. Solomon the [sic] overseer beat them with a big whip and massa look on. The niggers better not stop in the fields when they hear them yellin'. They cut the flesh most to the bones and some they was when they taken them out of stock and put them on the beds, they never got up again." -- Mary Reynolds, 100, former slave

From "American Slave Trade"

A slave having escaped from his master, in the state of North Carolina, within two or three years past, was seized and brought back, by a being, who, when requested by the master to name the reward he should render him for returning the slave, replied, that all the compensation he desired, was the satisfaction of flogging him.

This being granted, the slave was bound to a log, and the "resounding lash" applied, until the resentment of his executioner was satiated. The infatuated master then took the ensanguined lash himself, and was about to repeat the process of flagellation, when Death, not then a king of terrors, but a generous benefactor, a "friend in need" rescued him from the intended protraction of his excruciating torment."

In the state of Pennsylvania, a considerable number of years ago, the proprietor of a furnace took up a black boy, a few years old, and in the presence of his distracted father, wantonly thrust him into the flames and melted metal, where he was instantly consumed!"

***

The Jews honor their ancestors by reminding the world about their Holocaust. We owe it to OUR ANCESTORS to NEVER let the world forget about the suffering OUR ancestors endured during OUR African Holocaust.

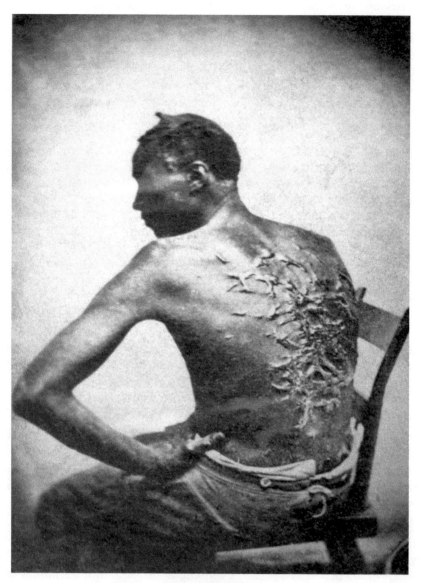

Peter, a slave, whipped by overseer

CHAPTER SIX

THE DESTRUCTION OF THE AFRICAN MALE SLAVE

Black Men Were Not Allowed To Protect Their Women Or Be Fathers To Their Children

Male slaves were forced to watch their women and children raped, tortured, and beaten, and were helpless to stop their suffering. The intent: *to destroy their confidence and self-respect as men.*

"I admit the black man is inferior. But what is it that makes him so? It is the ignorance in which white men compel him to live; it is the torturing whip that lashes the manhood out of him; it is the fierce bloodhounds of the South, and the scarcely less cruel human bloodhounds of the north, which enforce the Fugitive Slave Law." -- Harriet Brent, a slave who wrote the first autobiography written by a black woman "Incidents in the Life of a Slave Girl. (1813-1897)

Male slaves were not allowed to be fathers or husbands -- though many made the courageous but futile attempt to protect their women and children. This dealt the black male slave a terrible psychological blow.

"A poor slave's wife can never be true to her husband, contrary to the will of her master. She can neither be pure nor virtuous, contrary to the will of her master. She dare not refuse to be reduced to a state of adultery at the will of her master." -- Henry Bibb, in his 1849 autobiography, "Narrative of the Life and Adventures of Henry Bibb, An American Slave.

Due to the relentless sexual assaults by slave-owners, miscarriages, venereal diseases, and infections of the urinary tract were rampant among female slaves. *These conditions were RARE BEFORE the mass rapes of African males and females.* Dr. Jones, confirmed this FACT in his article in the Medical and Surgical Journal in 1838, wrote:

"...venereal disease and drunkenness among African slaves was rare."

The African male slave witnessing the sexual degradation of the African female slave planted the first POISONOUS seeds of contempt FOR the black female because of her terrible shame and her inability to maintain her honor as a woman of virtue.

The Slave Narrative of Josiah Henson (1796-1883)

Josiah Henson and Wife, Nancy

In his autobiography, Josiah Henson recalled how as a child he saw his father viciously punished for attempting to stop the plantation overseer from raping his wife (Josiah's mother):

"The day for the execution of the penalty was appointed. The Negroes from the neighbouring plantations were summoned to witness the scene. A powerful black-smith named Hewes laid on the stripes.

Fifty were given, during which the cries of my father might be heard a mile away, and then a pause ensured. True, he had struck a white man, but as valuable property he must not be damaged.

Judicious men felt his pulse. Oh! he could stand the whole. Again and again the throng fell on his lacerated back. His cries grew fainter and fainter, till a feeble groan was the only response to the final blows. His head was then thrust against the post, and his right ear fastened to it with a tack; a swift pass of a knife, and the bleeding member was left sticking to the place. Then came a hurrah from the degraded crowd, and the exclamation, "That's what he's got for striking a white man."

"Previous to this affair, my father, from all I can learn, had been a good-humoured and light-hearted man. His banjo was the life of the farm. But from this hour he became utterly changed. Sullen, morose, and dogged, nothing could be done with him. He brooded over his wrongs.

No fear or threats of being sold to the far south - the greatest of all terrors to the Maryland slave - would render him tractable. So off he was sent to Alabama. What was his fate neither my mother nor I have learned."
His autobiography, The Life of Josiah Henson (1849) was read by Harriet Beecher Stowe and inspired her best-selling novel, Uncle Tom's Cabin. The book was an instant hit in the North. Copies were sold all over the world.

Henson went to England and lectured on his life as "Uncle Tom," the slave. He published his autobiography, My life as Uncle Tom three times. "Father" Josiah Henson preached, lectured and wrote until his death in 1883.

A Little-Known Fact of Slavery:
The Rape Of The African Male

It is common knowledge that African slave women and girls were raped by slave-owners but very little has been said about the rape of African men and boys. Another little known FACT: homosexuality was nonexistent in African culture before European colonization and sexual domination/perversion.

Male homosexuality and raping the males of a conquered people is a EUROPEAN TRADITION that dates back to ancient Greek and Roman cultures. If this historical FACT is difficult to digest, consider the following:

What better way to "rape" a man of his MANHOOD and SELF-RESPECT than to RAPE HIM in front of his women and children?

The African female slave witnessing the RAPE of the African male slave planted the first POISONOUS seeds of contempt FOR the black male because of his terrible shame and his inability to protect his honor as a man.

Did The Rape Of African Male Slaves Plant The First Bitter Seeds Of Black Male Homosexuality?

We cannot afford to underestimate the catastrophic damage that was done to the manhood of African male slaves. At the risk of being labeled "homophobic," we will not waste valuable time being politically correct when it comes to the topic of "homosexuality."

It is crucial that the descendants of slaves UNDERSTAND the psychological trauma that male slaves endured -- because the SAME dehumanization and emasculation process of black males that took place during slavery is STILL happening today via the law enforcement, incarceration, education, and employment institutions in America.

Could the systematic psycho-sexual rape of African males over a 400-year period be the GENESIS (the root) of black male homosexuality today?

"During the past 400 years, Black men in the U.S. have been forced into passive and cooperative submission to white men. White men in this world area have at least a vague, perhaps unconscious, understanding that after 20 generations (400 years), male passivity has evolved into male effeminization, bisexuality, and homosexuality. These patterns of behavior are simply expressions of male self-submission to other males in the area of people activity called "sex."
-- Dr. Frances Cress Welsing, 'The Isis Papers,' (1991)

"The black woman was raped and sexually exploited like no other woman in the history of mankind." -- Richard Williams, Ed.D.

CHAPTER SEVEN

THE DESTRUCTION OF THE AFRICAN FEMALE SLAVE

The Rape Of The African Female

Contrary to some anti-historical "historians" -- and some misinformed black males -- African female slaves DID NOT have "sexual intercourse" with their slave-owners: **they were RAPED.** Female slaves did NOT "choose" to have "sex" with their slave-owners: **they had NO CHOICE.**

The word *"choose"* means the slave woman was able to "choose" her sexual partner AND the circumstances under which that sexual activity took place. Certainly, NO woman would ever "choose" to be a slave.

It is illogical, anti-historical, anti-humane, and RACIST to describe the serial rape of Sally Hemings, a slave female, by slave-owner, Thomas Jefferson, as a "romantic relationship." As long as Sally Hemings was a SLAVE, she had NO RIGHT to deny Jefferson sexual access to her body. She could NOT give CONSENT AS A SLAVE because she HAD NO CHOICE.

Anything short of FREE CHOICE is RAPE.

The mass rape of African girls and women also robbed African males of their ability to do what ALL MEN MUST DO TO BE CONSIDERED MEN: *to protect the honor and lives of their women.*

"Breaking-In" The African Female

Besides rape, the most common punishments for slave women were whippings with ebony brushes, which were described as being capable of "taking the skin off down to her heels."

Or the choice of a "whipping weapon" might be a whip made of plaited cow-skin, noted for being so strong that it could "take the skin off a horse's back" or "lay marks on a wooden board."

An observer of such a "whipping" said, the woman was "...lying down and groaning...her left side, where she had been whipped most, appearing in a most mortifying state, and almost covered with worms."

"In the state of New Jersey, a female slave, several years ago, was bound to a log and scored with a knife, in a shocking manner across her back, and the gashes were stuffed with salt! After which she was tied to a post in a cellar, where, after suffering three days, death kindly terminated her misery." -- from American Slave Trade.

Sexual Sadism Was Common Among Slave-Owners

"A master once made the comment that he would rather paddle a slave woman than eat food." -- from the slave narrative of Henry Bibb.

The punishments inflicted on slave women often had sexual overtones. The slave-owner or the overseer who inflicted "punishment," often experienced some sort of sexual satisfaction (sadism) from the pain and suffering of slave women.

Slave women who rejected the planter's sexual advances were often raped, flogged or both. Even when no offense had been committed. some slave-owners took delight in tormenting slave women. A slave narrative describes a slave woman, screaming, suspended by her wrists from a tree, and the slavemaster touching her with a stick of fire as she swayed back and forth.

Ladies Whipping Girls.   Page 109.

Slave Women Also Incurred The Deadly
Wrath Of The White Slave-Mistress

A woman who tried to repulse her master risked a beating, but one who gave in risked antagonizing the mistress of the household. One ex-slave told the story of a white woman who "slipped into a colored gal's room and cut her baby's head clean off because it belonged to her husband." (Source: 'America's women: 400 Years of Dolls, Drudges, Helpmates and Heroines' by Gail Collins).

"Severe beatings were the method most commonly used by slavemistresses to punish black female slaves. Often in a jealous rage, a mistress might use disfigurement to punish a lusted-after black female slave. The mistress might cut off a breast, blind an eye, or cut off another body part."
                                                    -- from a slave journal

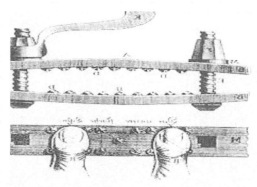

Thumbscrews (used to squeeze thumbs)

White Female Slave-Owners Just As Sadistic As White Male Slave-Owners

Historical accounts and slave narratives confirm that the white female slave-owner was just as sadistic as her male partner. An example given was a female slave-owner who used thumbscrews on the thumbs of slave women until the "blood gushed out;" or making them kneel on pebbles on their bare knees while washing the floor; or beating them with the heels of their shoes.

***

"I once saw a young slave girl dying soon after the birth of a child nearly white. In her agony she cried out, "O Lord, come and take me!" Her mistress stood by, and mocked at her like an incarnate fiend. "You suffer, do you?" she exclaimed. "I am glad of it. You deserve it all, and more too."

The girl's mother said, "The baby is dead, thank God; and I hope my poor child will soon be in heaven, too."

"Heaven!" retorted the mistress. "There is no such place for the like of her and her bastard."

The poor mother turned away, sobbing. Her dying daughter called her, feebly, and as she bent over her, I heard her say, "Don't grieve so, mother; God knows all about it; and HE will have mercy upon me."

Her sufferings, afterwards, became so intense, that her mistress felt unable to stay; but when she left the room, the scornful smile was still on her lips."

(SOURCE: Incidents in the Life of a Slave Girl. Written by Herself: Jacobs, Harriet A. (Harriet Ann), 1813-1897).

European Males Preferred "Importing" African Females Over European Females

"The Trans-Atlantic slave trade was the largest long-distance coerced movement of people in history and, prior to the mid-nineteenth century, formed the major demographic well-spring for the re-peopling of the Americas following the collapse of the Amerindian population.

*Cumulatively, as late as 1820, nearly four Africans had crossed the Atlantic for every European, and, given the differences in the sex ratios between European and African migrant streams, about **four out of every five females** that traversed the Atlantic were from Africa." (SOURCE: 'A Brief Overview of the Trans-Atlantic Slave Trade' by David Eltis)*

***

"No pen can give an adequate description of the all-pervading corruption produced by slavery. The slave girl is reared in an atmosphere of licentiousness and fear. The lash and the foul talk of her master and his sons are her teachers.

When she is fourteen or fifteen, her owner, or his sons, or the overseer, or perhaps all of them, begin to bribe her with presents. If these fail to accomplish their purpose, she is whipped or starved into submission to their will.

She may have had religious principles inculcated by some pious mother or grandmother, or some good mistress; she may have a lover, whose good opinion and peace of mind are dear to her heart; or the profligate men who have power over her may be exceedingly odious to her. But resistance is hopeless.

The white daughters early hear their parents quarrelling about some female slave. Their curiosity is excited, and they soon learn the cause. They are attended by the young slave girls whom their father has corrupted; and they hear such talk as should never meet youthful ears, or any other ears.

They know that the women slaves are subject to their father's authority in all things; and in some cases they exercise the same authority over the men slaves."

(SOURCE: 'Incidents in the Life of a Slave Girl. Written by Herself:' Jacobs, Harriet A. (Harriet Ann), 1813-1897)

In Celebration Of America's First Black "Bitches"

Frederick Douglass, (1818-1895), former slave, orator, social reformer, statesman, writer, and a leader of the abolitionist movement, tells of an incident where his aunt was found in the company of a black male without the slave-owner's permission:

"Before he [slavemaster] commenced whipping Aunt Hester, he took her into the kitchen, and stripped her from neck to waist, leaving her neck, shoulders and back, entirely naked.

*He then told her to cross her hands, and called her a "dead **bitch**." After crossing her hands, he tied them with a strong rope, and led her to a stool under a large hook in the joist, put in for the purpose. He made her get upon the stool, and tied her hands to the hooks. She now stood fair for his infernal purpose. Her arms were stretched up at their full length, so that she stood upon the ends of her toes.*

*Then he said to her, "Now you dead **bitch**, I'll learn you how to disobey my orders!" and after rolling up his sleeves, he commenced to lay on the heavy cowskin, and soon the arm, red blood (amid heart-rending shrieks from her, and horrid oaths from him) came dripping to the floor. I was so terrified and horror-stricken at the sight, that I hid myself in a closet, and dared not venture out till long after the bloody transaction was over."*

***

Fast-forward to the 21st Century: what is the most common word for a FEMALE DOG that is also used to refer to the black female?

BITCH

The Mass Rape Of African Females For Pleasure And Profit

The African female was essential to keep the engines of the slave economy humming. The slave-owner used the black female to increase the size (and value) of his (human) livestock by forcing her to reproduce (against her will) and produce children to be sold into slavery.

The female -- the mother -- of every race is SACRED because she is the FIRST teacher of the children, and instills her values (and fears) into her children. Breaking the slave mother almost guarantees a "broken' child who will submit to their enslavement.

Is this the main motivation behind the mass media's degradation of the black female today? To produce 'broken' black children?

An (Insane) "Celebration" Of Mass RAPE

African slaves deeply resented the children borne of rape because they were visible and painful reminders of the black male's inability to protect his women from a nation of rapists -- and the inability of black females to protect their honor. In sharp contrast, some blacks today are so enamored of "whiteness" (brainwashed), they DELIBERATELY breed with whites so their children will look "less black" (and less like their hated selves).

All political correctness aside, all people from all cultures are not the same. There are distinct differences in origins, behavior, genetics, and temperaments. Slave-owners were well aware of these differences when they deliberately bred different African tribes together then FORCIBLY injected their own European DNA into the mix via rape. The end result was mass cultural, psychological, and genetic confusion AND destruction.

This genetic and cultural confusion (destruction) along with a FORCE-FED diet of white supremacy programmed the descendants of slaves to value "whiteness" over their own genetically superior and powerfully melanated "African-ness."

Mass Confusion, Self-Hatred, And False Identities

In a white supremacy society (like America), there are only two classifications of people: *whites and non-whites.* Politically speaking, a black person, and a white person cannot produce a half-white, half-black, or a bi-racial child because this political classification DOES NOT EXIST.

The term **"bi-racial"** is a MANUFACTURED (false) identity designed to create an *imaginary "racial" caste line* between (inferior) blacks and (superior) whites.

These word and mind games may confuse non-whites but they do NOT confuse the white supremacists who deliberately created this skin color confusion to divide (and conquer) non-white populations.

Descendants of former slaves of the Pettway plantation

Cumberland Landing Slaves

CHAPTER EIGHT

THE DESTRUCTION OF THE AFRICAN SLAVE FAMILY

The Slave System Destroyed The African Family In America

Despite their best and desperate efforts, slaves were unable to establish stable families on the slave plantations. Males and females were not allowed to marry or show affection for each other, pass along their languages, religions, customs, or traditions to their children; or stop slave-owners from abusing, raping, or selling their loved ones.

Women who got pregnant in slavery were forbidden to ever speak the name of their child's father, and the fathers were not allowed to claim their babies as part of their blood kin. To add insult to extreme injury, when a slave girl got pregnant (after being raped by her slave-owner), she was condemned as "impure" in God's eyes!

The "Dark Deeds" Of American Slavery

"In due time we arrived safely in the slave pen at Natchez [Mississippi], and here we joined another large crowd of slaves which were already stationed at this place. Here scenes were witnessed which are too wicked to mention.

The slaves are made to shave and wash in greasy pot liquor to make them look sleek and nice; their heads must be combed and their best clothes put on; and when called out to be examined they are to stand in a row; the women and men apart; then they are picked out and taken into a room, and examined.

See a large, rough slaveholder take a poor female slave into a room, make her strip, then feel of and examine her as though she were a pig, or a hen, or merchandise. O, how can a poor slave husband or father stand and see his wife, daughters and sons thus treated!

Sometimes their little children are torn from them and sent far away to a distant country, never to see them again. O, such crying and weeping when parting from each other! For this demonstration of natural human affection the slaveholder would apply the lash or paddle upon the naked skin."

(From the "Life and Narrative of William J. Anderson, Twenty-four Years a Slave! Sold Eight Times! In Jail Sixty Times!! Whipped Three Hundred Times!!! or The Dark Deeds of American Slavery Revealed, 1857")

TO BE SOLD & LET

BY PUBLIC AUCTION,

On MONDAY the 18th of MAY, 1829,

UNDER THE TREES.

FOR SALE,

THE THREE FOLLOWING

SLAVES,

VIZ.

HANNIBAL, about 30 Years old, an excellent House Servant, of Good Character.
WILLIAM, about 35 Years old, a Labourer.
NANCY, an excellent House Servant and Nurse.

The MEN belonging to "LEECH'S" Estate, and the WOMAN to Mrs. D. SMIT

TO BE LET,

On the usual conditions of the Hirer finding them in Food, Clot in . and Medical ance,

THE FOLLOWING

MALE and FEMALE

SLAVES,

ROBERT BAGLEY, about 20 Years old, a good House Servant.
WILLIAM BAGLEY, about 18 Years old, a Labourer.
JOHN ARMS, about 18 Years old.
JACK ANTONIA, about 40 Years old, a Labourer.
PHILIP, an Excellent Fisherman.
HARRY, about 27 Years old, a good House Servant.
LUCY, a Young Woman of good Character, used to House Work and the Nursery.
ELIZA, an Excellent Washerwoman.
CLARA, an Excellent Washerwoman.
FANNY, about 14 Years old, House Servant.
SARAH, about 14 Years old, House Servant.

Also for Sale, at Eleven o'Clock,

Fine Rice, Gram, Paddy, Books, Muslins, Needles, Pins, Ribbons, &c. &c.

AT ONE O'CLOCK, THAT CELEBRATED ENGLISH HORSE

BLUCHER,

ADDISON PRINTER GOVERNMENT OFFICE

The Largest Slave Auction In Recorded History

On March 3, 1859, six years before slavery ended, 436 black men, women, children, and infants were brought to a racetrack in Savannah, Georgia on March 3, 1859, auctioned off and sold:

"Common as are slave-auctions in the southern states, and naturally as a slave may look forward to the time when he will be put up on the block, still the full misery of the event, of the scenes which precede and succeed it, is never understood till the actual experience comes.

"The first sad announcement that the sale is to be, the knowledge that all ties of the past are to be sundered, the frantic terror at the idea of being sent "down south," the almost certainty that one member of a family will be torn from another, the anxious scanning of purchasers' faces, the agony at parting, often forever, with husband, wife, child, these must be seen and felt to be fully understood.

"Young as I was then, the iron entered into my soul. The remembrance of the breaking up of McPherson's estate [the property of his first owner] is photographed in its minutest features in my mind. The crowd collected round the stand, the huddling group of negroes, the examination of muscle, teeth, the exhibition of agility, the look of the auctioneer, the agony of my mother. I can shut my eyes and see them all.

"My brothers and sisters were bid off first, and one by one, while my mother, paralyzed by grief, held me by the hand. Her turn came, and she was bought by Isaac Riley of Montgomery county. Then I was offered to the assembled purchasers.

"My mother, half distracted with the thought of parting forever from all her children, pushed through the crowd while the bidding for me was going on, to the spot where Riley was standing.

She fell at his feet and clung to his knees, entreating him in tones that a mother only could command to buy her baby as well as herself, and spare to her one, at least, of her little ones.

"Will it, can it, be believed that this man, thus appealed to, was capable not merely of turning a deaf ear to her supplication, but of disengaging himself from her with such violent blows and kicks as to reduce her to the necessity of creeping out of his reach and mingling the groan of bodily suffering with the sob of a breaking heart?

(continued on page 49)

Slave auction house in Atlanta, Georgia (1864)

"As she crawled away from the brutal man I heard her sob out, "Oh, Lord Jesus, how long, how long shall I suffer this way!" I must have been then between five and six years old. I seem to see and hear my poor weeping mother now.

"This was one of my earliest observations of men, an experience which I only shared with thousands of my race, the bitterness of which to any individual who suffers it cannot be diminished by the frequency of its recurrence, while it is dark enough to overshadow the whole after-life with something blacker than a funeral pall.

"Almost immediately, however, whether my childish strength at five or six years of age was overmastered by such scenes and experiences, or from some accidental cause, I fell sick, and seemed to my new master so little likely to recover that he proposed to R., the purchaser of my mother, to take me too at such a trifling rate that it could not be refused.

"I was thus providentially restored to my mother; and under her care, destitute as she was of the proper means of nursing me, I recovered my health and grew up to be an uncommonly vigorous and healthy boy and man." – Josiah Henson, former slave.

"A Mournful Scene Indeed"
The New Orleans Slave Market

"The slave auction was one of the most barbaric practices of the harsh system of slavery. The slave trade...destroyed families...especially after 1840. Planters could realize substantial profits selling enslaved people and New Orleans became the center of the trade.

"The resulting migration involved hundreds of thousands of African Americans. Some moved with their masters, but the migration also tore apart slave families residing on different plantations. Others were sold on the block." -- Solomon Northup remembers the New Orleans Slave Market in his "Twelve Years a Slave. Narrative of Solomon, a Citizen of New York, Kidnapped in Washington City in 1841.

After Slavery Ended Most Slaves Took Owner's Last Names

Prior to 1865, slaves had NO surnames; ONLY first names and the names of the people they "belonged" to. For example, *"Black Joe belongs to Mr. X (a slave-owner)."* The importance of surnames is critical because they are proof of IDENTITY, HERITAGE, OR KNOWLEDGE OF SELF.

"We didn't have a name. The slaves was always known by they master's last name, and after we was freed we just took the last name of our masters and used it. After we had got our freedom papers, they had our ages and all on them, they was lost so we guess at our ages." – Clayton Holbert, former slave

"My father was a slave, but I don't know where he was born, because he said when he knew anything he was in a house with the white people, and they never did tell him anything. Where I was born, it is a mighty fine country, and they was awful mean to the colored people in that country."

"My own pappy was named Stephany. I think he take dat name 'cause when he was little, his mammy call him 'Istifani.' Dat mean a skeleton, and he was a skinny man. He belong to the Grayson family and I think dat his master's name."

According to the 2000 U.S. Census, over 90 percent of the 163,036 people in the U.S. with the last name Washington were black. There are more black people with the same last name of the first U.S. President and slave-owner GEORGE WASHINGTON, than any other last name in America.

From Proud Africans To A Race Of "Non-People"

A **"non-people"** have NO KNOWLEDGE of self, of their (true) history, who they used to be, or where they came from. A non-people must rely on the manufactured identities of those who ROBBED them of their heritage.

Pure African bloodlines were destroyed as warring tribes were forced to breed under the terrible conditions of slavery. The slave-owners forcibly and deliberately injected their foreign genes into the racial mix to create maximum genetic destruction AND maximum psychological confusion.

This traumatic BLOOD MIX may explain the high level of psychological confusion AND conflict within the black collective, as our genetics, bloodlines, temperaments, and physical differences wage war from without AND from within.

Fast-forward to the 21st Century: what is the most common word for a MALE ANIMAL that mates with a female animal (a BITCH) that is also used to describe black males?

DOG (aka 'DAWG')

"Everything that is wrong with black people today, other than normal human frailties, was caused by our contact with Europeans (white people)."

-- Umoja

Recipe #2

500 Years of Justice DENIED

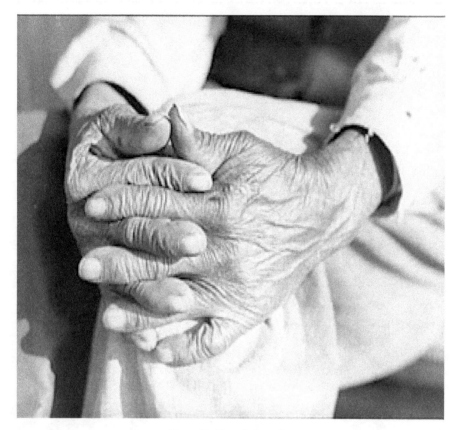

Female Slave's hands

"America has been the best country on earth for black folks. It was here that 600,000 black people, brought from Africa in slave ships, grew into a community of 40 million, were introduced to Christian salvation, and reached the greatest levels of freedom and prosperity blacks have ever known." -- Pat Buchanan, white male syndicated columnist (2008)

CHAPTER NINE

500 YEARS OF JUSTICE DENIED

If the Jews were compensated for 12 years of injustice, and the Japanese were compensated for three years of injustice, should the descendants of slaves be compensated for 400 YEARS of slavery?

Let the facts speak for themselves:

> *"I never know what it was to rest. I just work all the time from morning till late at night. I had to do everything there was to do on the outside. Work in the field, chop wood, hoe corn, till sometime I feels like my back surely break. I done everything except split rails." -- Sara Gudger, former slave from Burke County, North Carolina.*

FACT: American Slavery Did Not End With The Emancipation Proclamation Of 1865

After the Emancipation Proclamation was signed into law, and legal slavery "officially" ended, the slave-less south created NEW laws to overturn the rights of freed blacks to make up for the loss of FREE LABOR. Thousands of black men were falsely arrested and forced to work FOR FREE on prison chain gangs.

"Free" black men dug ditches, built America's roads, laid railroad tracks, and picked crops for wealthy white farmers. America's chain-gang "prisoners" were mostly black males, who put in 16-hour days, wearing 20 pound leg irons.

Rancid food, malnutrition, and "shackle poisoning," caused by the chains rubbing against their shackled ankles killed hundreds of prisoners each year. Chain gangs were abolished around 1955 -- *almost one hundred years after the end of slavery -- but slavery never ended on the back roads of America.*

Black Slavery In The Year 2010

> *"Blacks don't want to believe this (slavery) is happening in 2010...but (black) people are forced to stay on plantations in Glendora, Miss., Webb, Miss., Roseland, LA, and other places where (white) landowners use isolation and threats of violence to keep these Black workers under control."*
> *-- Antoinette Harrell, a black female researcher and genealogist, who has been tracking modern day slavery for a decade. (SOURCE: Final Call.com)*

African American convicts working with axes and singing on
a chain gang in a wood yard, Reed Camp, South Carolina, 1934

Blacks Picking Cotton At Louisiana's Angola Prison In 2008

*"On an expanse of 18,000 acres of farmland, 59 miles northwest of Baton
Rouge, LA, long rows of men, mostly African-American, till the fields
under the hot Louisiana sun. The men pick cotton, wheat, soybeans, and
corn. They work for pennies, literally. Armed guards, mostly white, ride
up and down the rows on horseback, keeping watch...the farm is called
Angola, after the homeland of the slaves who first worked its soil."*
-- (SOURCE: Maya Schenwar, www.truth-out.org)

Chain Gang street sweepers. From a real photo
postcard postmarked from Washington, DC in 1909

Parchman Farm chain gang, Louisiana, 1911

FACT: Slavery Existed In The North AND The South

Contrary to the MYTH that slavery only existed in the South, the center of slave trading in the North was New England's old colonies. While slavery never reached the numbers it did in the south, slaves were publicly auctioned in Philadelphia, Rhode Island, Virginia, New Jersey, Maryland, and New York.

THE EVIDENCE: Runaway Slave Advertisements as they appeared in print in Colonial Newspapers -- In The North!

The Boston Newsletter, July 23, 1716

This is to give notice that on the 16th of July, 1716, Runaway from his Master, David Lyell, an Indian Man named Nim, he lately belonged to Mr. James Moore, he is about one and twenty years of Age and is short broad shouldered Fellow his hair hath lately been cut off, he has a swelling on the back of his right hand, and can do something in the Carpenters trade, he hath with him two new shirts, a new waistcoat, and breeches of white course linen, and the same blew striped; a homespun Coat, wears a Hat, Shoes, Stockings. 'Tis believed he endeavours to get on board some Vessel. Whoever takes up the said Indian in the Jerseys, and brings him to his said master shall have forty shillings and charges and if in any other government Five pounds if they give but notice where he is, so that his Master may have him again. Direct to David Lyell in New York.

The American Weekly Mercury, November 15, 1722.

Runaway from William Yard of Trenton in West-Jersey, the Fifth Day of this Instant November, a Negroe Man named Fransh Manuel, but commonly called Manuel, of a pretty tall stature, and speaks indifferent english. He wears a dark coloured homespun coat, an Ozenbrig Jacket, old Leather breeches, Sheep-russet Stockings, new Shoes and an old Beveret hat. He pretended formerly to be a Freeman and had passes; but he did belong to one John Raymond of Fairfield in New England and I bought him of said Raymond. And the said Negro boy has told since he has run away, Whoever takes up the said Negroe, secures him and brings him to Mr. William Bradford of New York, or to Mr. William Burge of Philadelphia or to his said Master at Trenton, shall have forty shillings reward, beside all reasonable charges, paid by me, William Yard.

The American Weekly Mercury, May 1, 1729.

These are to be given notice that on the first day of this instant May, 1729, was taken up a Negroe man, about forty-three years of age and put into the goal at Burlington, for stealing from several persons sundry sorts of goods; the Negroe man saith he belongs to one Roger Mathews living in Baltimore County in Maryland, The said negroe man formerly belonged to Governeur Markham and was sold down at Maryland by Mr. Reneir, Attorney at Law.

Even Abraham Lincoln's family owned slaves.

FACT: Ninety percent of slaves lived on plantations and farms and labored from sun-up to sun-down, providing skilled and unskilled labor on plantations in the South and contributing to the labor demands of the North.

"The conch shell blowed afore daylight and all hands better git out for roll call or Solomon bust the door down and get them out. It was work hard, git beatings, and half fed. They brung the victuals (food) and water to the fields on a slide pulled by a old mule. Plenty times they was only a half barrel water and it stale and hot, for all us niggers on the hottest days. Mostly we ate pickled pork and cornbread and peas and beans and taters. They never was as much as we needed. The times I hated most was picking cotton when the frost was on the bolls. My hands git sore and crack open and bleed. We'd have a li'l fire in the fields and iffen the ones with tender hands couldn't stand it no longer, we'd run and warm our hands a li'l bit. -- Mary Reynolds, former slave, interviewed in the 1930s.

FACT: Slaves Were Literally "Worked To Death"

New York City, 1991 -- Construction workers digging a foundation for a skyscraper unearthed an 18th century slave graveyard, revealing the remains of 427 bodies. African-Americans waged a fierce political fight to preserve the site as a sacred place. After losing the battle, and after months of negotiation, the skeletons were sent to Washington, D.C.'s Howard University for examination by biological anthropologists. The startling conclusion: *African slaves not only built early New York; they were literally worked to death while doing it.*

Half the bodies found were children; many infants under 6 months old. The high infant mortality rate tells researchers that the living conditions of enslaved Africans were inhumane. After scientists at Cobb Laboratory studied the defects in muscle attachments and fractures on the remains of the buried slaves, they concluded that slaves were *"pressed to the very margins of human physical capacity."*

FACT: Slaves Demanded Compensation For Their Labor

Slaves were not the brainless mass of sub-humanity that western history books and Hollywood films depicted. Many slaves were well aware of the value of their labor. At the end of the Civil War, some demanded compensation for creating so much wealth for white slave-owners.

"We has a right to the land were we are located. . . Our wives, our children, our husbands has been sold over and over again to purchase the lands we now locates upon; that the reason we have a divine right to the land... didn't we clear the land, and raise the crops of corn, of cotton, of tobacco, of rice, of sugar, of everything?" -- from a speech in 1866 by former slave Bayley Wyat at Yorktown, Virginia on behalf of freedmen's land claims.

Abraham Lincoln: Emancipator OR Racist Manipulator?

"I will say then that I am not, nor ever have been in favor of bringing about in anyway the social and political equality of the white and black races - that I am not nor ever have been in favor of making voters or jurors of negroes, nor of qualifying them to hold office, nor to intermarry with white people; and I will say in addition to this, that there is a physical difference between the white and black races which I believe will forever forbid the two races living together on terms of social and political equality.

And inasmuch as they cannot so live, while they do remain together there must be the position of superior and inferior, and I as much as any other man am in favor of having the superior position assigned to the white race.

I say upon this occasion I do not perceive that because the white man is to have the superior position the negro should be denied everything."

-- Abraham Lincoln (1809 - 1865)

CHAPTER TEN

WILLIE LYNCH
NOTWITHSTANDING

Contrary to the Willie Lynch legend, slavery ALONE is NOT responsible for the conditions of blacks today. Even 400 years of brutality and murder could NOT extinguish the RESILIENT AFRICAN SPIRIT.

During AND after chattel slavery, blacks greatly valued our family units. Newly freed slaves traveled thousands of miles to find loved ones, spouses, and children. We had a strong sense of community, and in some areas, geographically and socially, we surpassed whites.

We ran for political office -- and won – since blacks were the majority of registered voters in Alabama, Florida, Georgia, Louisiana, North Carolina, and South Carolina. Former slaves started businesses that rivaled, and often exceeded, those of whites, and were patronized by black and white customers.

However, this brief period of "freedom" and prosperity for newly freed slaves came to a screeching halt for the following reasons:

THE RECONSTRUCTION ERA (1865 - 1877)

In the aftermath of the Civil War the South, which was heavily dependent on slave labor, was in shambles. To solve this "problem," President Andrew Johnson (a former slave-owner) gave Southern whites all the power to define freedom for former slaves. Blacks -- who had been promised freedom after fighting in the Civil War for that freedom -- were denied any say in the process.

When these new "governments" passed the 'Black Codes' in 1865, the rights of former slaves as "free citizens" as defined by the U.S. Constitution were abolished. They had no legal rights, no right to own land, and were forbidden from working and earning the same as whites. Even though land was in plentiful supply, newly freed slaves were forced back to the plantations to work as share-croppers for FORMER plantation owners, and had to buy seed, tools, and supplies from the "landlords."

This new form of slavery, which in some parts in the South STILL exists, allowed former slave-owners to grow rich off the labor of blacks, and guaranteed a life of hardship and poverty for former slaves and their descendants.

THE 'BLACK CODES' (1865)

To control the labor, migration and freedoms of newly freed slaves, the Southern States passed laws known as the 'Black Codes,' which were put into effect IMMEDIATELY after the Civil War to ensure cheap black (slave) labor would remain in plentiful supply.

1865

Examples of 'Black Codes' AFTER Slavery Ended

Mississippi:

"Negroes must make annual contracts for their labor in writing. If they should run away from their tasks, *they forfeited their wages for the year.* Whenever required, they must present licenses (in a town from the mayor; elsewhere from a member of the board of police of the beat) citing their places of residence and authorizing them to work. Fugitives from labor were to be arrested and carried back to their employers.

"Minors were to be apprenticed, if males until they were twenty-one, if females until eighteen years of age. Such corporal punishment as a father would administer to a child might be inflicted upon apprentices by their masters. *Negroes might not carry knives or firearms unless they were licensed to do so.* It was an offense, punishable by a fine of $50 and imprisonment for thirty days, to give or sell intoxicating liquors to a negro. When negroes could not pay the fines and costs after legal proceedings, *they were to be hired at public outcry by the sheriff to the lowest bidder.*"

South Carolina:

In South Carolina persons of color contracting for service were to be known as "servants" and those with whom they contracted, as "masters." On farms the hours of labor would be from sunrise to sunset daily, except on Sunday. The negroes were to get out of bed at dawn. Time lost would be deducted from their wages, as would be the cost of food, nursing, etc., during absence from sickness. Absentees on Sunday must return to the plantation by sunset. House servants were to be at call at all hours of the day and night on all days of the week.

Illinois:

Laws were passed to discourage blacks from coming to Illinois. Blacks were denied the right to vote and denied most rights given to white men. Blacks required a 'certificate of freedom' to travel between states, and had to register that certificate or suffer the fate of the "runaway slaves" -- which could be a sentence of thirty-five lashes. Blacks were forbidden from assembling in groups of three or more could be jailed and whipped.

The "Black Law" of 1853, no black person from another state could stay in Illinois for more than ten days, or was subject to arrest, a fine, a jail term, and removal from the state. If the "offender" was unable to pay the fine, the sheriff could auction the offender to a (white) bidder willing to pay the fine in exchange for free labor.

The Black Codes drew "public outrage" from the *hypocritical North,* which had passed its own discriminatory laws against blacks. In 1866, the South was put under military rule. New elections were held; blacks and poor whites were allowed to vote; and the new government repealed all the Black Codes. In reality, former slaves were still bound by the 'Black Codes,' which are still in effect today.

Black Codes: Yesterday VS Today

1865	2011
Slaves forbidden to learn to read or write	Inferior black schools
"Free" slaves endured corporal punishment from "employers"	Police brutality
No legal rights or justice for blacks	All-white juries = no juries of peers = false convictions = harsher sentences for black defendants
Blacks not allowed to carry firearms	Strict gun bans in most cities with large black populations
Blacks had to show a "pass' to travel from town to town	Black drivers racially profiled by police while traveling from town to town
"Free" blacks forced by law to return to the plantations and work for former owners	"Free" blacks still held captive on plantations in Mississippi and Louisiana in 2010.
"Free" blacks work for free on chain gangs	Black prisoners provide labor for corporate America for 90 cents/hr
Slaves taught to worship and fear a white God	Majority of blacks still worship the same religion (and white God) slaves worshipped.
"Free" blacks deprived of right to vote	One million black votes not counted during the 2000 presidential election
Whites allowed to maim or murder blacks without fearing consequences	Whites cops and citizens allowed to maim, rape, and murder blacks without fearing consequences

JIM CROW (1876 - 1965)

Jim Crow was a set of state and local laws in the U.S. created to replace the repealed 'Black Codes' that mandated 'separate but (un)equal,' status for all blacks in America. Jim Crow laws remained in effect from 1876 to 1965, and were designed to turn freed slaves into PERMANENT NON-CITIZENS (SLAVES).

Examples Of Jim Crow Laws

Alabama:

"All passenger stations in this state operated by any motor transportation company shall have separate waiting rooms and separate ticket windows for the white and colored races."

Georgia:

"All persons licensed to conduct a restaurant, shall serve either white people exclusively or colored people exclusively and shall not sell to the two races within the same room or serve the two races anywhere under the same license."

Louisiana:

"Any person who shall rent any part of any such building to a Negro place or a Negro family when such building is already in whole or in part in occupancy by a white person or white family, or vice versa when the building is in occupancy by a Negro person or Negro family, shall be guilty of a misdemeanor."

Maine:

"A Constitutional amendment was passed in 1893 requiring electors to be able to read the Constitution in English and write his name." (Since slaves were not allowed to learn to read or write, this "requirement" prevented most blacks from voting).

Maryland:

"All railroad companies and corporations, and all persons running or operating cars or coaches by steam on any railroad line or track in the State of Maryland, for the transportation of passengers, are hereby required to provide separate cars or coaches for the travel and transportation of the white and colored passengers."

North Carolina:

"Books shall not be interchangeable between the white and colored schools, but shall continue to be used by the race first using them. The state librarian is directd to fit up and maintain a separate place for the use of the colored people who may come to the library for the purpose of reading books or periodicals."

The Psychological Wages
Of 'Whiteness'

"It must be remembered that the white group of laborers, while they received a low wage, were compensated in part by a sort of public and psychological wage.

They were given public deference and titles of courtesy because they were white. They were admitted freely with all classes of white people to public functions, public parks, and the best schools.

The police were drawn from their ranks, and the courts, dependent on their votes, treated them with such leniency as to encourage lawlessness. Their vote selected public officials, and while this had small effect upon the economic situation, it had great effect upon their personal treatment and the deference shown them.
White schoolhouses were the best in the community, and conspicuously placed, and they cost anywhere from twice to ten times as much per capita as the colored schools. The newspapers specialized in news that flattered the poor whites and almost utterly ignored the Negro except in crime and ridicule."

-- "Black Reconstruction in America," W. E. B. DuBois (1935)

'HONORARY WHITES' KEPT BLACKS 'IN THEIR PLACE'

"The Irish, who, at home, readily sympathize with the oppressed everywhere, are instantly taught when they step upon our soil to hate and despise the Negro...Sir, the Irish-American will one day find out his mistake."
-- Frederick Douglas, May 10, 1853

In the first half of the 19th century, over three million Irish emigrated to America to escape the Potato Famine (1845-1855), and oppression at the hands of the Anglo-Irish Anglicans. The 'Penal Laws' used against the oppressed Irish Catholics in Ireland were similar to the 'Black Codes' against blacks in America.

The desperately poor Irish immigrants were the most despised of all free laborers. They had no skills, and although they spoke the English language, the vast majority could not read or write it. Since they were not seen as "white" by the White Anglo Saxon Protestants (WASPs) elites, Irish immigrants were forced to labor side by side with blacks or worked as overseers on slave plantations.

This "closeness" may explain why so many blacks have IRISH LAST NAMES, such as Smith, Murphy, Moore, Boyce, Butler, and Banks.

In contrast, most slaves were forced to learn a trade, and were the master builders, carpenters, ironworkers, farmers, seamstresses, and cooks that provided most of the skilled labor in the South -- ***the same skilled slave labor that built the White House.***

To keep freed blacks in an inferior position, the WASPS struck a deal with the Irish, the largest immigrant group in America. In exchange for being "white," the Irish had to embrace racism and serve as the "foot soldiers" of the white supremacy elite. In return, the Irish were rewarded with monopolies on the most dangerous blue-collar jobs: fire, police, and construction, and were paid a generous wage to ensure they would always be more prosperous than blacks.

The predominantly Irish police force became a TOOL of the white elite to intimidate and terrorize blacks to keep them from rebelling against a racist system. Blatant police abuses against blacks served another purpose: it was visible "proof" to the lower-caste whites that even while they were being exploited, they were ***still more privileged than*** (and superior to) blacks. This cemented their LOYALTY to an economic system that allowed even the poorest whites to feel superior.

One only has to check the ethnic roster of most major city fire, police, and construction unions; their resistance to blacks joining the trade unions, police, and fire departments; and today's rampant police brutality against blacks to see the DEAL between the white elites and their "honorary white" foot-soldiers ***is still in effect.***

THE KU KLUX KLAN (KKK)

Founded in 1865 in Pulaski, Tennessee by Confederate Army veterans (the losers of the Civil War), the KKK terrorized, robbed, raped, and murdered blacks to keep them "in their place" and was largely successful, especially in the South.

BLACK WALL STREET (1908 - 1921)

Despite the relentless violence and oppression against former slaves, blacks made phenomenal gains shortly after legal slavery ended. The Land Run of 1880 allowed blacks to acquire "free" land, and many former slaves fled the South and took advantage of this unique opportunity. From 1865 to 1920, Oklahoma had over 50 independently functioning, all-black towns.

These all-black towns were an oasis for blacks from the brutal racism found in racially-mixed parts of the country. According to Arthur Tolson, a historian of blacks in Oklahoma, many blacks turned to *"...idelologies of economic advancement, self-help, and racial solidarity."*

The most famous example was Tulsa, Oklahoma, better known as **"Black Wall Street,"** an all-black town that boasted a thriving business district, a bus line, 21 restaurants, a library, a bank, a hospital, 21 churches, two movie theaters, a newspaper, excellent schools, a half dozen private airplanes, law offices, and a post office. This was an amazing feat for a people just a few decades from being slaves.

Unfortunately, Black Wall Street drew the wrath of less prosperous white towns. An envious white mob, fueled by the fictitious story of a black boy raping a white girl; and aided by the KKK, local law(less) enforcement, and the U.S. military looted and fire-bombed the all-black town from the air.

Over 3,000 black men, women, and children were murdered. Twelve hours after one of the worst race riots in U.S. history, Black Wall Street was no more. The Great Depression dealt the final deathblow to most all-black towns and blacks began to migrate west and north to find employment. The white "rape victim" later confirmed she hadn't been raped after all.

Massive Injuries On Top Of Massive Injuries

Jim S. is walking down a dark country road when he is struck by a hit-and-run driver, and sustains serious injuries. He crawls into the road to get help but it is pitch black outside. The bus driver doesn't see him until it is too late, and Jim is run over by the bus. Jim was NOT "destroyed" by the first set of injuries. He was young and strong, and had he received the help AND the time he needed to heal, **he would have survived his injuries**. However, a second set of equally devastating injuries on top of his **unhealed injuries** effectively sealed Jim's fate.

If slavery had destroyed African slaves, there would have been no need to for whites to create the Black Codes or Jim Crow laws. Had former slaves been allowed to HEAL from the damage caused by slavery **without sabotage from whites,** they could have **completely recovered from slavery.** However, 150 years of post-slavery racism literally threw the descendants of former slaves UNDER THE BUS.

If whites had NOT had 500 years of SUPERIOR educational, economic, and social ADVANTAGES, they would NOT be in a (superior) position over blacks. **Perhaps, it is this secret knowledge in the hearts of whites collectively that continues to fuel today's racism.**

'Black Wall Street' (before the riots)

The imaginary "crime" that sparked the Black Wall Street Massacre

If former slaves were able to build a "Black Wall Street" only THREE DECADES AFTER SLAVERY, one could only imagine what Black America could have become WITHOUT any racist interference and sabotage. It is highly possible AND highly probable there would have been THOUSANDS of prosperous, independently-run black cities all over America.

Slaves working on cotton gin

Slaves working on sugar cane plantation

CHAPTER 11

DO BLACKS DESERVE REPARATIONS?

"The fact is, you can't brutalize a people massively and then just tell them to get over it. That will never work -- just as it would never work in our personal lives." – Donna Lamb, C.U.R.E. (Caucasians United for Reparations and Emancipation)

The idea of reparations for slavery is nothing new. Neither is the outrage against racist injustice and oppression.

Walker's Appeal (Published September, 1829)

In 1829 David Walker, a black slave, published "Walker's Appeal," a 76-page pamphlet that condemned white Christians for not opposing racism and slavery. Walker encouraged slaves to rebel by any means necessary, including violence, in order to win their freedom. In his "Appeal," Walker stated that blacks suffered more than any other people in the history of the world did:

"The whites have had us under them for more than three centuries, murdering, and treating us like brutes..."

"Walker's Appeal" Identified Four Causes For The "Wretchedness" Of Slaves:

1. Slavery
2. A submissive and cringing attitude towards whites (even among free blacks)
3. Indifference by Christian ministers, and
4. False help by groups such as the American Colonization Society, which promised freedom from slavery only on the condition that freed blacks would be forced to leave America for colonies in West Africa.

Walker vigorously opposed the idea of leaving a country that was built on the backs of slaves:

"Let no man of us budge one step, and let slave-holders come to beat us from our country. America is more our country, than it is the whites — we have enriched it with our blood and tears. The greatest riches in all America have arisen from our blood and tears: — and will they drive us from our property and homes, which we have earned with our blood?"

Unfortunately, Walker didn't live long enough to see slavery abolished. He was mysteriously poisoned, allegedly by whites.

Black Manifesto (1969)

"If we can't sit at the table [of democracy], let's knock the fucking legs off!" -- James Forman, black civil rights leader and author of the "Black Manifesto" (1969)

As a part of his Black Manifesto, James Forman demanded $500 million in reparations and a percentage of the assets from white churches and other racist institutions to make up for injustices blacks had suffered over the centuries. The original ten-point "program demands" outlined in the Black Manifesto:

"We call for the establishment of a southern land bank to help our brothers and sisters who have to leave their land because of racist pressure and for people who want to establish cooperative farms but who have no funds. We have seen too many farmers evicted from their homes because they have dared to defy the white racism of this country. We need money for land. We must fight for massive sums of money for this southern land bank. We call for $200,000,000 to implement this program."

"Why We Owe Them" By Carol Chehade, C.U.R.E. (Caucasians United for Reparations and Emancipation)

"Stop living in the past and move on after slavery!" This is what we often tell African Americans. Well we certainly forced them to move on. We moved on to Black Codes, Jim Crow, lynching, de facto segregation. We moved on to White knights hiding behind ghosts of themselves while religiously lighting crosses in praise of a Satan they were fooled into thinking was God.

We moved on to the cities of Tulsa, St. Louis, and Rosewood where we, apparently, were unaffected by the burned and seared flesh of Black people. We moved on to laws that upheld racial oppression over and over again. We moved on to the many Black men placed on death row because they fit the description. We moved on and made sure that Emmett Till would not be the last fourteen-year-old Black child whose unrecognizable corpse was the price paid for supposedly whistling at a White woman.

We moved on to exclude African Americans from rights of democracy by blocking avenues to employment, education, housing, and civil rights. In the final decade of the last century the slow, consistent racial apocalypse started showing signs of even more things to come when a Black man's head was seen rolling behind a pick up truck in Jasper, Texas.

By the time we racially profiled our way from Texas to New York, we find a city plagued with plungers and forty-one bullets. Every time Black people have tried leaving the shackles of slavery behind, we find that we were the ones that couldn't stop living in the past."

Let No Man Budge One Step

Ray W., 48, was having his usual lunch; sitting alone, reading, and eating a sandwich he'd brought from home. He always sat in a corner of the company cafeteria at the smallest table to discourage company. He was known as a loner, a strange black man who worked in the solitary confinement of the copier room and always had his nose buried in a book.

Ray found it hard to relate to his coworkers, even the black ones. Most people lived in their small boxes and had little interest in anything that did not affect them personally.

He learned to keep his thoughts to himself, do his job, be cordial to all comers, and then go home to his wife and three kids. Ray was so engrossed in his newest literary acquisition, a copy of *"Walker's Appeal,"* he didn't notice O'Brien, a payroll clerk from accounting, peering over his shoulder.

"You're always reading," said the forty-something red-haired man.

Ray slowly closed his book. This white man made reading sound like a crime. Maybe it was for a black man. Ray knew some of his coworkers were puzzled by a black man who didn't chase tail, cheat on his wife, talk a lot of jive, or constantly grin like a damn fool.

Ray assumed his strange ways were responsible for his failure to be promoted out of the copier room, despite a bachelor's degree in accounting. After a decade of working for corporate America, Ray had lost his taste for ambition, and had settled for earning enough of a living to keep a roof over his family's head and food on the table.

Annoyed, Ray glanced at his watch. In fifteen minutes, his lunch would be over. He didn't relish wasting it, talking about nothing with a man who didn't speak when they passed in the hallway.

"What's that you're you reading?" O'Brien asked, eyes reaching across the table.

"Walker's Appeal."

"Appeal? You studying to be a paralegal?"

"Walker's Appeal was written almost two hundred years ago by a slave." Ray stopped short. He knew from experience that whites weren't interested in any history but their own – and only the parts that painted them in a flattering light.

"I thought slaves couldn't read." O'Brien looked skeptical.

"David Walker," Ray repeated firmly. "Wrote an appeal condemning slavery. He said slaves should fight for their freedom by any means necessary, and that slaves deserved their share of the wealth they helped create."

"You're one of those." O'Brien folded his arms across his chest.

"Those who?" Ray frowned.

"You think blacks should get reparations."

"I *know* we should," Ray said without hesitation.

"Why should I pay? My family never owned any slaves. "

"Blacks didn't put Jews or Japanese in concentration camps, but we paid."

"That's different."

"How?"

"You want reparations, ask the African chiefs who sold you."

"Because slavery didn't make Africa the richest nation on earth."

"You think slaves made America rich?" O'Brien's eyes widened in disbelief.

"Do you know how much wealth was generated by millions of people working for free for 400 years?" Ray asked. "All the work back then had to be done by hand. You didn't have no machines to do it. That's why slaves was so valuable. We never got our 40 acres and a mule. You know how much 40 acres is worth today?"

"What's that got to do with you? Were you a slave?"

Ray almost said he still was. If he had any doubts, all he had to do was think back a week ago when two white cops pulled him over and frisked him in broad daylight, while the other drivers slowed down to watch. After no drugs or guns were found, they let him go. Without one word of apology.

"Maybe some plantation owners got rich from picking cotton," O'Brien conceded. "That didn't make America rich."

Ray couldn't resist the opportunity to educate this ignorant white man. A lot of people -- blacks and whites -- thought all slaves did was pick cotton, when in reality, slaves were the biggest pool of skilled workers, ironworkers, carpenters, planters, inventors, cooks, and baby-raisers in the South. Hell, slaves built the damn White House!

"Say you started a small company that made widgets," Ray continued, ignoring the tight-lipped expression on O'Brien's face. "Somehow -- it doesn't matter how -- you got ten million people to work for your company for free. They didn't get any salaries, no medical benefits, no pensions, nothing. They worked from sunup to sundown, never took a day off, never took off sick, and worked until the day they literally dropped dead. Then their kids and grandkids took their place--"

"I know where --"

"Let me finish," Ray said. "You got all the credit for the work they did, even the inventions they created to make their work easier, since they were doing all the work, anyway. Four hundred years later your company's the biggest widget maker in the world. Nobody could compete with you because nobody else had free labor. Your kids, granddaddies, and great grandkids are super rich because they inherited the company and all the inventions. How in the world could you fix your mouth to say 400 years of free labor didn't make your family rich?" The question hung unanswered as the two men stared at each other in silence.

"You act like we never did nothing for the blacks." O'Brien finally said, in a tone ringing with resentment.

"We who?" Ray's laugh was harsh. "*We* did everything for you."

"What about civil rights, affirmative action, welfare—"

"Who's talking about welfare?" A small voice in the back of Ray's head warned him to let it go. He'd noticed the curious looks they were getting as people passed by the table, pretending not to eavesdrop, but he couldn't stop himself. He was sick and tired of eating Jim Crow and choking down white denial.

"I never been on welfare a day in my life, I pay taxes the same as you. Didn't nobody give black people civil rights, we died fighting for those rights, the same way me, my daddy and my granddaddy fought overseas for this country. You ever been in the military?"

"You got all the answers, you tell me."

"You asked a question, I answered it," Ray said. That's right, he was a smart nigger. The kind of nigger O'Brien's kind had no use for.

"You people need get over yourselves." O'Brien's chair scraped the floor as he shoved it back. "Nobody's gonna pay for something that happened before you was born. It's ridiculous."

"*You people* ?"

"That's right, you poor black people, we're so sorry we kidnapped you from Africa where you were starving and brought you to America so you could live in the greatest country on earth, and here's the key to the U.S. Treasury. Just take what you think we owe you.'"

"Don't worry, we plan to." Ray didn't know how but he was working on it.

"You want reparations?" O'Brien jammed a hand in his pocket. "Start with this."

Ray sat as still as a statue as the quarter rolled across the table and bounced off his book. Everything in him wanted to reach out and choke the shit out of that white man for all the David Walkers who had come before him – and for all the black men who were still treated like dirt. He opened his book, and tried to focus, but the words swam in his blurred vision. O'Brien stood up, and leaned on the table, palms flat, eye-to-eye with Ray.

"If you hate America so much," O'Brien said quietly. "Why don't you leave?"

"Because we earned the right to be here." Ray stared into the hard blue eyes without blinking. "More than you and anyone else in this room."

After O'Brien left, Ray couldn't help wondering if he would be looking for a new job soon. He uncapped the neon yellow highlighter with a trembling hand and swept it across a passage:

"Let no man of us budge one step, and let slave-holders come to beat us from our country. America is more our country, than it is the whites — we have enriched it with our blood and tears. The greatest riches in all America have arisen from our blood and tears..."

THE END OF STORY

FACT: America would NOT be the nation it is today without 500 years of free slave labor, economic exploitation, and the cultural, medical, and scientific contributions, and ingenuity of black people.

A Short List Of American Corporations That Profited From Slavery:

1. North American Continent
2. Aetna, Inc.
3. American International Group (AIG)
4. Lloyd's of London
5. New York Life Insurance Company
6. FleetBoston Financial Corporation
7. JP Morgan Chase Manhattan Bank
8. Lehman Brothers
9. RJ Reynolds Tobacco Company
10. Loews Corporation (Lorrilard)
11. Canadian National Railway
12. CSX Corporation
13. Norfolk Southern
14. Union Pacific Railroad

Reparations Paid By The U.S. Government

1971	$1 Billion + 44 acres	Alaska Native Land
1980	$81 Million	Klamaths of Oregon
1985	$105 Million	Sioux of South Dakota
1985	$31 Million	Chippewas of Wisconsin
1985	$12.3 Million	Seminoles of Florida
1986	$32 Million	Ottawas of Michigan
1990	$1.2 Million	Japanese Americans
2001	$56 Million	Seminoles of Oklahoma

Reparations Paid By Other Governments

1952	German	$822 Million to German Jewish survivors
1988	Austria	$25 Million to Holocaust survivors
1990	Canada	$230 Million to Japanese

Do Blacks deserve reparations?

Hell Yes

And we should keep demanding what is DUE us until we get what is OWED us.

"Labor was the first price, the original purchase. It was not by gold or silver, but by labour, that all the wealth of the world was originally purchased."

-- Adam Smith (1723-1790)

Recipe #3

Racial Memories

The Slave's Dream by Henry Wadsworth Longfellow (1807-1882)

Beside the ungathered rice he lay,
His sickle in his hand;
His breast was bare, his matted hair
Was buried in the sand.
Again, in the mist and shadow of sleep,
He saw his Native Land.

Wide through the landscape of his dreams
The lordly Niger flowed;
Beneath the palm-trees on the plain
Once more a king he strode;
And heard the tinkling caravans
Descend the mountain-road.

He saw once more his dark-eyed queen
Among her children stand;
They clasped his neck, they kissed his cheeks,
They held him by the hand!--
A tear burst from the sleeper's lids
And fell into the sand.

And then at furious speed he rode
Along the Niger's bank;
His bridle-reins were golden chains,
And, with a martial clank,
At each leap he could feel his scabbard of steel
Smiting his stallion's flank.

Before him, like a blood-red flag,
The bright flamingoes flew;
From morn till night he followed their flight,
O'er plains where the tamarind grew,
Till he saw the roofs of Caffre huts,
And the ocean rose to view.

At night he heard the lion roar,
And the hyena scream,
And the river-horse, as he crushed the reeds
Beside some hidden stream;
And it passed, like a glorious roll of drums,
Through the triumph of his dream.

The forests, with their myriad tongues,
Shouted of liberty;
And the Blast of the Desert cried aloud,
With a voice so wild and free,
That he started in his sleep and smiled
At their tempestuous glee.

He did not feel the driver's whip,
Nor the burning heat of day;
For Death had illumined the Land of Sleep,
And his lifeless body lay
A worn-out fetter, that the soul
Had broken and thrown away!

CHAPTER 12

RACIAL MEMORIES

Racial memory touches upon a peculiarity of humankind. We continue to be gravely upset by the frightening events, which occurred repeatedly to our numerous ancestors. These racial impressions are a powerful factor in determining the behavior and well-being of large groups of people."
– James C. Thomson, (1950)

What Is A "Racial Memory?"

According to Carl Jung, a Swiss psychiatrist, and the founder of analytical psychology, **"racial memory"** is a *"reservoir of the experiences of our species"* and a form of *"our collective unconscious."*

The American Psychological Association (APA) gives another definition for racial memory: *"The feelings, patterns of thought, and fragments of experience that have been transmitted from generation to generation in all humans that deeply influence the mind and behavior."*

Is It "Déjà Vu" Or A 'Racial Memory?'

We have all heard a relative say a particular child has the same "ways" (personality traits) of a deceased family member. Some of us have had a déjà vu moment where something that shouldn't be familiar, somehow is.

We might recall a childhood nightmare that haunted our dreams; or we fear what can't be explained; love who we shouldn't love; or exhibit certain personality traits that have been with us for as long as we can remember.

It's possible that some of our personality traits were passed along from our ancestors, from one generation to another. This doesn't mean we are carbon copies of our ancestors; it means our mental and emotional characteristics are influenced by the racial memories and experiences -- of our ancestors.

The collective unconscious may contain the experiences, emotions, and memories of our ANCESTORS that are present at birth in the genetic material of every individual. Our DNA-based racial memories may be responsible in part for the Black Gender Wars between black males and females.

Is Talent A Form Of Racial Memory?

Our "collective unconscious" may explain the ability some children display at an early age, in math, music, art, or science. An example is singer extraordinaire, Whitney Houston.

Her mother, Cissy Houston, is a Grammy Award-winning gospel singer, and her cousin, Dionne Warwick, is an international musical legend. Is their combined musical genius just a lucky family coincidence? Or can the ability to sing be inherited and passed from one generation to the next as a form of racial memory?

Are Phobias A Form Of Racial Memories?

Phobias are an irrational, intense, and persistent fear of certain situations, activities, things, or people. Psychologist Martin Seligman conducted experiments on phobias that led him to conclude that **certain objects may have a GENETIC PREDISPOSITION** (from birth) to being associated with fear.

Seligman believed heredity and genetics, combined with life experiences, played a major role in developing anxiety disorders and phobias.

Many behavioral psychologists believe phobias are be a throwback to some traumatic event one of our ancestors may have experienced, and that it is possible to inherit those fears and other emotional disorders, like depression, schizophrenia, alcoholism, and anti-social personality disorders, the same way we inherit the color of our skin or the shape of our noses.

For example, Cynthia, 22, is diagnosed with "pogonophobia" – the fear of men with beards. Cynthia has never had a traumatic experience with a bearded man, but her phobia could suggest she inherited the racial memory of an ancestor who had. Is it possible that her fear of men with beards became a genetic "thumbprint" (memory) on her DNA?

If ONE traumatic experience can create a genetic "thumbprint," can millions of the same traumatic experiences over a 400-year period create a GENETIC "blueprint" that afflicts an entire race?

Is Fear Of the Unknown Caused By Racial Memory?

Tim, a 43-year-old black male who never experienced the horrors of slavery, remembers having childhood nightmares of being brutally whipped by a white male. As an adult, he is prone to mood swings, paranoia, and avoids unfamiliar places and people – especially white people.

Some call Tim 'anti-social,' but his 87-year-old aunt swears Tim has the same ways as her grandfather, Solomon, who was lynched by a white mob in 1919 -- before Tim was born. Is it possible that Tim inherited his nightmares (racial memories) from his great grandfather's brutal murder?

Can Racial Memories Directly Affect Our Behavior?

"It was remarkable to see their physical disposition. They walked into the room with their heads held low, shuffled in...for lack of a better word, {they looked like} slaves. They had lost their way, and there was no light in their eyes whatsoever." -- Dr. Joy DeGruy Leary, after talking to an audience of black male prisoners at Riker's Island, New York's largest jail.

Why do so many young black males view prison as a "rite of passage into manhood?" Once we examine the PHYSICAL and SPIRITUAL CONNECTION between today's prisons and yesterday's slave plantations, the answer is clear.

"My oldest son called me today from prison. He says he wants to transfer to a prison in another state so he can have a private cell and his own TV. He don't care that he's gonna be farther from home. He's getting too damn comfortable with his situation. They make prison life so easy for black males some of them don't mind being locked up." -- George S., 43.

Some slaves were afraid to leave the plantation because as bad as slavery was, the unknown was even more terrifying. They had become so dependent on the slave-owner, they didn't believe they could survive on their own in a hostile white world. For similar reasons, young black males are reluctant (terrified) of leaving their poor crime-ridden neighborhoods (plantations) because the unknown may be worse than what is familiar.

The onslaught (psychological war) by the supremacy entertainment/economic/educational system has programmed some black males to believe the only thing they can be successful at is FAILURE. Once they are convinced they are destined to fail, it is easier (and safer) to waste their lives behind bars.

America's prison systems are modern-day plantations for a million black males and females trapped in a pre-1865 reality.

Can Stress Trigger Racial Memories?

Some behavioral scientists believe genetic tendencies toward certain mental illnesses can be TRIGGERED by environmental stress:

"In most cases, an inherited factor needs to be present for schizophrenia to develop. However, without severe environmental stresses the illness may not appear in those who have a predisposition to it." -- Dr. David Rosenthal

If Dr. Rosenthal is correct, could "severe environmental stresses" like poverty, violence, police abuses, and racism trigger the INHERITED mental illnesses CAUSED by 400 years of slavery?

Racial Memories May Explain The Hostility (Some) Whites Exhibit Toward The Descendants of Former Slaves

Why would the (white) descendants of the Victimizers despise the descendants of the Victims? Part of the answer may be a psychological condition known as **projection** -- a psychological DEFENSE mechanism where a person unconsciously (or consciously) PROJECTS their own UNDE-SIRABLE thoughts, feelings, actions, and character flaws onto other people to obtain ACQUITTAL by his or her CONSCIENCE.

Extreme guilt is often transformed into resentment -- even hatred -- because the Victimizers cannot stand the reflections in their own mirrors, and MUST PROJECT their own bad behavior and character flaws onto their Victims. Those flaws are then transformed into the "natural" character traits of their Victims.

For example, the wanton (and savage) slaughter of Native Americans by European invaders was TRANSFORMED into Indian savages scalping and murdering Europeans. The mass rape of African females was TRANS-FORMED into sexually loose and hot-blooded female slaves, and black male slaves were TRANSFORMED into black males raping white females.

Racial memories (guilt) may be partly responsible for the high rates of drug addictions, mental illnesses, depression, and suicide among the white collective in a futile attempt to self-medicate away, or escape the pain of a shameful past and an equally shameful present regarding non-white people.

Another possible explanation for the irrational hatred some whites feel toward blacks may be a GENETIC PREDISPOSITION (mental illness) to hate/harm non-white people, along with an **UNDEVELOPED MORAL CONSCIOUS and a genetic INABILITY to empathize, feel guilt, shame, or be remorseful towards those who look "different."**

In short, the pathological need to practice racism is a mental, emotional, psychological, and spiritual disorder/disease.

Racial Memories And White Supremacy

The "racial memories" of whites may also explain the white collective's overall DISREGARD for black suffering, police brutality against blacks, discrimination, even the loss of black life because it was not so long ago that blacks were considered property AND less than human.

There may be another (rarely discussed) explanation for the white collective's barely disguised glee toward black suffering:

Their OWN DNA-deep racial memories of the days when Africans enslaved their European ancestors.

Why Whites Loved The Movie "Precious" And Blacks Hated It

"Do you know how many thousands of years whites were dominated by Africans or people of African descent? I think they (whites) get some kind of abject pleasure from these pleading, lamentable scenarios of their Negroes of the sort of "Ha, ha, look at you now."

Do you realize the wealth that was seen as an African birthright in the old days? Europeans on average did not even eat fruit or taste the sweetness of sugar and their meats were salted or sour. Their growth was stunted on average and nutritional disorders were rampant. Infant mortality was through the roof. These conditions existed to the late 1500s.

And the Africans were tall and strong and they wore woven fabrics colorful with rich textures. Their meats were sweet and fruit was plentiful, and the African gold, there was no other metal so beautiful! This is not some kind of Black fantasy I'm talking about. This account is real and no one will contest the veracity, thereof. I guess for these reasons our pain is so sweet." -- D. B., historian

Recipe #4

Slave Traditions

"The clever combatant imposes his will on the enemy but does not allow the enemy's will to be imposed on him."

-- Sun Tzu, 'The Art of War' (544-496 BC)

CHAPTER 13

SLAVE TRADITIONS

What Are "Slave Traditions?"

A "tradition" is a set of behaviors and beliefs that are passed from one generation to the next. Traditions provide the tools to civilize (or uncivilize) a group of people, and establish order (or disorder).

The best traditions promote prosperity (economic survival), and build strong families (genetic survival). All human societies -- whether "primitive" or "advanced" -- are bound by TRADITIONS.

All human beings -- if given free choice -- will establish the kind of traditions that benefit their group. However, when a group's natural traditions are destroyed and new traditions are created by their enemies, the predictable end result is *disorder and chaos*.

After African slaves were forced to abandon their original (civilizing) traditions, they had to adapt to the unnatural, barbaric traditions of the slave-owners that were DESIGNED to keep them ENSLAVED.

The Ugly Words Blacks Use Against Blacks Are Slave Traditions

It is unheard of for a white person to insult another white person by saying, "...*with your white, ugly self*," OR for a Japanese person to say to another Japanese person, "...*with your Japanese, ugly self*," BUT it is very common to hear a black person say, "...*with your black, ugly self*" to another black person.

For some blacks the words -- "*black and ugly*" -- go together like "*snow and white*" even to the extent that one of the most popular "black" shows in television history -- Sandford and Son -- was built around blacks degrading the physical features and intelligence of other blacks. Why? **It's a SLAVE TRADITION.**

Blacks Mistreating Other Blacks Is A Slave Tradition

When slaves were tortured and killed for trying to protect each other, it is easy to understand why some blacks still feel it is UNNATURAL to trust, protect, OR cooperate with other blacks. **It's a SLAVE TRADITION.**

When black authority on the plantation represented slaves brutalizing other slaves (doing the slave-owner's dirty work), it is easy to understand why so many blacks still distrust "black authority" and are still fearful of "white authority." **It's a SLAVE TRADITION.**

When slaves were forced to witness the suffering of their loved ones and were helpless to stop it -- *which is still happening to blacks in the 21st century* -- it is easy to understand why some blacks today have become NUMB towards the suffering of other blacks. **It's a SLAVE TRADITION.**

Blacks Fearing Whites Is A Slave Tradition

After 500 years of BRUTALITY against slaves AND freed blacks in a white society where even the most impoverished white civil servant (a policeman or security guard) can take a black life (commit murder) without suffering any consequences, it is easy to understand why blacks still fear "white authority." **It's a SLAVE TRADITION.**

Blacks Appeasing And Pleasing Whites Is A Slave Tradition

When slaves were forced by white slave-owners to call other slaves "niggers," it's easy to understand why so many blacks today feel it is NATURAL to degrade other blacks in the presence of whites. **It's a SLAVE TRADITION.**

When slaves were forced to speak in broken English, and were forbidden to read or write to reassure whites they would remain intellectually inferior, it's easy to understand why blacks collectively are behind in the 500-year educational game compared to whites. **It's a SLAVE TRADITION.**

Black Dependency And Poverty Is A Slave Tradition

According to a 2010 study by Brandeis University in Massachusetts, the typical white family is five times richer than its black counterpart of the same class. The typical assets of black families averaged just $5,000, compared to white families who averaged $100,000.

In nearly every black community in the nation, blacks own a tiny minority of the businesses there. We are NOT only totally dependent on whites for all our necessities -- food, transportation, clothing, shelter, utilities, police and fire protection -- we are just as dependent on the non-white immigrants who have literally just stepped off the boat.

The majority of blacks in America are consumers NOT producers, and the vast majority of that majority see nothing wrong with that picture. In spite of the hard, cold evidence of Hurricane Katrina just five short years ago, too many blacks still believe white America will feed, house, and clothe its black population even in the event of an economic collapse. Why do we cling to this (obviously false) belief? **It's a SLAVE TRADITION.**

'Soul Food' Is A 'Slave Tradition'

"What yo' gwine do when de meat give out? What yo' gwine do when da meat give out? Set in de corner wid my lips pooched out! Lawsy!"
                                                    -- Lucinda Davis, former slave.

Slaves had two choices: to eat the parts of animals and plants that whites considered unfit for human consumption OR STARVE. They used their creativity and plenty of seasoning to create what is known today as "soul food." Due to its scarcity, food became a source of comfort for slaves.

When food is scarce, **it becomes a status symbol and a source of security** for those deprived of a plentiful supply. It is not surprising every occasion or celebration in the black community centers around excessive food consumption. Why? **It's a SLAVE TRADITION.**

Avoiding Emotional Intimacy Is A Slave Tradition

When the parents of slave children were unable to protect their children from predatory slave-owners, it is easy to understand why so many black parents today still feel they cannot protect their children from street or law enforcement predators. **It's a SLAVE TRADITION.**

When black males and females were forbidden to love each other, and lived with the daily terror that their loved ones could be sold to another plantation and never seen again, it is easy to understand why some blacks are still afraid of loving each other too much AND why it's so easy to "love" someone white because *we have no real emotional or spiritual attachment to them. It's a SLAVE TRADITION.*

Beating And Whipping Our Black Children Is A Slave Tradition

Black mothers (and fathers) beating and cursing their children in public is a common sight in many black communities. Slave mothers used to beat and curse their children in front of the slave-owner to prove their children needed no further punishment. Why do so many black parents today STILL feel it is in their children's best interests to abuse them? **It's a SLAVE TRADITION.**

Black Males NOT Supporting, Protecting, Or Giving Their Children Their Last Names Is A Slave Tradition

Black male slaves were not allowed to father OR claim their children. Why do some black males today **voluntarily** abandon their children, refuse to sign birth certificates, and "breed" children with multiple females they cannot support financially or emotionally? **It's a SLAVE TRADITION.**

Blacks Breeding With Whites To "Whiten" Their Offspring Is A SLAVE-OWNER'S TRADITION

When lighter-skinned slaves were treated better than dark-skinned slaves, it is understandable why some blacks favor lighter-skinned children. **It's a SLAVE-OWNER'S TRADITION.**

Believing The Topic Of Slavery Should Be Gone And Forgotten Is A SLAVE-OWNER'S TRADITION

Blacks who claim slavery has nothing to do with the present condition of black people today are practicing the SAME SLAVE TRADITIONS of those who claim blacks are "inferior" due to genetics, NOT because of 500 years of racist oppression. Why? **It's a SLAVE TRADITION.**

"So you call for the same God he calls for. When he's putting a rope around your neck, you call for God and he calls for God.

And you wonder why the one you call on never answers you."

-- Malcolm X (1925 - 1965)

Blacks Celebrating National Holidays That Promote White Supremacy Is A SLAVE-OWNER'S TRADITION

"Holidays" celebrate the heroes and traditions of a people. Almost every American holiday -- with the exception of Dr. King's birthday -- is founded on the promotion AND justification of white supremacy. Five examples:

1. *Christopher Columbus Day:* credits Europeans invaders for "discovering" a country that was ALREADY OCCUPIED by the original indigenous non-white population (what is known today as Native Americans).
2. *George Washington's birthday:* celebrates the birth of the first U.S. president -- who **OWNED African human beings**.
3. *Abraham Lincoln's birthday:* celebrates the 16th president as an emancipator of black slaves, when in reality, he believed blacks were inferior and should be treated as such. His family also OWNED SLAVES.
4. *Thanksgiving:* a time to give "thanks" was, in reality, a "celebration" of the bloody slaughter (genocide) of Native Americans by Europeans.
5. *Christmas:* marketed as a pseudo-religious holiday, when in fact, it is based on the MYTH that Jesus was born on December 25th, and is more about excessive materialism, courtesy of a *white* Santa Claus.

Most American holidays celebrate the enslavement, abuse, exploitation, and murder of non-white people. Why? It's a WHITE SUPREMACY TRADITION.

Blacks Who Practice The *Same* Religion Slave-Owners Taught Slaves DURING Slavery Are Practicing A Slave Tradition

Slave-owners used Christianity and the image of a white God and a white, blue-eyed Jesus to BRAINWASH slaves to believe they would displease God (aka the WHITE MAN) if they ran away OR rebelled against their enslavement. A slave-owner, in a speech given to his slaves, said:

"You are rebellious sinners. Your hearts are filled with all manners of evil. 'Tis the devil who tempts you. God is angry with you, and will surely punish you, if you don't forsake your wicked ways. Instead of serving your masters faithfully, which is pleasing in the sight of the your heavenly master, you are idle, and shirk your work. God sees you. You tell lies. God hears you.

Instead of engaging in worshipping him, you are hidden away somewhere feasting on your master's substance; tossing coffee-grounds with some wicked fortune teller, or cutting cards with another old hag. Your master may not find out, but God sees you, and he will punish you!" (SOURCE: "Incidents in the life of a slave girl").

Murdering Blacks Is An American Slave Tradition

In the book, *'Without Sanctuary,'* author James Allen presents an extraordinary (and revealing) collection of photographs and postcards that were kept **as souvenirs** at the lynchings of black men, women, and children -- **as young as 10 years old** -- by murderous white mobs.

Lynching of Redmond, Roberson and Addison

Black woman lynched (1911)

Black man lynched (1889)

Ruben Stacy Lynched

William Brown Lynched and Burned

Lynching of Jesse Washington

"Nationally, homicide is the leading cause of death for black young men ages 10-24, and the second leading cause of death for black women ages 15-24." -- Black On Black Crime Coalition, www. hhscenter.org

Role Call: A Very Short List Of Murder-By-Cop Victims

The long list of UNARMED BLACK MALES AND FEMALES includes LaTanya Haggerty, Donta Dawson, Michael Byoune, Moses DeJesus, Robert Russ, Joseph Gould, Tyisha Miller, Amadou Diallo, Kathryn Johnston, Sean Bell, and Oscar Grant.

This very short, very incomplete list of potentially tens of thousands of black victims leads to an important question: *Why do so many blacks -- especially young black males -- believe their lives and the lives of other black people have so little value?*

Because Murdering Blacks Is An American Tradition

It is **well past time** for the descendants of slaves to abandon the "slave traditions" that celebrate the slaughter and enslavement of our ancestors and other non-white people, and RE-CREATE the kind of historically and morally correct traditions that reflect KNOWLEDGE OF AND RESPECT FOR SELF.

Strange Fruit

Southern trees bear a strange fruit,
Blood on the leaves and blood at the root,
Black body swinging in the Southern breeze,
Strange fruit hanging from the poplar trees.

Pastoral scene of the gallant South,
The bulging eyes and the twisted mouth,
Scent of magnolia sweet and fresh,
And the sudden smell of burning flesh!

Here is a fruit for the crows to pluck,
For the rain to gather, for the wind to suck,
For the sun to rot, for a tree to drop,
Here is a strange and bitter crop.

Lewis Allen (1939)

Recipe #5

The Secret Shame of Slavery

"To accept one's past – one's history – is not the same thing as drowning in it; it is learning how to use it. An invented past can never be used; it cracks and crumbles under the pressures of life like clay in a season of drought."
— *James Baldwin (1924-1987)*

CHAPTER 14

THE (SECRET) SHAME OF SLAVERY

The Hollywood Myth Of The "Childlike, Happy Slave"

Why did Hollywood films during the early-to-mid 1900s portray blacks as savage, stupid, cowardly, lazy, and less-than-human beings? ***To justify the LIE that blacks were not intelligent or deserving enough to be free from slavery and racist oppression.***

"I was raised in Chicago but spent my summers with relatives in Missis-sippi. One of my uncles would drive up to Chicago and pick me and my brothers and sisters up in a big white Cadillac! My momma always fixed us a big shopping bag of fried chicken, potato salad, and chips, and an ice cooler filled with pop for the road.

I was too young and ignorant to know why we had to take enough food for a whole day, or why we had to pee in the bushes by the road. I didn't know blacks couldn't eat in restaurants or use public bathrooms in the South. When my uncle took us to the movies, we sat in the balcony and the whites sat downstairs, but I was afraid to ask why, like I knew it would embarass my uncle.

We didn't talk about those things in those days, or maybe the adults talked about it when we wasn't around. Maybe they was too ashamed to let us kids know how bad the whites treated them and how much shit they took off them.

I think this has a lot to do with why blacks avoid our history. Nobody wants to admit their people were slaves, and didn't or couldn't do anything about it. Maybe, we were afraid we let white people make fools of us because we really were inferior." -- Samuel, 63, postal worker

For Samuel's sake -- and for all the countless black children and adults who grew up being ashamed of our tragic past -- we'd like to set the record straight:

FACT #1: Slaves Were NOT Docile, "Happy," Or Submissive

Some slaves submitted to the daily brutality of slavery, but there were many others who REFUSED to bend or break under the lash of the overseer's whip. Some slaves poisoned their slave-owners with arsenic and ground up glass. Some attacked slave-owners with axes, knives, and anything that could be used as a weapon. Some burned down houses, and destroyed livestock and crops.

SLAVES RESIST!

Excerpt From The Black Chronicle article (published in 1831)

Slaves are not happy, docile servants. In the manner of livestock, they are usually worked unmercifully, then kept in huts or shackles until their service is required again. But despite their suffering and deprivation, these human beings resist, and resist daily.

Black Chronicle is fortunate to have spoken with several escaped slaves. They expressed deep resentment for their "masters," the men who reaped the benefits of their work.

To resist, we were told, slaves will do almost anything. Planters report losing over half their tobacco crops because their slaves slow down during the best picking seasons.

When worked beyond endurance, slaves often flee to the swamps, returning when their demands for better conditions are met. Occasionally, they simply refuse to work.

"In working niggers," one plantation owner has said, "we always calculate that they will never labor at all, except to avoid punishment, and they will never do more than 'just enough' to save themselves from being punished."

We were told that black overseers do not even attempt to stop slaves from destroying their "master's" property. They let cattle wander in fields of ripe crops, leave gates open so animals can escape, and destroy tools as rapidly as they are replaced.

Slaves sometimes injure themselves rather than obey the man who calls himself their owner. In the greatest act of resistance, some slaves commit suicide and others kill members of their family.

"I had 13 children," boasted one black woman. "Every one I destroyed with my own hands rather than have them suffer slavery."

Slaveholders know that such frustration could lead to their destruction. "The least unusual noise at night alarms them greatly," said one slave. "They cry out, What is that? Are the boys all in?"

"The above is intended to represent the horrid Massacre of the Whites in Florida in December 1835. Near 400, including women and children fell victim to the barbarity of the Negroes and Indians." (text excerpted from a 1835 newspaper article)

$100 REWARD !

Ranaway from Richards' Ferry, Culpeper County, Va., 23rd instant, ABRAM, who is about 30 years old, 5 feet from 8 to 10 inches high, and weighs from 175 to 180. His complexion is dark, though not black, and hair long for a negro. He is a very shrewd fellow, and there is reason to believe he is attempting to get to a free State. I will give the above Reward if taken out of Virginia—$50 if taken 20 miles from home, or $20 if taken in the neighborhood. WM. T. J. RICHARDS, *Adm'r of Jas. Richards, Dec'd.*
Sept. 24.

Harriet Tubman (far right in white) with rescued slaves

"There was one of two things I had a right to, liberty, or death; if I could not have one, I would have the other; for no man should take me alive.

I should fight for my liberty as long as my strength lasted, and when the time came for me to go, the Lord would let them take me."
-- Harriet Tubman, an escaped slave who was active in the Underground Railroad and risked her life and freedom to lead many other slaves to freedom. (1820-1913)

An 1895 photograph of Harriet Tubman. The scar from her childhood head injury is still visible.

FACT #2: Slaveowners Lived In Constant Fear Of Their Slaves

Slaveowners in the South lived in constant fear of runaway slaves, property and crop damage, sabotage, slave rebellions, and of being attacked or murdered in their sleep. Some slaves refused to bow, smile, be subservient or submissive. Others resorted to work slowdowns; committed suicide, and thousands ran away each year.

"They did this so often that it is nothing short of amazing that the myth of the docile Negro persists." -- writes Lerone Bennett Jr. in 'Before the Mayflower: A History of the Negro in America 1619-1964.' *"They poisoned masters and mistresses with arsenic, ground glass, and spiders beaten up in buttermilk. They chopped them [slaveholders] to pieces with axes and burned their houses, gins and barns to the ground."*

Contrary to the racist Hollywood myth of the happy-go-lucky slave who was content with his (or her) "circumstances," thousands of slaves resisted and fought back against their enslavement!

Historian Herbert Aptheker calculated over 200 separate slave revolts took place between the 1600s to 1865. That's comes to approximately one revolt per year -- proof that slaves violently resisted their enslavement.

THREE HUNDRED DOLLARS REWARD.

RANAWAY from the subscriber on Monday the 17th ult., three negroes, named as follows: HARRY, aged about 19 years, has on one side of his neck a wen, just under the ear, he is of a dark chestnut color, about 5 feet 8 or 9 inches hight; BEN, aged aged about 25 years, is very quick to speak when spoken to, he is of a chestnut color, about six feet high; MINTY, aged about 27 years, is of a chestnut color, fine looking, and about 5 feet high. One hundred dollars reward will be given for each of the above named negroes, if taken out of the State, and $50 each if taken in the State. They must be lodged in Baltimore, Easton or Cambridge Jail, in Maryland.

ELIZA ANN BRODESS.

Near Bucktown, Dorchester county, Md. Oct. 3d, 1849.

☞ The Delaware Gazette will please copy the above three weeks, and charge this office.

Nat Turner Slave Rebellion

Discovery of Nat Turner

Nat Turner's Slave Rebellion (1831)
(an actual recount by the Anglo-African Magazine, Dec 1859, New York)

Nat Turner attacked Virginia from within, with six men, and with the determination to spare no life until his power was established. We must pass over the details of horror, as they occurred during the next twenty-four hours. Swift and stealthy as Indians, the black men passed from house to house -- not pausing, not hesitating, as their terrible work went on.

In one thing they were humaner than Indians, or than white men fighting against Indians: there was no gratuitous outrage beyond the death-blow itself, no insult, no mutilation; but in every house they entered, that blow fell on man, woman, and child -- nothing that had a white skin was spared.

From every house they took arms and ammunition, and from a few money. On every plantation they found recruits: those dusky slaves, so obsequious to their master the day before, so prompt to sing and dance before his Northern visitors, were all swift to transform themselves into fiends of retribution now; show them sword or musket, and they grasped it, though it were an heirloom from Washington himself.

The troop increased from house to house -- first to fifteen, then to forty, then to sixty. Some were armed with muskets, some with axes, some with scythes, some came on their masters' horses. As the numbers increased, they could be divided, and the awful work was carried on more rapidly still. The plan then was for an advanced guard of horsemen to approach each house at a gallop, and surround it till the others came up.

The outbreak lasted for but forty-eight hours; but, during that period, fifty-five whites were slain, without the loss of a single slave. These negroes had been systematically brutalized from childhood; they had been allowed no legalized or permanent marriage; they had beheld around them an habitual licentiousness, such as can scarcely exist except under slavery; some of them had seen their wives and sisters habitually polluted by the husbands and the brothers of these fair white women who were now absolutely in their power.

Yet I have looked through the Virginia newspapers of that time in vain for one charge of an indecent outrage on a woman against these triumphant and terrible slaves. Wherever they went, there went death, and that was all. Mrs. Stowe's picture of Dred's purposes is then precisely typical of his: "Whom the Lord saith unto us, 'Smite,' them will we smite. We will not torment them with the scourge and fire, nor defile their women as they have done with ours. But we will slay them utterly, and consume them from off the face of the earth."

"True Stories" Hollywood Will Never Tell
A (Very) Short List of Slave Rebellions

1663 -- First major slave revolt

1712 -- New York slave revolt (9 whites killed)

1730 -- Norfolk, VA slave revolt

1733 -- St. John Slave Revolt

1739 -- Stono Rebellion in South Carolina (25 whites killed)

1741 -- New York City slave revolt

1760 -- Tacky's War (Jamaica)

1773 -- Slaves in Massachusetts petitioned legislature for freedom

1791 -- Slave revolts in Haiti led to the Haitian Revolution

1800 -- Prosser Slave Revolt, led by Gabriel Prosser and 1,000 slaves

1805 -- Chatham Manor, Virginia

1811 -- Louisiana slave revolt was the largest slave revolt in US history

1815 -- George Boxley, Virginia

1816 -- 300 slaves took over Fort Blount until US troops attacked

1822 -- Denmark Vesey slave revolt involved thousands of slaves

1829 -- Slave revolt in Cincinnati, Ohio

1831 -- Nat Turner slave revolt (over 60 whites killed) An insurrection has broken out in Southampton. By the last accounts, there were 60 whites killed and the militia was retreating. It was reported that 300 militia were retreating before 600-800 rebels, Southampton, VA

1835-- Black Seminole Slave Rebellion

1839 -- Amistad slave revolt/mutiny

1841 -- Slaves overpowered crew on slave ship "Creole" and sailed to the Bahamas where they were granted asylum (freedom)

1842 -- Slave Revolt in the Cherokee Nation

1849 -- Harriet Tubman's escape from slavery. She returned to South 19 more times and freed 300 slaves.

1857 -- Escaped slaves Fight Pursuers. 12 fleeing slave fugitives surprised their ten pursuers by turning on them and waging a furious battle. When the slave hunters retreated to plan another attack, the slaves ran into the forest. This is the third confrontation in Chester, Penn. in recent months. (March 5, 1857)

1859 -- John Brown, along with 5 slaves and 13 whites led a slave revolt.

FACT #3: Over ONE MILLION European Christians were enslaved by North African (black) Muslims between 1530 and 1780, according to a new study by Robert Davis, a professor of history at Ohio State University.

Apparently, black people aren't the ONLY people stamped with the "shame of slavery."

"Blessed are those who struggle
Oppression is worse than the grave
It's better to die for a noble cause
Than to live and die a slave."

— The Last Poets

Recipe #6

The Post Traumatic Slavery Syndrome

"When the white Columbine kids got killed, the whole country felt sorry for them. Black kids get killed every day and nobody cares. The only time we get any attention is when we mess up. Nobody asks us if we are messed up because of all the killings we seen, they just lock us up and throw away the key." -- Jamal, 17, Chicago

"Over 605 black children have been shot and/or killed in Chicago from 2007 to 2009 — more than the total number of soldiers from Illinois who have died in the Iraq or Afghanistan wars COMBINED." -- Phillip Jackson, The Black Star Project, Chicago, IL (2009)

CHAPTER 15

BUILDING THE CASE FOR THE "POST TRAUMATIC SLAVERY SYNDROME" (PTSS)

"To understand the present, you must embrace your past." -- Umoja

Post Traumatic Stress Disorders Are Not New

Webster's Dictionary defines the *"Post Traumatic Stress Disorder"* as a psychological reaction that occurs after a highly stressful event, like witnessing a murder or being the victim of a violent crime. The term, *Post Traumatic Stress Disorder (PTSD),* is so widely accepted by the medical and psychiatric community that it has become a household name.

The medical community and the entire nation empathized with the survivors of youth-related tragedies like the Columbine (1999) and Virginia Tech (2008) shootings, because they recognize that ONE TRAUMATIC EVENT can permanently damage an individual. Researchers found even a minor trauma, like getting stuck in an elevator, created PTSD symptoms in some white college students.

Post Traumatic Stress Disorders Can Affect The Offspring Of The Survivors

According to an article by the American Academy of Experts in Traumatic Stress (AAETS), www.aaets.org, the emotional wounds of Jewish Holocaust survivors may have *"seeped into the psyches of many of their children."*

The article also stated that the children of Holocaust survivors were at greater risk for depression, anxiety, and PTSD symptoms because of their exposure to **their traumatized parents**. Another study in 1998 found that the children of Holocaust survivors reported *"Holocaust-related thoughts and images as their primary traumas."*

The total lack of interest by the mainstream media, law enforcement, and the white collective in general in the almost daily murders of black children in America may explain their callous dismissal of the **"Post Traumatic Slavery Syndrome"** (PTSS), and why this term cannot be found in any Webster's dictionary.

In this chapter, the authors will attempt to do what the mainstream media, the medical/psychiatric communities, and the guardians of Webster's dictionary refuse to do: *acknowledge the Post Traumatic Slavery Syndrome as a LEGITIMATE DISORDER, and demonstrate how PTSS is the SINGLE BIGGEST CAUSE of BLACK GENDER WARS between the black male and female.*

"We are still slaves. The chains are inside us now. They turn our spirits mean, our hearts into metallic chambers...They render our memories empty, our vision short, our song coarse, our fathers broken, our mothers bereaved."

-- Randall Robinson, author of 'The Reckoning."

CHAPTER 16

THE POST TRAUMATIC SLAVERY SYNDROME (PTSS) IS THE FOUNDATION FOR TODAY'S BLACK GENDER WARS

Let's begin at the beginning by defining the "Post Traumatic Slavery Syndrome."

Q: What is the Post Traumatic Slavery Syndrome (PTSS)?
A: PTSS is the psychological TRAUMA of the **Transatlantic Slave Trade,** and 150 YEARS of post-slavery racism.

Q: What is the 'Transatlantic Slave Trade?'
A: *"Transatlantic"* refers to the transport of African slaves via the Atlantic Ocean from Africa to North America, Europe, Brazil, and the Caribbean.

Q: If slavery has existed since the beginning of time, what makes American slavery so different?
A: Prior to the TransAtlantic Slave Trade, slavery had NEVER involved the *deliberate psychological destruction* of the slaves.

We know this happened to African slaves in America because there are *historical documents, photographs, audio recordings, and living witnesses who told their stories before they died.*

Q: Isn't Post Traumatic Slavery Syndrome just an excuse so blacks can avoid taking responsibility for their present condition?
A: The descendants of slaves -- who are still oppressed by modern-day racism -- DO NOT have to make ANY excuses for being victims anymore than a rape victim has to make excuses for being raped over and over.

The RAPIST is always responsible for his crime, regardless of how "easy" or how "hard" the victim or victims fought back.

Q: Isn't it disrespectful to Jews to use the word "Holocaust" to describe the Transatlantic Slave Trade?
A: The Jewish Holocaust lasted 12 years (from 1933 to 1945). The African Holocaust lasted over 400 years (from approximately 1441 to 1865). *The answer should be obvious.*

Q: Doesn't teaching slavery teach blacks to hate whites?
A: When Jews teach their children (and the world) about the Jewish Holocaust, are they accused of teaching hate? Not only do blacks have the RIGHT to teach our children (and the rest of the world) about OUR African Holocaust; *we have an obligation.*

It is NOT the history of slavery that creates racial animosity toward whites; *it's the lack of respect for that history.* It is the unwillingness of the white collective to admit slavery was a crime against humanity, and their refusal to acknowledge the wealth that black labor contributed to America. Most of all, it is the CONTINUATION of racism/white supremacy 150 years after slavery that creates the MOST racial animosity toward whites. Until the victims are made whole, whites will continue to be on the defensive (and in denial), and (conscious) blacks will continue to be OFFENDED.

Q: Why should whites who never owned any slaves be held accountable for something that happened over 100 years ago?
A: It doesn't MATTER if the ancestors of a few, some, or all whites owned slaves. ALL whites have benefited from a white supremacy system that was built on the backs of millions of African slaves who contributed 400 years of FREE LABOR. Even whites who did NOT own slaves still PARTICIPATED in the oppression of blacks via the economic, educational, and employment discrimination that started during slavery and continues to this day.

Q: Why don't blacks blame the African chiefs who sold their ancestors into slavery?
A: (1) African chiefs DID NOT SHIP ONE AFRICAN OUT OF AFRICA. (2) Africans did not own the ships that sailed to America. (3) Africans did not benefit from 400 years of FREE labor. (4) African slave labor did NOT make Africa one of the RICHEST nations on earth. (5) the ones who profited the MOST, and did the most psychological damage are the MOST TO BLAME -- not the African chiefs who sold the losers of their tribal wars.

Q: Is Post Traumatic Slavery Syndrome a ploy to get reparations by making whites feel guilty?
A: It is MORE important to repair the bond between the black male and female than it is to induce "white guilt." Guilt is non-productive for the victims of racism because it rarely results in a change of behavior of those who benefited from the injustice. In fact, too much guilt actually increases resentment and the tendency to justify one's behavior rather than correct it.

Q: Why should whites recognize PTSS if they do not benefit?
A: Whenever a group commits a great injustice against another group, and sincerely make AMENDS for their crimes, they make the world safer for everyone -- including themselves. However, when a group commits an injustice BUT refuses to acknowledge it OR make amends, they LOSE their humanity and put themselves, their group, and their nation *at great spiritual risk.*

Q: What about the immigrants who faced ethnic discrimination when they came to America? Do they deserve reparations?

A: Comparing immigrants who came to America VOLUNTARILY with slaves who were KIDNAPPED and ENSLAVED for 400 years is as LOGICAL as comparing an apple to an elephant.

However, if any immigrant group feels their experience is equivalent to 400 YEARS OF SLAVERY, let them PRESENT THEIR HISTORICAL EVIDENCE, in the form of documents, photos, audio recordings, witnesses, slave journals, etc -- to back up their claims. If they CANNOT present **any historical evidence** then the following statements are logical and true:

1. NO OTHER ETHNIC GROUP -- including immigrants -- was brought to America chained together in the holds of slave ships.

2. NO OTHER ETHNIC GROUP in America -- including immigrants -- was raped, lynched, burned, tortured, dismembered, and murdered for SPORT and for PROFIT for 400 years.

3. NO OTHER ETHNIC GROUP in America -- including immigrants -- was stripped of their religion, culture, language, identity, and history.

4. NO OTHER ETHNIC GROUP in America -- including immigrants -- stood naked on slave auction blocks to determine their "market value."

5. NO OTHER ETHNIC GROUP in America -- including immigrants -- contributed 400 years of free labor and *received nothing in return.*

6. **NO OTHER ETHNIC GROUP in America lost 12 MILLION SOULS in a Transatlantic Slave Trade.**

Comparing Slaves With Immigrants

Cultural "Assets"	Descendants of Slaves	Immigrants
Identity	Destroyed	Intact
Language	Destroyed	Intact
Religion	Destroyed	Intact
Customs	Destroyed	Intact
Family Structure	Destroyed	Intact
History/Family Tree/Origin	Destroyed	Intact

Q: What about all the government "reparations" for blacks, like welfare, food stamps, and affirmative action?

A: Social services are NOT reparations. Whites receive the vast majority of benefits from all government entitlement programs like welfare, food stamps, college grants, social security, Medicare, farm subsidies (to big farmers), bank bailouts, and huge tax breaks for corporations (corporate welfare).

Most blacks (like most non-blacks) work and pay taxes. Blacks have fought in EVERY WAR America has ever fought, from the Revolutionary War to Iraq and Afghanistan -- even while being denied our basic human rights. Despite the long history of slavery, service, and sacrifice to America, blacks are STILL accused of getting a free ride at the (white) taxpayers' expense.

Some Americans are more outraged over the tiny monthly sum poor black women and children receive than they are about the (white-owned) multinational corporations that pay ZERO income taxes, and ship American jobs overseas.

Even if some blacks receive welfare that has NOTHING to do with reparations for 400 YEARS of FREE LABOR, anymore than US "aid" to Israel wipes out the demands for reparations for the Jewish Holocaust.

Q: What about all the progress blacks have made in America? Doesn't that contradict the existence of PTSS?
A: Whatever "progress" blacks have made in America, it was HARD WON. The TRUE LACK of "progress" can be easily seen in the GROWING inequality between blacks and whites. According to a new study by Brandeis University in May 2010, the typical white family is *five times richer* than its black counterpart of the same class. Tom Shapiro, one of the authors of the report stated:

> *"...there are greater opportunities and less challenges for low and moderate income families if they're white in comparison to if they're African-American or Hispanic."*

This study reveals the HIGH FINANCIAL COST of integration on the economic UN-development of black people: *"...wealth among the highest-income African-Americans has actually fallen in recent years...while among white counterparts of similar class and income it has surged..."*

> *"The gap between Black and white household wealth quadrupled from 1984 to 2007, totally discrediting the conventional wisdom that the U.S. is slowly and fitfully moving towards racial equality, or some rough economic parity between the races.*
>
> *Like most American myths, it's the direct opposite of the truth. When measured over decades, Blacks are being propelled economically downward relative to whites at quickening speed, according to a new study by Brandeis University." -- www.blackagendareport.com*

Q: Does PTSS explain why blacks are so inferior?
A: There's a huge difference between being in an **INFERIOR POSITION and being INFERIOR.** It is illogical to think or to expect black people, collectively, to be "equal" to whites after we were denied equal educational, social, economic, and political opportunities for over 500 years.

Q: Isn't this black generation a little too far removed to be able to attribute our behaviors to slavery? To segregation, racism, socioeconomic disparities, of course, but I can't even trace an ancestor who had a master." -- black female college student, 21

A: That's correct to an extent. Slavery ALONE is NOT responsible for the condition of blacks today. It was the massive damage of slavery COMBINED with the massive damage from 150 years of racist oppression that are responsible for the conditions of blacks today.

It is illogical (and self-defeating) to minimize 400 years of slavery and only focus on the 150 years after slavery. Slavery laid the FOUNDATION for mass black dysfunction but was NOT totally responsible for the end result. If blacks were TRULY inferior, why was new legislation needed to HALT BLACK PROGRESS? The answers should be OBVIOUS.

Q: Does the "Post Traumatic Slavery Syndrome" mean black people are permanently damaged?"
A: No, but it is impossible for blacks to fully recover from PTSS in a black-hating, white supremacist society, just as it is impossible to recover from tuberculosis if you are trapped inside a TB ward and constantly re-infected.

Q: Is there a "cure" for PTSS? If so, what is it?
A: There are *ONLY two permanent cures for PTSS*

1. the total elimination of racism/white supremacy from the planet.

2. for blacks to separate *completely* from the white supremacist culture, "white values," *and white people.* Once black people have been returned to an environment and culture where it is normal AND desirable to be black, our natural African instincts BURIED UNDER 500 YEARS OF WHITE SUPREMACY PROGRAMMING will return.

Q: If "PTSS" is a legitimate psychological disorder, why doesn't the medical and psychiatric community recognize it as such?
A: There are four possible reasons:

1. The American the medical/psychiatric community is a REFLECTION and an EXTENSION of the white supremacy system.

2. 400 years of FREE SLAVE LABOR would qualify MILLIONS OF BLACK DESCENDANTS for **massive reparations** from America and Europe, since BOTH nations participated in AND profited greatly from slavery.

3. Acknowledging PTSS as a legitimate syndrome would remove the stigma (lie) of BLACK INFERIORITY from the descendants of slaves; and would CORRECTLY place the majority of the blame for mass black dysfunction where it rightfully belongs: *on the white supremacy system.* However, in a white supremacy system, this "admission" would be intolerable and completely unacceptable.

4. Recognizing PTSS as a legitimate disorder would make it OFFICIAL that slavery was *a massive crime against humanity*; and it would PUBLICLY IDENTIFY the criminals who COMMITTED those crimes, and WHO is obligated to pay for those CRIMES. It would also establish ONE more indisputable FACT: *That most of America's and Europe's wealth came from 400 YEARS of AFRICAN SLAVE LABOR.*

Q: How should blacks respond when the Post Traumatic Slavery Syndrome is ridiculed or dismissed?
A: By NOT wasting our precious time and energy trying to convince anyone of what we KNOW TO BE TRUE: that 500 years of repeated trauma has damaged our entire race. What is MORE important *is understanding how PTSS still affects blacks 150 YEARS AFTER slavery "officially" ended.*

Once we understand what the Post Traumatic Slavery Syndrome is, and how it is STILL affects our thinking and behavior, we can take *corrective actions to neutralize its effects.*

We DO NOT NEED PERMISSION OR APPROVAL to break the financial and psychological chains of slavery. *It is time to STOP asking for it.*

The Victims should NEVER make the feelings of their Victimizers a priority – or even a CONSIDERATION.

Q: The Post Traumatic Slavery Syndrome sounds so doom and gloom. Are there any positive lessons to be learned from it?
A: Absolutely! Enslaved Africans SURVIVED the WORST that mankind and womankind could conceive, *and their descendants are STILL STANDING.*

The list of accomplishments by black inventors, scientists, surgeons, scholars, and builders is too long for one book, so we will not attempt to list them here.

That being said, the survival skills developed during slavery are the SAME survival skills many blacks draw upon today to overcome racism and poverty. By learning the lessons from our past, we CAN rebuild the black male/black female relationship and will be able to say -- with confidence:

Never again!

CHAPTER 17

PTSS AND 'THE STOCKHOLM SYNDROME'

"We (blacks) just can't get enough of them (whites). It's the Stockholm Syndrome. We love people who are over you and put you down, it's some sort of freaky love. It's something innate inside of us that makes us want to forgive." -- Paul Mooney

The '**Stockholm Syndrome'** was coined by criminologist Nils Bejerot, after the 1973 Norrmalmstorg robbery in Stockholm, in which several bank robbers held four bank employees hostage for six days (August 23 to August 28, 1973).

By the time the victims were freed from their six-day ordeal, they had become so emotionally attached to their victimizers, they were defending them. According to Bejerot, the **Stockholm Syndrome** is more likely to develop when the captives are in a situation where their captors have complete control over their basic needs for survival and whether they live or die.

The Psychological Effects Of Stockholm Syndrome On Its Victims

1. Once the captives are isolated from the outside world, they will become totally dependent on their captors for their basic survival needs. The captives will develop a sense of gratitude toward their captors for ALLOWING THEM TO LIVE, and will begin to view their world (and their reality) from the captors' perspective.

2. The captors may occasionally use violence to prove they can kill the captives any time they choose, thus persuading the captives that it is safer to endure captivity than to resist and risk serious injury or death. However, the captors know excessive cruelty will make their captives hate them and rebel against them, so the most cunning captors perform occasional acts of kindness to encourage their Victims to focus on their "good side."

3. Once the captives believe their captors are their benefactors (the good guys), they will develop a sense of LOYALTY that is stronger than their loyalty to other captives -- or even themselves. The survival instinct makes the captives reluctant to hate or even dislike their captors because *they are too dependent on them.*

A Recent Example of Stockholm Syndrome

In 1991, 11-year-old Jaycee Lee Dugard was kidnapped, raped, and held captive for 18 years by Phillip Garrido. In 2009, when the parole officer of her abductor became suspicious, Dugard tried to PROTECT her ABDUCTOR by posing as a battered wife hiding from an abusive husband instead of revealing her identity and obtaining her freedom. Her description of her rapist/kidnapper? *"A great person who was good with her kids."*

The Most Profound And Overlooked Example Of Stockholm Syndrome: The 400-Year TransAtlantic Slave Trade

1. Once the slaves are isolated from the outside world, they will become totally dependent on slave-owners for their basic survival needs. The slaves will develop a sense of gratitude toward the slave-owners for ALLOWING THEM TO LIVE, and will begin to view the world (and their reality) from the slave-owners' perspective.

2. Slave-owners occasionally use violence to prove they can kill the slaves any time they choose, thus persuading slaves that it is safer to endure captivity than resist and risk serious injury or death. However, the slave-owners know excessive cruelty will make their slaves hate them and rebel against them, so the most cunning slave-owners perform occasional acts of kindness to encourage their slaves to focus on their "good side."

3. Once the slaves believe their slave-owners are their benefactors (the good guys), they will develop a sense of LOYALTY that is stronger than their loyalty to other slaves -- or even to themselves. FEAR and the instinct for SURVIVAL makes the slaves reluctant to hate or even dislike the slave-owners because **they are too dependent on them.**

4. Even 150 years after slavery, many blacks (secretly) view the small privileges we receive -- like getting service with a smile at a white-owned restaurant or store; or being able to sit next to whites on a bus, train, or airplane -- as a "kindness" rather than a HUMAN RIGHT.

   As long as blacks receive the smallest courtesies, we are MORE LIKELY to overlook the more devastating (and more telling) acts of cruelty and racism that are being committed against black people on a daily basis, including employment and housing discrimination, inferior schools, predatory lending, incarceration, police brutality, and "entertainment terrorism" against blacks.

5. If four bank employees in Stockholm, Sweden can be psychologically traumatized after a six-day ordeal, it is LOGICAL to assume that a black human being who is TRAUMATIZED by racism from cradle to grave is by BIRTHRIGHT *a lifetime candidate for the Stockholm Syndrome.*

CHAPTER 18

PTSS AND 'LEARNED HELPLESSNESS'

The Martin Seligman Experiment (1967)

Martin Seligman, an American psychologist and a world-renowned authority on abnormal psychology, made an unexpected discovery while he was conducting experiments on depression. These experiments led to **the "Theory of Learned Helplessness,"** which refers to a human being (or an animal) who is conditioned to think he cannot change his circumstances even when the opportunity presents itself.

The Learned Helplessness Experiment: Part One

Three groups of dogs were placed in identical harnesses. **Group 1 dogs** were released after being restrained for a set period of time. **Group 2 and Group 3 dogs** were yoked together in pairs. The **Group 2 dogs** were given an electric shock, which the dogs could stop by pressing a lever. The **Group 3 dogs** received an identical shock but could not stop the shock even if they pressed the lever.

The **Group 1** and **Group 2 dogs** recovered from the experience. The **Group 3 dogs** had already "learned" that ending the shocks was out of their control, and as a result, became depressed, hopeless, and *"helpless."*

The Learned Helplessness Experiment: Part Two

The same three groups of dogs were put into a box-like apparatus. The dogs could escape the electric shocks by jumping over a low partition. The **Group 1 and Group 2 dogs** escaped the shocks, but the **Group 3 dogs** that had "learned" previously that nothing they did would stop the pain *lay down and whined.* Even though **Group 3 dogs** could have followed the examples of **Group 1** and **2 dogs** and escaped, they had been CONDITIONED to feel so "helpless," *they didn't try.*

The lesson: If a person has been repeatedly abused and have tried and failed to stop the abuse, he or she will become demoralized, numb, apathetic, depressed, and HELPLESS.

The best example of "learned helplessness" in a human population are the descendants of African slaves. After 500 years of slavery and oppression many blacks deep down believe that no matter how hard they try they cannot eliminate the "pain" of racism -- and eventually "learn" to FUNCTION as a "helpless" population.

The good news: One-third of the **Group 3 dogs** eventually escaped the shocks -- PROOF that it is possible to UNLEARN the syndrome of "learned helplessness" *and release ourselves from our paralyzed condition.*

Recipe #7

Racism/ White Supremacy

127

"If you do not understand White Supremacy (Racism), what it is, and how it works, everything else that you understand, will only confuse you."

Neely Fuller, Jr. (1971)

CHAPTER 19

WHAT IS RACISM/WHITE SUPREMACY?

"Racism is white supremacy. White supremacy is racism. There is no other form." -- Neely Fuller, Jr.

Let's Begin At The Beginning By Defining The Words:

1. **White Supremacy** -- a social, economic, and political system based on the belief that whites are superior to non-whites. (the Foundation).
2. **Racism** -- the systematic discrimination (the denial of rights and benefits) by whites against non-whites in all areas of human activity: (1) economics, (2) education, (3) entertainment, (4) labor, (5) law, (6) politics, (7) religion, (8) sex, and (9) war. (the Behavior).

Q: Why is it called "Racism/White Supremacy?"
A: Because this describes exactly WHO is practicing racism. For one group to practice racism that group must have MORE POWER than another group. Since whites control **ALL** the major areas of human activity in America -- housing, education, health, entertainment, economics, politics, law, and religion -- it is accurate to define all "**racism**" as "**white supremacy.**" We must be accurate so the victims of racism do not become confused.

Q: Isn't all racism the same, regardless of who is practicing it?
A: There is only ONE kind of racism: **white supremacy**. White people are the only group in America with the POWER to discriminate (deprive or punish other ethnic groups), and the systems and institutions to maintain the imbalance of power.

For example, rich people are more powerful than poor people. Rich people have the POWER to discriminate against poor people by depriving them of income, promotions, jobs, housing, land, justice, and any other rights – if they choose to do so.

In America, whites have the POWER to discriminate against blacks (and other non-whites) by depriving them of income, promotions, jobs, housing, land, justice, and any other rights – if they choose to do so. It doesn't matter that some whites are poorer than some blacks.

In all things and in all places in America, whites are **collectively** more powerful than blacks are **collectively**. This imbalance of (white) power creates the opportunity and the ability to practice racism against non-whites.

Racism is not empty rhetoric (words) or mindless emotion. Racism is economic, political, institutional, and systematic POWER. Since whites control all the institutions and systems of power in America, only whites have the power to practice racism.

Q: Why are people referred to as "groups" instead of "races?"
A: Because there is ONLY ONE RACE: *the white race.* To prove this statement, let's look at the TRUE meaning of "race." In ancient civilizations tens of thousands of years ago (before Europeans inhabited the planet), the world's people identified themselves by bloodline, birthplace, and culture – but NEVER by the artificial construct (concept) of "race."

What is the "black race" in real terms? It does NOT describe the place where black people were born because there is no such place as "black land," (or red, yellow, brown, or white land). Race does not describe a person's religion because there is no such thing as a black, red, brown, yellow, or white religion.

Race does not describe a person's culture (except in false, stereotypical terms), and it does NOT define biology, ethnicity, or nationality. Race does not describe skin color because the so-called "black race" includes people whose complexions range from the palest pink to the purest blue-black. Therefore, "race" is a false, manmade concept.

Q: If "race" is a false concept, why was it created?
A: Race was created for ONLY one purpose: *to practice race-ism* (*racism*). To practice "racism," whites had to separate themselves from other groups of people by artificially creating different "races."

Q: Why was "racism/white supremacy" created?
A: Dr. Frances Cress Welsing, a black psychiatrist and the author of *'The Isis Papers: The Keys to the Colors'* (1991), states that White Supremacy is practiced by the global "white" minority on the conscious and unconscious level to ensure their genetic survival by any means necessary. (Pg. 353)

Because of their "numerical inadequacy," whites may have defensively developed *"an uncontrollable sense of hostility and aggression"* towards *people of color, and developed a social, political, and economic structure to give blacks and other 'non-whites' the appearance of being inferior."*

Q: Who decides what "race" a person will be?
A: The same (white) people who created the concept of race. If the ONLY purpose of "race" is to practice racism, and whites are the only group or "race" (in a white supremacy system) that can practice racism, then it is logical to assume there is ONLY ONE RACE: *the white race.*

Q: If the white race is the only race, what are the other 'groups' called?
A: There are three types of people in a white supremacist system:

1. Non-white people
2. White people (Racist Suspects)
3. White Supremacists (Racists)

Q: What is a "Non-White" person?
A: Anyone who is NOT classified as "white." This includes all black, red, yellow, and brown people aka "people of color."

Q: What is a "Racist Suspect?"

A: ANY white person who is CAPABLE of practicing racism against non-whites. Since all whites are able to practice racism in a white supremacy system if they choose to do so, it is correct (and logical) to use the term "racist suspects" to identify whites who do not openly function as white supremacists (racists). This is not a hateful, unjust, or racist statement, but it is a **logical statement**.

Q: What is a "White Supremacist?"

A: A white person (a racist) who practices racism against non-whites. Being a white supremacist has nothing to do with income, title, or status. It does not mean a white person belongs to the KKK, the Aryan Nation, or is covered with Nazi tattoos.

A white supremacist can be a soccer mom, a businessman, or a US Senator if they are practicing racism against non-whites. Another term for a white supremacist is "racist white man" and "racist white woman."

Q: How can a non-white person determine if a white person is a racist?

A: Non-whites cannot always determine who is a racist, and who is not, because it is impossible to monitor (or judge) all the individual actions and words of any white person at all times. To illustrate this point:

Case Of The Stolen Wallet

There are five people in a room when a wallet that belongs to a sixth person (who is not in the room) is stolen. All five are "suspects" because every person in the room had the ability and the opportunity to take the wallet. This does not mean all five are thieves NOR does it mean all five are not thieves, because any of them could have stolen something at an earlier time.

As it turns out, two of the five people in the room CONSPIRED to steal the wallet by breaking into the sixth person's locker. The other three saw it happen, did not participate in the crime, did not care that the wallet was stolen, and did and said nothing to stop it from happening.

The sixth person – the owner of the wallet -- has no idea who stole it, if anyone saw what happened, or how many participated in the theft. All he knows is has been the VICTIM of a crime because his wallet is missing.

The two people who stole the wallet are guilty of "commission" – they actually **committed the crime**. The three witnesses are guilty of "omission" since they **witnessed the crime, said nothing and did nothing to stop it, and refused to help the victim with the information they had.**

The next day the two thieves treat the three witnesses to lunch, paying for it with the money from the stolen wallet. The witnesses did not steal the wallet but are knowingly or unknowingly benefiting from the theft. The three witnesses are not **legally liable**, but they are **morally liable,** and are correctly viewed as **"suspects" by the victim.**

Racism operates the same way. There are whites who:

- are practicing racism against non-whites at a particular moment
- are not practicing racism at that moment but have practiced it at a previous time, or will practice it at a later time
- are not practicing racism at that moment, but say and do nothing to stop those who are
- are not practicing racism at that moment, but have no problem with other whites practicing racism (don't care
- are benefiting from the crime of racism even if they are not practicing racism at that moment
- refuse to tell WHO is practicing racism; HOW racism is being practiced; and refuse to help the victims with the information they have
- oppose racism by exposing and opposing whites who practice it

Another Example:

Mr. X, a black management trainee, is looking for an apartment closer to his new job. He calls an upscale rental complex near his office, and asks if they have any one-bedroom apartments. The rental agent, a young white male, says there are two one-bedroom apartments available, takes Mr. X's name and phone number, and asks him to stop by and fill out an application.

The next day Mr. X stops by the complex after work. A different rental agent, Mrs. W, a middle-aged white female, greets him in the reception area. She says she's sorry, but there are no apartments available.

She suggests he fill out an application so they will have his information on file, and assures Mr. X that he will be the first one she calls when a one-bedroom becomes available.

Mr. X is immediately suspicious, but he fills out an application anyway. On his way home, he replays the conversation with the rental agent. Mr. X has no way of knowing if the first rental agent made an honest mistake, or if he has just been a victim of racial discrimination. His gut tells him it was the latter.

The Crime
When Mrs. W saw Mr. X was black, she used the same line she always used with black applicants. Later, she warns the new rental agent -- who talked to Mr. X over the phone – to never rent to blacks or Hispanics.

The Victim
Like the man whose wallet was stolen, Mr. X is the victim of a crime. The problem is, Mr. X can't be sure a crime was even committed, which makes it more difficult for him to protect himself from being victimized in the future. It is this kind of confusion that wreaks the most psychological damage on black people who run a DAILY risk of being victimized by racism – without being able to prove they were victimized.

The Criminals

Mrs. W is guilty of commission (practicing racism). The new rental agent is guilty of omission because he said and did nothing, and refused to help Mr. X with the information he had (that another white person, Mrs. W, was practicing racism).

It is the *crime of commission AND omission* that allows the system of racism/white supremacy to function so effectively. The system does not require all whites to practice racism at all times, but it does require that **the majority of whites say and do nothing when racism is occurring and allow themselves to benefit from the victimization of non-whites.**

Those benefits include better jobs, housing, food, medical care, education, police protection, justice, etc., than non-whites. If the majority of whites were opposed to racism/white supremacy, it would NOT be the most powerful social, economic, and political system on the planet.

It is LOGICAL to assume that the majority (or possibly all) white people have made a DELIBERATE DECISION to do one or all of the following:

- practice racism
- do nothing and say nothing to stop others from practicing racism
- deny racism is being practiced even when they know it is happening
- refuse to help the victims of racism with the information they have

That's why simple-minded thinking is useless when determining which white person is a racist and which one is not. It cannot be determined by a white person's sexual behavior. White slave owners had sexual relations with male and female slaves but they were still white supremacists (racists).

Whites have engaged in sexual relations with black people, but that doesn't mean they are not racists. Whites who have black friends, wives, husbands, or children are still "racist" if they are practicing racism against non-whites. It cannot be determined by observing the words or the actions of a particular white person, who may or may not be practicing racism at that particular time. It cannot be determined by a random (or deliberate) act or acts of kindness toward a non-white person. Mass child-murderer John Gacy was "kind" to children when he performed in his clown costume. There were slave-owners who were "kind" to their slaves, but not kind enough to stop selling human beings.

AXIOM #1: YOU CANNOT OPPOSE SOMETHING AND KNOWINGLY BENEFIT FROM IT AT THE SAME TIME.

It is LOGICAL in a white supremacist society to assume the **majority of whites** are either practicing racism (the act of commission), or are cooperating with those who are, by saying and doing nothing to stop them, refusing to help the victims of racism with the information they have (the act of omission), and are *benefiting* from the practice of racism.

Q: Do non-racist whites benefit from White Supremacy?

A: ALL whites benefit from white privilege in a white supremacy system, even if they are not practicing racism at that moment. It does not matter if they are rich or poor; or whether they admit there is such a thing as white privilege.

Anyone who is classified as "white" in a white supremacy system will always have advantages over someone who is not. Just as a black person in a black supremacy system (if one existed) would have advantages over someone who is not black.

Q: Aren't some white people opposed to racism?
A: Only if they are saying and doing something to oppose it. For example, John Brown, a white male, encouraged armed insurrection by slaves as a means to end slavery, and as a result, was charged with treason and hanged. However, that does not mean John Brown did not practice racism at an earlier time OR would not have practiced it at a later time had he lived.

Q: Aren't white anti-racists opposed to racism?
The self-annointed, white anti-racist activist offers little more than LIP SERVICE. They sacrifice NOTHING, take NO risks, and reap MORE financial rewards than the black activists fighting in the (real) trenches.

The white anti-racist actually creates MORE confusion by creating the FALSE illusion that the devastated black masses can be liberated from racism by sitting in a church, auditorium, or conference room listening to a white person -- who is STILL enjoying his or her white privileges -- making anti-racism speeches.

It is UNLIKELY that the same white anti-racist activists who PROFIT from writing books and giving speeches about racism -- have any real desire (or intent) to destroy the same white supremacy system that allows them to oppose it without losing a single 'white privilege.'

There may be whites who are sincere about replacing the system of white supremacy with a system of justice, *but that number is so statistically small, it is insignificant.*

Q: When blacks mistreat whites, isn't that "racism/black supremacy?"
A: No, because black supremacy does not exist. If black people were collectively more powerful than whites collectively, blacks would have the power to practice racism. Logically speaking, that would mean the end of white supremacy.

AXIOM #2: BLACK SUPREMACY CAN EXIST ONLY IN THE TOTAL ABSENCE OF WHITE SUPREMACY. WHITE SUPREMACY CAN EXIST ONLY IN THE TOTAL ABSENCE OF BLACK SUPREMACY. THE TEXTBOOK DEFINITION OF "SUPREMACY" IS:

THE HIGHEST RANK OR AUTHORITY.

THIS MEANS ONLY ONE THING CAN BE "SUPREME" OR OCCUPY THE "HIGHEST RANK" AT A TIME.

If blacks and whites had equal power and resources, there could be no black supremacy OR white supremacy. Our ability (power) to discriminate against (mistreat) each other would be cancelled out, leaving only two options: *coexist peacefully or destroy each other.*

CHAPTER 20

HOW WHITE SUPREMACY DAMAGES BLACK PEOPLE

Given our painful 500-year history of white oppression, do blacks hate whites?

A better question: can blacks -- who depend on white institutions and systems for survival -- afford to hate whites? It would be less confusing if all whites were openly racist, but that is not the case.

Black Paranoia Is A Natural By-Product Of Racism/White Supremacy

Whenever we are denied a job, a promotion, are stopped by the police, followed by store security, denied a loan, told there are no apartments available, or are seated at a table near a swinging kitchen door, it is difficult to tell if race was a factor. Today's racism is more refined and more subtle, which makes it more psychologically and financially devastating because the victims become confused.

If we attempt to be reasonable, we wonder if we have been the victim of discrimination or if we just had an unpleasant encounter with a disagreeable human being who just happened to be white.

If we are angry, bitter, and tired – an understandable reaction to living black in a white supremacist society -- we may feel that *everything* is about skin color, and that every white person who denies us something we want or says something we don't like is a racist.

This is why our focus MUST BE on understanding how the system of white supremacy works, and all the different faces it wears. If we judge racism solely on our pleasant or unpleasant interactions with whites, or by individual whites we like (or love), we will confuse ourselves and draw faulty conclusions.

For example, we might assume that a white person who is nice to us can't be a racist (untrue), and a white person who is not nice must be practicing racism (untrue).

It is the collective AND individual behaviors of white people who function as racists AND racist suspects that results in systemic racism/white supremacy.

The answer to the question -- do blacks hate whites – is no. Do blacks fear, resent, and distrust whites? Absolutely -- whether we admit it or not. It is natural to distrust a member of a group that has a history of mistreating your group.

It is natural to fear someone who has the power to abuse you and get away with it. It is natural to resent someone who benefits from your mistreatment, knows you are being abused, but says and does nothing to stop the abuse.

This is NOT the definition of "hate;" this is the law of physics. *For every action, there is a reaction.*

To accuse blacks of being "as racist as whites" -- when whites, collectively, have the power and a 500-year history of practicing racism against blacks – makes as much sense as comparing the schoolyard bully to a bullied child who now fears and dislikes the bully because of the way the bully has treated him.

"I am quite certain that there will never be healing between blacks and whites in this country until whites face up to the crime we as a people committed against people of African descent and begin to set it right. That's the only way Blacks will ever be able to genuinely respect us.

And, odd as it may seem, it's the only way we'll ever be able to respect them, because no one can feel clean, at ease with and respectful with someone they've robbed and brutalized and then felt they got away with it.

Working toward mutual respect is the only way to bring about true racial harmony. Anything else is divisive." -- Donna Lamb, C.U.R.E. *(Caucasians United for Reparations and Emancipation).*

AXIOM #4: IN A SYSTEM OF WHITE SUPREMACY, IT IS NATURAL FOR BLACK PEOPLE COLLECTIVELY TO FEAR AND RESENT WHITE PEOPLE COLLECTIVELY.

The consequences of speaking openly and honestly about racism can be severe, so many blacks remain silent. Out of fear and confusion, we allow ourselves to be drawn deeper into a false and dangerous sense of security, forgetting there is NO security for black people within a black-hating society.

To survive (and advance) in a predominantly white workplace, blacks often feel they must wear a compliant mask in the presence of whites for the same reason an employee hides his feelings from a boss he does not like or trust.

"I keep my voice even and low in meetings because if I raise it, the white people get scared," said one black male Hollywood insider, who preferred to remain anonymous. "I can't afford to be perceived as an 'angry black man,' but the truth is, I'm angry most of the time. People think my job is glamorous but they have no idea how racist this business is."

The Dangers Of Black Denial

When we hide our true feelings about racism, we're not protecting white people; we're protecting ourselves from the wrath of white people. We've learned from the painful (and sometimes fatal) experiences of others who have dared to speak out, that many whites cannot handle an honest dialogue about racism, and will deny racism is happening even when it is happening right under their noses.

It is understandable why blacks feel we must mask our anger and outrage in order to function in a white supremacist society. The real danger comes from wearing our masks in private, when we're alone. Our denial of our true reality creates a weak psychological foundation that can easily crack under pressure.

Instead of confronting (and correcting) the source of our pain, we self-medicate with food, alcoholism, and drug addictions, violence, ego trips, risky sexual behaviors, infidelity, promiscuity, poor parenting, obesity, overspending, materialism, violence, irrationality, and over-emotionalism.

The psychiatric community defines depression as rage turned INWARD. What then is the deadly manifestation of rage turned INWARD AND OUTWARD? Is it a form of racial schizophrenia?

The misdirection, suppression, and self-medication of rage accounts for a majority of high blood pressure, stroke, cancer, mental illness, schizophrenia, drug and alcohol addiction, depression, suicides, and murders that plague the black community.

Many blacks avoid examining their true feelings about racism because they are terrified that once they do, they won't be able to continue functioning (smiling, grinning, tap-dancing, denying, and pretending) as an inferior person within a white supremacist, black-hating society.

We are reluctant to face the truth because once we face our real problem -- racism/white supremacy -- we can no longer avoid the responsibility for fixing it. Without realizing it, our ineffective coping strategy (surrender) actually *extends* the life and the power of the white supremacist system.

Black Amnesia Is Anti-Historical And Self-Genocidal

We must stop being naïve about racism. Racism is not about whites liking or disliking blacks, or about blacks liking or disliking whites. Racism is not about blacks and whites knowing each other better. Racism is not about more blacks living next door, or going to the same schools as whites, or any such nonsense. Increasing the crossover appeal of black entertainers will not end racism. As a famous black comedian (with huge crossover appeal) once observed:

"I don't understand what goes on some times, right, 'cause here we are in this theater, we getting along just fine. We go outside and the shit changes." – Comedian Richard Pryor speaking on racism

Sammy Davis, Jr. was one of white America's favorite entertainers during the 1950s and 1960s yet this rich and famous black man could not stay in the same hotels where he received standing ovations. We forgot (or didn't understand) that even the most rabid monkey-hater will pay a fortune to see a monkey sing, talk, and tap dance.

We forgot that in the segregated Deep South, whites and blacks lived next door to each other, and played together as children but that did not eliminate racism. Southern whites certainly "knew" the black women who cleaned their houses; raised their children; cooked their food; and nursed white infants at the black woman's breast.

Black domestics workers were "just like family" to their white employers, but this did not protect them from being victimized by the same racist segregation laws that were condoned by their white pseudo "family members."

Racial sensitivity and diversity training will not end racism. Blacks and whites living, learning, working, or eating together in the same neighborhoods, schools, workplaces, or restaurants will not end racism.

Racism will NOT end until white supremacy ends. White supremacy will NOT end until non-whites in every part of the world CHANGE THEIR RESPONSES to it.

"Hence I have no mercy or compassion in me for a society that will crush people, and then penalize them for not being able to stand up under the weight."

Malcolm X (1925-1965)

Recipe #8

Integration

"No, there is plenty wrong with Negroes. They have no society. They're robots, automatons. No minds of their own.

I hate to say that about us, but it's the truth. They are a black body with a white brain. Like the monster Frankenstein. The top part is your bourgeois Negro. He's your integrator. He's not interested in his poor black brothers.

He's usually so deep in debt from trying to copy the white man's social habits that he doesn't have time to worry about nothing else. They buy the most expensive clothes and cars and eat the cheapest food. They act more like the white man than the white man does himself."

-- Malcolm X

CHAPTER 21

INTEGRATION: AMERICAN DREAM OR AFRICAN NIGHTMARE?

In a materialistic society like America, where resources are plentiful but are unequally and unjustly distributed, greed and selfishness are the predictable by-products. A culture that defines "success" as accumulating more things than we need instead of sharing our excess with those in need, will breed a population that believes it is normal -- even desirable -- to be greedy and selfish.

An epidemic of materialism and selfishness is systematically destroying our friendships, relationships, marriages, families, and communities. We were not this way PRIOR to INTEGRATION.

BEFORE INTEGRATION

The civil rights movement was a living testimony to our willingness to make personal sacrifices for the common good of all black people. Even though slavery had destroyed the "African family," the family STILL meant everything to former slaves and their descendants.

The strength of the black family was our extended families of aunts, uncles, grandfathers, grandmothers, sisters, cousins, nieces, nephews, and neighbors who were just like family. It was common in black families for two or three generations to live in the same home or on the same street.

In 1925, **only three percent of black families were headed by women**. The marriage rate for blacks during the Great Depression was higher than the marriage rate for whites, even though blacks were more likely to be poor than whites.

During the depression, white vagrants often relied on the generosity of poor, rural blacks for a hot meal or a handout, even when they could not count on their own kind. Despite our limited resources, black people once had a reputation for being the most generous and forgiving people in the nation.

In the pre-integration South, there were no "latchkey kids." There was always a neighbor or a relative willing to fill in where the parents left off so no child came home to a cold, empty house.

Before integration, black men and women -- regardless of income and education -- knew they NEEDED EACH OTHER, and KNEW there was SAFETY in numbers. We had to rely on and cooperate with each other because we did NOT have the option of moving to a "white suburb."

Before integration, black men and women knew the importance of family, and would have REJECTED the programming of trash-talk shows and their degrading (and racist) baby-momma-daddy-dramas.

Before integration, the vast majority of black men had to get married if they wanted a home, children, respectability, and regular sex.

Before integration, our children reaped the benefits of experience and wisdom that spanned two or three generations, from grandpa and grandma to the elderly Mr. and Mrs. Jones, who lived down the block. Black children learned to respect their elders *because no one gave them a choice.*

Despite all our "progress" in America, the black marriage rate is lower today than it was during the Great Depression, and our divorce rate is the highest it has ever been. Over seventy percent of black children live in single female-headed households; and MTV, BET, VH-1, gangster rappers, and the streets are the values-creators for much of today's black generation.

What Happened To Us? INTEGRATION

We adopted the (white) majority culture's materialistic and non-spiritual value systems and began to worship money and material things instead of our Creator. Some of us got a taste of the "good life" and began to embrace (poisonous) individualism, forgetting that our safety and prosperity in a hostile white nation ALWAYS came from us STANDING TOGETHER.

Thanks to the 24-hour, 7-days-a-week mass-media machine, we were bombarded by fraudulent images of happiness, sexiness, status, and success -- always defined in white, materialistic terms. The rampant materialism of celebrities, athletes, and an increasing number of handpicked "showcase" blacks with their non-black spouses taught us what "real success" looked like -- and it didn't look like BLACK LOVING BLACK.

We began to define our black self-worth by what we owned instead of who we were.

The more we assimilated into (and surrendered to) the white majority culture, the more materialistic, self-centered, black-hating, and black-self-disrespecting we became. Those of us who managed to carve out a bigger slice of the American pie began to look down on those who hadn't. Some of us bought into the myth (lie) that poor blacks were poor because they wanted to be poor.

Many first-generation, college-degreed, white-collar, and business-suit-wearing black males and females began to separate themselves psychologically and physically from the black masses. *"I wear a suit and tie) to work, so I'm better than someone who is poor or gets their hands dirty."*

We began to value each other less -- OR more -- depending on the material "goodies" our potential partners brought to the table, and how well they "measured up" by white standards.

Character and kindness fell sharply on our "gotta have" lists and we focused more on competing with the kinds of lifestyles we saw whites leading on and off-screen. As the number of successful and professional blacks increased, so did our egos, vanity, materialism, arrogance, white-identification, and broken black families.

Blacks -- who were once the most SEXUALLY CONSERVATIVE people in the nation -- eagerly embraced the dominant culture's sexual immorality and perversity. We started "swinging" and "swapping" spouses because white people were doing it, and some of us started swinging *both ways.* Our new mantra became: *"If it feels good, DO IT, and worry about the consequences later,"* even if our children were the ones who paid for our bad behavior.

We *"integrated"* (surrendered) our round black (African) identities to fit into a square, black-hating white culture, and some of us desperately sought racial redemption in a pair of white arms, and told ourselves we were living the "American Dream."

We began to believe (and act like) we didn't need each other. Some of us put all our faith in the illusion of inclusion and believed that since we were part of White America, we didn't need to develop a Black America.

We took inordinate pride in the tiny number of "showcase blacks" who dazzled us with their high-profile positions, fame, thousand-dollar suits, and million-dollar homes. We were awed by their ability to mix, mingle, date, and mate with whites, even while the so-called best and brightest blacks ignored the RISING POVERTY AND DESPAIR of the their own people. We didn't understand that celebrating another "first black" after 500 years in America wasn't a sign of progress -- it was PROOF OF A LACK OF PROGRESS.

And -- we forgot our enemies always put aside their "individualism" to move against us as a unified, well-organized, and well-financed group.

Lessons We Can Learn From Non-White Immigrants

Forty years after integration, the black collective -- regardless of education or income -- is MORE DEPENDENT on whites than we were FIFTY YEARS AGO. To make matters worse, we are just as dependent on the non-white immigrants who JUST GOT OFF THE BOAT for the majority of goods and services sold in the black community.

These non-white immigrants focused on ECONOMIC POWER, not on assimilating with whites. They STUCK TOGETHER, WORKED TOGETHER, and *built strong ethnic families, communities, and mega-businesses together* -- usually right within the DIS-UNIFIED black community.

Non-white immigrants know ETHNIC UNITY and STRONG FAMILIES are the KEYS to economic prosperity. They seldom seek social acceptance (validation) from whites because *they know they will never get it* (because they will never be white). They know it is BAD BUSINESS to get a "good job" in someone else's company instead of building their own. Instead of resenting their success, we should be **studying and imitating them.**

If we could turn the civil rights clock back 45 years, which one would we choose: Social integration OR economic empowerment? The answer can be found in the economically successful, tight-knit, non-white immigrant communities in America.

"The Negro is like a man on a luxury commuter train doing ninety miles an hour. He looks out of the window, along with all the white passengers in their Pullman chairs, and he thinks he's doing ninety, too.

Then he gets to the men's room and looks in the mirror—and he sees he's not really getting anywhere at all. His reflection shows a black man standing there in the white uniform of a dining-car steward. He may get on the 5:10, all right, but he sure won't be getting off at Westport."

-- Malcolm X (1925-1965)

CHAPTER 22

THE CURSE OF BLACK SKIN AND WHITE EYES: THE WHITE-IDENTIFIED BLACK

"It is impossible to achieve equality when one group has the power to deny rights to another group. Until we understand that distinction, we will not understand the difference between tolerance and acceptance."
                                                                              -- Umoja

What Is A "White-Identified" Black?

A black person who views the world through a "white lens," and judges most or all events, people, places, actions, and things from a **white perspective**.

What Is The "White Perspective?"

The beliefs, opinions, behaviors, and value systems of whites as a group. The **white perspective** is based on what is normal, desirable, and beneficial for white people collectively. An example is the Rodney King beating case. In spite of VIDEOTAPED evidence of police brutality, an all-white jury decided collectively that what benefited the white police officers benefited white people collectively. That perceived "benefit" resulted in an acquittal.

Had it been the other way around – an unarmed white male beaten by black police officers -- it is certain that an all-white jury would have convicted the black officers. The white collective would have (correctly) viewed an unarmed white person's beating by black policemen as potentially dangerous to ALL white people collectively – because that meant it could happen to ANY white person. The white collective would have acted in their collective best interest by punishing the black officers.

In a racially divisive society (like America), it is NORMAL for the white collective to set standards that benefit their group, and affirms their self-worth as white people collectively. This does not mean all white people think the same, or share the same perspective in all things.

What Is The "Black Collective" Perspective?

The black collective operates on a similar principle; that black people collectively (should) view most or all events, people, places, actions, and things from a perspective that assumes whatever benefits or harms a black person benefits or harms all blacks collectively. This does not mean all blacks think the same, or share the same perspective in all things.

From the black collective perspective, the beating of an unarmed black man by white police officers would have been (correctly) perceived as harmful to ALL black people – because the same thing could happen to ANY black person. Therefore, a black jury would be more likely to convict the white officers.

The OJ Simpson trial is another example of how the white collective and the black collective perceive their self-interests differently. The white collective assumed OJ Simpson was guilty (even before any evidence was heard), while the black collective saw Simpson's acquittal as justice for all blacks, not just Simpson.

This does not mean all blacks believed that OJ was innocent, or that all whites believed OJ was guilty. An individual may not agree with the group perspective on any or every issue, but it is undeniable this kind of group mentality exists within a racist society.

It is NORMAL for the black collective to set their own standards, according to what benefits black people and affirms their self-worth as black people. However, due to black-inferiority programming, which was accelerated by the integration and assimilation into a black-hating white culture, the black collective often acts against its own self-interest without understanding why they are doing it.

It also explains most of the black collective's self-destructive behaviors. This inferiority programming is the main reason many blacks refuse to identify with the black collective -- because *it is the black collective*.

AXIOM #7: A GROUP WHOSE COLLECTIVE ACTIONS PENALIZES THEIR OWN GROUP (AND REWARDS ANOTHER GROUP) IS SELF-DESTRUCTIVE AND SELF-GENOCIDAL.

For this reason, the white-identified black is a liability, NOT an asset, to the black collective. Before we go further, let's define what a white-identified black is NOT.

What A White-Identified Black Person Is Not

This is not a condemnation of blacks who are often unfairly labeled as not "black enough." All (or most) blacks are white-identified to a smaller or a greater degree, because we were raised in a white-supremacist culture (America). It is the degree of white-identification that determines the degree of the problem.

Being white-identified does not mean you prefer Beethoven to Beyonce, or Madonna to Master P. It is not about our tastes in food, music, art, or literature. It is not about the way we dress; wear our hair, walk, talk, sing, or dance.

It is not about our level, income, or education, or the type of work we do. It is not about being smart, or educated, or speaking standard English, or several languages that makes us white-identified.

ALL people – regardless of race – have a wide range of talents, interests, skills, and tastes, and are capable of enjoying a wide range of things for the simple sake of enjoyment. Black people are not monolithic (the same), nor are all white-identified blacks the same.

What Is A 'White-Identified' Black?

A white-identified black person is a black person who views the world through a white perspective *even when* it conflicts with his or her own self AND group interests. A white-identified black pursues interests, activities, and relationships *primarily because white people are associated with them* – and often avoids or looks down on certain people, places, and things *primarily because black people are associated with them.*

White-identified blacks can be found anywhere, at every income level, from the most exclusive gated community or Ivy League campus, to an inner-city housing project. How a black person sees black people, talks about black people, treats black people, feels about being a black person, and treats white people determines *the degree* of white-identification.

White Supremacy Is The Foundation For The "White Perspective"

The white collective perspective is based on the following principles:

1. white is superior to non-white
2. white life is more valuable than non-white life
3. white people created everything worth creating
4. white is the most normal (the standard) for ALL human beings

If white is the most **normal**; black **must be the most abnormal**. For those who doubt that this white standard exists, there is one INDISPUTABLE piece of evidence that can be found in every medicine cabinet in America: **the 'flesh-colored' Band-Aid.**

In other words, the "normal" color for human flesh is the color closest to the skin color of white people. What does this say to the non-white person? *That their skin color is NOT normal because they are NOT as human.*

AXIOM #8: BLACK NORMALCY CANNOT EXIST IN A SYSTEM OF WHITE SUPREMACY.

White-Identified Blackness = Psychological Suicide

By viewing the world through "white eyes," white-identified blacks are in the unenviable position of embracing their own inferiority and abnormality, and have no choice but to be anti-black – and ANTI-SELF.

If the white-identified black is observed interacting with whites or blacks, he or she will eventually reveal their OWN racial bias and inferiority complex by the things they say or do.

Their confusion comes from trying to straddle the precarious line between the black world and white world, by serving two opposing masters at the same time: **white supremacy and black normalcy.**

It is **unnatural and perverted** for a race of people to adopt a perspective and a set of standards that does NOT benefit their group AND denies their own NORMALCY and self-worth as members of that group. Unfortunately, this kind of distorted thinking is exactly what has led to the personality disorders and self-hatred issues that plague the black population.

Curing The 'Disease' Of Black Abnormalcy

If whiteness is the norm; blackness must be the disease. The ONLY cure is the assimilation of (inferior) blacks into a (superior and normal) white value system in order to reduce their "black abnormalcy." This fear of being "abnormal" is the main reason some blacks become assimilated (white-identified), so they will be **"normal"** by white standards. Unfortunately, white-identified blacks will never be as normal as white people because they will **never be white**.

By accepting the (false) premise that white is the most 'normal,' the white-identified black is confirming his or her own genetic and intellectual inferiority.

The white-identified black person will never admit to being white-identified, but will do anything to avoid being perceived as too "black." When pro-golfer Tiger Woods created a new term -- **"Cablinasian"** (coined from the words **Ca**ucasian, **Bl**ack, American-**In**dian, and **Asian**) – to describe his racial heritage, some people wondered why a man with a black father and an Asian mother would put "Caucasian" first in the racial pecking order.

Ironically, despite Woods' attempt to racially reclassify himself, he is still known as a "black golfer." In a white supremacist society, non-whites cannot racially reclassify themselves. Those who choose to forget this fact will be abruptly reminded.

A blatant reminder occurred in 2008, when a solution was proposed by Kelly Tilghman, a white female sports anchor, for younger golfers who wanted to challenge Tiger's title as the world's No. 1 golfer. She suggested that they, *"Lynch him in a back alley."*

Tiger's response: *"Kelly and I did speak. There was no ill intent. She regrets saying it. In my eyes, it's all said and done."*

The real question is not whether Tilghman had ill intent; it's whether the word "lynching" would have been used to refer to a white golfer. It is similar to Fuzzy Zoeller's comment at the 1997 Masters tournament when he called Tiger *"that little boy"* and told him not to serve *"fried chicken or collard greens."*

The irony is these blatant "racial reminders" make the white-identified black more uncomfortable than the whites who had an unfortunate slip of the tongue. White-identified blacks are quick to forgive these kinds of comments because they are desperate to reassure whites that they are not "angry" blacks – even when they are being mistreated.

This kind of behavior is more common for black males than black females, since showing anger is taboo for black males who want to succeed with the white public. The downside of allowing racist comments to appear innocent is the black masses -- who do not have millions of dollars to insulate themselves from everyday racism – are expected to suffer the same racist treatment without protesting:

"Look at that black XYZ celebrity. He doesn't make a big deal out of a harmless comment about lynching (niggers), so why should you (an ordinary nigger) get upset?"

A columnist for a major sports magazine also casts some doubt on the wisdom of Tiger's response:

"Woods doesn't have to become a civil-rights spokesman, but he could have at least acknowledged that he understands the meaning of the word, and how powerful and hurtful it remains."
-- Farrell Evans, Writer-Reporter, Sports Illustrated

Their desperate desire to distance themselves from themselves (and their despised blackness) is the emotion that drives many white-identified blacks to deliberately seek out a white or Asian spouse to rid their offspring of the racial 'abnormalities' that exist within themselves. This is why it is critical to recognize the symptoms of black denial and self-hatred, so their "disease" will not infect us.

The Poisonous Effect Of White-Identified Black Celebrities

White-identified black celebrities are extremely dangerous to other blacks because they VALIDATE black inferiority/white superiority by the kinds of lifestyle and romantic choices they make. These "successful" white-identified black celebrities are more likely to be rewarded by the white supremacy system with lucrative book deals, talk shows, movies, and TV shows **because they are the best advertising white supremacy can buy.**

Their fame, awards, and desperation to be embraced by the white elite and the white collective sends a DEADLY MESSAGE to the black masses -- especially to black youth: **if you want to be rich and successful, be less black.**

The white-identified black person is the ADULT victim of the black doll/ white doll experiment. White-identified blacks understand how tragic it is for the little black girl or boy to pick the white doll as the nicer doll, but cannot see how damaged they must be to do the SAME THING.

If blacks are "inferior," how does the white-identified black exempt him or herself from the same judgment?

Some white-identified blacks adopt external gimmicks to maintain the illusion (and delusion) of "black pride" -- like wearing African clothing, coconut beads, dreadlocks, and talking incessantly about the "black struggle," all while imitating, (secretly) identifying with, sexing, and loving *white.*

Because white-identified blacks usually get more crumbs from the "white" table than their black-identified peers, they are convinced that their external achievements (and white validations) are proof of their internal self-esteem, when in reality, it is just the opposite.

Wealth, fame, status, titles, material things, or wearing dreadlocks and African clothing, have nothing to do with **SELF-ESTEEM**. However, **SELF-ESTEEM** does require RESPECT for the truth:

AXIOM #9: A NON-WHITE PERSON CANNOT BE EQUAL TO OR THE SAME AS A WHITE PERSON IN A WHITE SUPREMACY SYSTEM.

To maintain the level of self-deception and denial needed to maintain their (false) white identity, the white-identified black person must create even more delusions (lies) as to their TRUE status as a black person (a nigger) in a white supremacy system.

This is why white-identified blacks are more vulnerable to the emotional devastation caused by racism -- because they don't think they will ever be victims of it.

CHAPTER 23

THE COLOR OF SUCCESS

Miranda is a senior software programmer for a Fortune 500 company and earns a six-figure salary. She drives a luxury car, lives in a downtown condo just blocks from her job, eats out twice a day, and is always stylishly attired. Five foot-six, and attractive; Miranda maintains her trim 140-pound frame by exercising three times a week at the pricey health club in her apartment building.

Miranda avoids interacting with the black copy clerks, messengers, and secretaries at her firm since she has nothing in common with them. She has a handful of black friends and associates -- all Ivy League grads like herself -- who work for other Fortune 500 firms.

She attends most company functions, and occasionally joins her white coworkers for happy hour at the bars near their office. She dated a white consultant for a few weeks the previous year but they went their separate ways after he said he "wasn't looking for anything serious." She hasn't met anyone since, and is dateless most weekend nights.

Miranda has dated only a few black men over the last fifteen years; but after one or two dates, they never called again, which led her to assume black women of her caliber intimidated black men.

This was confirmed (in her mind) after one black jerk said, at the end of their first and only date, that if he wanted to date a white woman, he'd find a real one. Miranda took that as a compliment. If Mr. Right turned out to be white, she was okay with that.

The truth is, Miranda feels more comfortable around whites, which is why she lives in a predominantly white area. She grew up in a predominantly white neighborhood and attended predominantly white schools where she had been one of a handful of blacks. She hadn't stayed in touch with her black classmates, and only occasionally wondered what had become of them.

Although Miranda's midwestern city is one of the most segregated cities in the nation, she swears she has never personally experienced racism, except for the occasional white ignoramus who disliked blacks. Shoot, there were plenty of blacks she didn't like herself!

She refuses to be manipulated by all that "brother" and "sister" crap blacks use as a crutch. All blacks had to do to overcome white misgivings and negative stereotypes, was to be more prepared and work harder than their white peers. It was just that simple.

Either a person was up to the challenge, and if they weren't, they had no one to blame but the person in the mirror. If they succeeded, the rewards were well worth it. Her impressive career was proof.

More proof was the retirement party three weeks ago for the black vice-president of public affairs. The company bigwigs went all out for McCabe. A rented hotel ballroom, a catered five-course meal, a six-piece jazz band, balloons, and champagne. Miranda had never seen anyone -- let alone a black man -- get such a royal send-off. It definitely beat a 30-year pin from the post office.

When Miranda announced to a small group at the retirement party that she was a proud, card-carrying Republican and had never once voted Democratic, she was secretly pleased by their surprised reactions. It was a prudent career move, she added, since the firm's biggest client was a staunch Republican. The truth was, Miranda despises being typecast as a black Democrat. She hated the patronizing way the Democrats threw out an occasional ham hock to get the black vote. Just what had Democrats done for black people like her lately?

What was even more aggravating was the way the Republican Party ignored the thousands of blacks who thought the way she did. People who were educated, successful, intelligent, and understood the value of an unregulated free market, free trade, and minimal government regulation. Her lifestyle and stock portfolio was living proof of how well it worked.

When the firm eliminated an entire division last year – mostly blue-collar jobs -- Miranda saw nothing wrong with it. Every company had the right to find cheaper labor, even if that meant outsourcing jobs. Management had an obligation to maximize profits for the company and for stockholders—like herself. Any workers who were displaced had to find new jobs. *It was just that simple.*

On the day Miranda receives an outstanding job review, the firm announces plans to cut another 10,000 jobs to boost profitability. Since the firm employs over 61,000 workers worldwide, Miranda isn't too worried, but assumed the people junior to her should be. Miranda is the only black person in her department, but that small detail hardly causes a wrinkle in her powder-smooth forehead. After chatting with a Human Resources manager, a black woman she was only marginally friendly with, Miranda discovers that she is the only one in her department with a Master's degree.

It feels good to know her job is secure; not that she ever doubted it for one second. Miranda feels appreciated at the firm, gets along well with her coworkers and boss, and always gets excellent performance reviews. She is confident they see her as an equal and a valuable team member.

The following Friday pink slips are handed out in her department, and there is one with Miranda's name on it! Her entire department is being downsized, and the rumor is their jobs are being outsourced to India. No explanations or apologies were issued with the separation package that included three months severance pay. Miranda packs her belongings in boxes under the watchful eyes of a security guard. She is furious, humiliated, and profoundly confused because she never saw the hammer coming.

A few weeks after she was laid off, Miranda runs into one of her former coworkers, Beth, an accountant who still works for the firm. She tells Miranda that the programmers in Miranda's department had been transferred to other branches.

Miranda is stunned. Why wasn't she offered a job when she had the most experience? And why didn't the sister in Human Resources warn her? The look of pity on Beth's face stops Miranda cold before the questions slip out.

Then Beth says something that catches Miranda completely by surprise. She says Miranda should file an EEOC suit against the firm. Two of the senior black accountants in Beth's area were laid off while she and three of the least experienced accountants were shuffled into different jobs. Miranda didn't ask if the three were white. She didn't have to. Beth was.

Eight months after losing her job, Miranda is still unemployed. The few job offers she receives pay a third of what she used to make. Miranda refuses to consider them but is too proud to pound the pavement for a new job, even after her unemployment benefits run out.

Eventually, the headhunters stop calling. A year later Miranda is still unemployed, 35 pounds overweight, and is taking medication for depression. Her savings are exhausted so she is forced to give up her condo and move back home to live with her bewildered parents.

An Epidemic Of Mirandas

Miranda is a classic case of the white-identified black professional. She did everything right. She went to college, graduate school, remained childless and single, and associated with the "right" (white) people. Miranda's false sense of security allowed her to be blind-sided and her career to be permanently derailed.

There are tens of thousands of male and female Mirandas in America, some of who were raised in predominantly white environments; attended predominantly white schools; and their closest friends and romantic partners -- if they were lucky enough to have any -- were white.

It is understandable that these blacks identify with whites, however, this is a problem for three reasons: (1) They are NOT white, (2) They will NEVER be white, and (3) They believe they are equal to whites (which is never true in a white supremacy system).

White-identified blacks are often fooled by the ease in which they sometimes move about in predominantly white settings. In reality, they are such a small minority, they pose no threat (or competition) to whites.

Unfortunately, white-identified blacks can't tell the difference between tolerance and acceptance. They are so determined to fit in, whites find their admiration and imitation flattering, and thus allow them to be in their company.

This doesn't mean blacks and whites cannot form friendships however, these friendships usually depend on the black person **remaining white-identified**.

Since most white-identified blacks believe whites are the ONLY people who can validate them, they will do whatever it takes to get white approval and distinguish themselves from the (unwashed) black masses, even if that means reinforcing racial stereotypes against other blacks (and themselves).

Miranda believed the extravagant retirement party for the black vice-president was proof that blacks were equals at her company. She didn't know McCabe had been forced into premature retirement, or that the firm used the bad economy as an opportunity to eliminate the affirmative action positions -- including hers -- created to secure government contracts.

Miranda didn't know about the countless humiliations McCabe had suffered at the hands of his white colleagues. She didn't know that the day after his first promotion a decade ago, McCabe came to work the following morning and found his desk had been moved into a small closet by the white supervisors who resented sharing their office space with a black man.

She never knew McCabe's eternal smile, which earned him the (dubious) nickname of "Smiley," had almost cost him his health and his marriage.

The male and female Mirandas do not understand (or accept) that **skin color always overrides** education, degrees, professional credentials, cars, clothes, white lovers, and white spouses when it comes to the CORE pecking order in a white supremacist society.

That's why, when they encounter racism, they have a tendency to ignore it unless they are forced to deal with it. They interpret this denial as confidence and strength, but it is just the opposite. *Denial is the height of weakness.*

The Good Black Is The Most Delusional Of All Blacks

Despite the mountains of overwhelming evidence to the contrary, 'good blacks" like Miranda believe MORE education, degrees, designer clothing, fancier homes, addresses, manners, cars, white spouses, and biracial offspring will accomplish what Michael J. with all his millions failed to do: *Erase the imaginary stigma of being black.*

'Good blacks' refuse to accept that no one – least of all, white supremacists – respects a black man or woman who is willing to do anything, say anything, be anything, or betray anyone to belong to a club that doesn't want them as a member.

A Healthier, Black-Loving Perspective

The psychological opposite of the "white-identified" black is the **black-identified black**. The black-identified individual sees the world as it really exists and does not blame black people for being the victims of racism. Since they are NOT in denial about racism, they are seldom caught completely off guard because they keep their expectations at a reasonable and realistic level.

They understand that getting along with whites in the workplace does not mean whites see blacks as their equals. This is why most black-identified blacks seldom pursue friendships or relationships with white coworkers outside of work — to the relief of their white coworkers -- and rely on black males and females for their psychological, emotional, and romantic needs.

CHAPTER 24

THE ZEBRA AND THE LIONS:
A TALE OF POISONOUS INDIVIDUALISM

"OJ Simpson Guilty of Armed Robbery, Kidnapping." (10/4/2008)

One day, Horace, the Zebra, got the craziest notion in his large, elongated head. He decided he didn't want to be part of a herd any longer. He was tired of grazing where all the other zebras grazed. He was tired of the smells, and the endless grunting and snorting. Zebras were absolutely disgusting!

Horace spent most of his days staring for hours at his reflection in the river. He was the most handsome zebra in the herd; too handsome to be an ordinary zebra. Whenever one of the more comely females flicked her skinny tail in his direction, Horace turned his big snout up in the air. He wasn't about to bring any more smelly zebras into the world.

Horace wandered away from the herd toward a shady grove of trees. To his delight, there was the sweetest green patch that had not been burned brown by the blistering African sun. Horace looked back at the rest of the herd chewing blissfully on the dry tufts underneath their hooves and snorted loudly in contempt. Look at those dumb zebras, eating dry grass like manna from zebra heaven.

Horace moved deeper into the grove and faced the herd so he wouldn't be seen but could see them if they came too close. If they discovered his tasty find, there would be less for him.

Unbeknownst to Horace, fifty yards from the shady grove was a pack of lions; one male and three females. As Horace came closer, they strategically kept their distance. They wanted the zebra to think he was safe, so far away from the herd.

"What a dumb zebra," they growled deep in their throats with amusement. The pack licked their huge teeth in anticipation. The zebra was nice; thick around the middle with a big, fat ass.

"He doesn't do much running," one lioness chortled with contempt. She had no use for a lazy male of any species, and was looking forward to ripping that striped hide with her sharp teeth until the blood flowed.

"He's such a stupid zebra," a second lioness agreed, "to wander off by himself. Doesn't he know there are hungry lions in the fields just waiting to take him down?"

"Ho, look at him," roared the male lion, shaking his magnificent, golden-brown mane. "Chowing down like there's no tomorrow—and there won't be after we rip his striped ass apart."

The lions laughed quietly, so they wouldn't alert the blissfully grazing zebra. They were in a good mood. There was nothing predators loved more than a big-headed, stupid animal, so arrogant it forgot its own safety lay in unity of the herd.

In a herd, the zebras' stripes created an optical illusion that confused the lions. To make matters worse, the more devious zebras would zigzag back and forth in front of the herd to make it more difficult to single one zebra out. Together, the zebras were smarter than they looked – but apart – they became a lion's happy meal.

Oblivious to the danger beyond the trees, Horace ate until his big belly bulged. A shifting wind rippled the bristly hairs along his ridged back. His head jerked up and around. In an instant, he recognized the scent. *Lions!* He sniffed again, taking in large gulps through his flared nose. They must have seen him hiding in the trees!

Horace trotted out of the shady grove and paused on trembling legs. Nervously, he looked back and spotted the top of a magnificent brown and gold mane moving low through the grasses – coming in his direction!

Horace broke into a full gallop, his big belly swaying from side to side, toward the herd grazing in the distance. His eyes widened with terror when he looked back and saw the lions, four deep, in hot pursuit.

Horace brayed at the top of his lungs, calling the herd's attention to his plight. When the other zebras lifted their heads, and saw the lions., they took off, leaving Horace in a huge cloud of dust.

Horace couldn't believe these cowardly zebras weren't willing to risk their lives when he needed their help! How could they abandon such a proud, stately, handsome zebra like himself? Wasn't he just like them – only better?

Before Horace could make another sound, one of the lionesses leaped in the air and landed on his back, followed by another, bringing him crashing down on his front forelegs. The male lion rushed in, snapped his powerful jaws around the thrashing zebra's neck, and clamped down until the zebra suffocated.

By the time the last tremors rippled through Horace's body, the lions were already feasting. One lioness tore off a bloody chunk of zebra flesh and chewed happily. Poisonous individualism sure made one hell of a tasty meal!

The End of Story

"Even the weak become strong when they are united."
– Johann Friedrich Von Schiller (1759-1805)

Integration was the worst thing that could have happened to black people.

You can't "integrate" into a culture that despises you.

You can't "integrate" when you have to ask (beg) for everything you need.

That's not integration, that's subjugation.

And if you don't know the difference between being equal and wanting to be equal, you never will be.

Umoja

Recipe #9

False Beauty Standards

"Once you convince someone to hate the reflection in their mirror, you can convince them of anything." -- Umoja

CHAPTER 25

THE BEAUTY CON GAME

The old cliché -- "Beauty's in the eye of the beholder" – is no match for the power of white supremacy. Under this system, beauty has become a zero-sum equation for whites and non-whites, which states:

1. If whites are the most attractive, non-whites are the least attractive.
2. If light skin is a sign of (racial) beauty, dark skin is a sign of (racial) ugliness.

Black Inferiority Complexes Are Rooted In Our Mirrors

This (false) man-made concept of beauty is used to instill the FIRST seeds of self-hatred and inferiority in non-white children -- in particular, the darkest-skinned (of African descent). It is critical that we understand how the **second weapon of Mass Mind Destruction – BEAUTY** – functions so we will understand why so many non-whites despise the person in their mirrors.

Debunking White Supremacy Beauty Myths

MYTH #1: We Should Take Credit For An Accident Of Birth

We have no control over the parents we have, the genes we inherit, or the color of the womb that delivered us into this world. Giving ourselves credit for being born white, black, red, or green; light or dark-skinned; six-foot-two or four-foot-one; blue-eyed or brown-eyed; is the same as taking credit for having two hands and two feet.

Our skin color is an accident of birth; a random toss of the genetic dice. To base our superiority on something we had no control over is foolish. We should only take credit for what we have personally accomplished.

MYTH #2: God Made Whites Superior To Blacks

If this is true then the following must also be true:

1. God CANNOT be all-powerful and all-knowing because He made the African man and woman the first people on earth. (He made a mistake).
2. Two inferior human beings (the African man and woman) can produce two superior offspring (the European man and woman).

MYTH #3: *Mother Nature Is Clueless And Incompetent*

Mother Nature – the physical manifestation of GOD – gave every species – including humans -- the physical traits needed for survival. Europeans have straighter, longer hair that provides protection in a cold climate. Pale skin and light eyes indicates that whites have less melanin than more melanated people (of color), and also indicates a native environment where there was less exposure to intense, direct sunlight.

Mother Nature chose Africa as the birthplace of all humankind and chose the African man and woman to be the first people on earth. She equipped Africans with dark eyes, tightly spiraled hair, and the most melanin, which makes dark skin ideal for Africa's climate and intense heat and sunlight.

Light skin, hair, and eyes are more desirable in a cold climate with less intense sunlight since melanin blocks the absorption of sunlight. Bottom line, the differences in skin color for whites evolved due to natural selection, genetics, and environment, NOT racial or intellectual superiority.

MYTH #4: *One Beauty Standard (European) Fits All (Races)*

False. The physical differences between different ethnic groups are determined by genetics, the environment, and other biological factors. It is illogical (and insane) to judge all human beings by ONE beauty standard, just like it is insane (and illogical) to expect a Rottweiler to look like a Great Dane just because both are DOGS.

MYTH #5: *The European Beauty Standard Is A Universal Standard*

False. It is ILLOGICAL (and insane) for the white minority (10% of the people on the planet) to be the standard for what is normal or desirable for the other non-white 90%. In fact, today's (European) beauty standards are the exact opposite of the beauty standards that existed hundreds of years before white supremacy infected the planet:

Pre-Modern Asian Ideas On Race

The text below is reprinted directly from the article, "Universal preference of whiteness over blackness" - courtesy of colorq.org (www.colorq.org/articles/article.aspx?d=1999&x=blackwhite)

"Standards of beauty in South and Southeast Asia: Marco Polo reports on the Dravidians of South India: "It is a fact that in this country when a child is born they anoint him once a week with oil of sesame, and this makes him grow much darker than when he was born.

In the Chinese record Nan tsi Chou, a Chinese traveler to Southeast Asia wrote of the people: "...they consider black the most beautiful."

Prior to European colonization, the ancient Visayans of the Philippines considered the very opposite of high noses and oval faces handsome. Visayans, as well as some other Austronesian peoples in Malaysia and Indonesia, compressed their babies' skulls to achieve broad faces and flat noses.

Old Chinese Views On Caucasians

The text below is reprinted directly from the article, "Universal preference of whiteness over blackness" -- courtesy of www.colorq.org

> By traditional Chinese opera conventions, a black face is considered nobler. Actors wear masks that denote the character's qualities. A predominantly black face indicates courage, righteousness, and incorruptibility. A predominantly white face indicates craftiness, deceit, and knavery.

> Ming Dynasty China records even state that Caucasians, especially blondes, are physically unattractive: "Huihui are shaggy with big noses, and Qipchags have light hair and blue eyes. Their appearance is vile and peculiar, so there are those (Chinese) who do not wish to marry them."

This distaste for blondes is a stark contrast to the worship of European standards of beauty so prevalent among modern Asians today.

The Character And Beauty Of Ethiopians Admired By Ancient Europeans

The text below is reprinted directly from the article, "Universal preference of whiteness over blackness" -- courtesy of www.colorq.org

> "The Ethiopians," wrote Herodotos, "are said to be the tallest and best-looking people in the world." (In ancient Roman/Greek writings, the term "Ethiopian" is loosely used to refer to all black Africans).

> Greek writer Diodoros wrote of the Ethiopians: "Their piety has been published abroad among all men, and it is generally held that the sacrifices practiced among the Ethiopians are those which are the most pleasing to heaven." (Sources and links for pp 164-165 found on website).

If Europeans were living back in ancient times, they would be searching for cosmetic remedies to darken their skin and kink up their hair – like the millions of whites today, who flock to beaches and tanning salons to darken their skin; to plastic surgeons to thicken their lips, and enlarge breasts and buttocks; and to hair salons to perm, wave, kink, and curl their hair.

MYTH #6: Africans Worshipped The First Europeans As "Gods"

False. Contrary to the racist delusions of Hollywood moviemakers, Africans did not think the first Europeans were gods (or goddesses). Some Africans believed Europeans were white because they had been skinned alive. Some Africans believed Europeans were white because they had been skinned alive. Others, like Olaudah Equiano, were terrified by the appearance of the white men who kidnapped him from his African village and brought him to the New World on a slave ship in 1756.

After ten years of enslavement, Olaudah purchased his freedom and wrote his autobiography, describing the horrors of slavery, the cruelty of slave-owners, and how he fainted with fright the first time he saw the *"white men with horrible looks, red faces, and long hair."*

In pre-colonial Africa, a skin-color inferiority complex was nonexistent. Africans took pride in their skin, hair, and features because it was desirable (normal) to look like their fathers, mothers, siblings, and grandparents.

Africans never knew they were "inferior" **until the Europeans colonized (conquered) Africa,** and used physical differences to justify enslaving, robbing, raping, and murdering them. Only after four centuries of being FORCE-FED these artificially created (false) European beauty standards, Africans, and their descendants, learned to hate what they saw in the mirror.

MYTH #7: It Is Normal For One Race To Think A Different Race Is More Attractive (Superior)

False. It is ABNORMAL to view another race as more attractive, just like it is ABNORMAL to look into a mirror and see ugliness. A black child will not automatically think pale skin is superior to his skin, any more than a white child thinks his pale skin is inferior. Every child – regardless of race -- has a healthy amount of self-esteem until he or she is *taught* to feel inferior.

What Happened To "Black Is Beautiful?"

The slogan, "Black is beautiful," which became popular in the 1970s, was little more than a good idea turned bad fad. By the time non-black merchandisers, the blax-ploitation filmmakers, and the media made a fortune from *Super Fly* hats, high-heeled shoes, idiotic films, and afro combs, "black and proud" became synonymous with "black and foolish."

We did not understand why such a wonderful slogan had been doomed from the start. We did not understand that we had to scrape off the rusted paint of self-hatred and inferiority before we applied a new paint job. We did not understand that in order to REDO, we first had to *UNDO.*

The telltale sign of past or present European colonization of a non-white nation: the people become self-hating.

If European (white supremacy) beauty standards had not been literally rammed down the throats of millions of Asians, it is doubtful a single Asian woman would correct a NONEXISTENT flaw by undergoing eye surgery to make her slanted eyes rounder, and more "Western" (European).

If European (white supremacy) beauty standards had not been literally rammed down the throats of Africans (and their descendants), it is doubtful a single African man or woman would even think of using bleaching creams and swallowing poisonous pills, risking skin cancer, leukemia, thyroid disorders, and leprosy to lighten (destroy) the most age-resistant skin on earth.

MYTH #8: *Whites Benefit From White Supremacy Beauty Standards*

The BEAUTY CON GAME has boomeranged on the very ones it was supposed to benefit by breeding an unhealthy obsession with the exterior rather than the more important interior. This obsession is the primary reason there is so much unhappiness within the white collective over minor (and nonexistent) flaws in their own appearances.

Ironically, even though whites are supposed to be the most attractive people on the planet (in a system of white supremacy), they are also the most dissatisfied with their own appearance -- and the MOST INSECURE.

This predominantly white obsession with appearance (perfection) can be seen in the endless snake-oil advertisements for the billion-dollar beauty industry. For the promise of whiter (perfect) teeth, perfect noses, chins, thighs, abs, stomachs, lips, hair, skin, bigger breasts, wrinkle-free skin, potions, lotions, and the promise of staying young forever, millions of Americans swallow billions of pills and voluntarily go under the knife.

This obsession with perfection is also apparent in the epidemic of eating disorders that are most common among the white female population, who ironically, are also held up as the standard of feminine beauty for non-white females.

Truth Is Stranger Than Fiction (In A White Supremacy System)

Despite the inferiority programming of non-white females, black and Asian women generally have a more positive body image than Caucasian females, according to a Washington University study. In addition, black women with **a strong sense of racial identity** actually rated themselves more attractive than pictures of supposedly beautiful white fashion models, and 40% of moderately and severely overweight black women rated their figures to be attractive or very attractive.

Other research indicates that this may be because black women are more flexible in their concepts of beauty than their white counterparts, who express rigid ideals and greater dissatisfaction with their own body-shape. Another survey found black girls were more self-confident in high school than either white or Hispanic girls, and that white girls lost their self-confidence at an earlier age than Hispanic girls. How can this be true in a white supremacy system where the black female occupies the bottom rung of the beauty totem pole?

Is the obsession to be "perfect" (superior) undermining the white female's self-esteem rather than building it up?

Black girls with **a strong sense of racial identity** do not define themselves by (false) white beauty standards. Nor are they totally dependent on looks for self-esteem, but rely on other factors like personality, style, and intelligence. They know there is nothing inherently wrong with being black; and are less likely to mutilate or surgically alter their bodies. Which explains why so many black females view the eating disorders (like bulimia and anorexia) that afflict the white female population with puzzlement and contempt.

Black females, in general, do not long for rail thin arms and legs or tiny butts. Their opinion of a sexy body is far more generous and forgiving since perfection is never a requirement. Black females also have less of a tendency to obsess over minor flaws in their appearance. However, if a black female is white-identified, she may mimic the self-hating behavior of her white peers, although seldom to the same extreme degree.

White Beauty Standards Are Contemptuous Of ALL Women

Would a culture that truly values its females create a beauty standard that demoralizes and penalizes them? The answer is clear: it does not value them; but in fact, secretly despises, even hates them. This contempt is obvious, given the widespread slaughter of white females **for entertainment and for profit in television, movies, and in real life.**

The white supremacy "beauty standards" actually demonstrate MORE contempt for white females than admiration. A culture that promotes a media-manufactured body ideal -- tall, long-legged, blonde, and bone-thin with zero-body-fat (a boy's body) -- that drives white girls and women to literally starve themselves to death is ANTI-WOMAN -- not woman-loving or woman-respecting.

This is NOT about empathizing with whites, who are victims by their OWN HAND. This is NOT about empathizing with white females who use the same racist standards to elevate themselves above non-white females. *This is about exposing the BLATANT CONTRADICTIONS of a white beauty standard that even the WHITE CREATORS do not and cannot measure up to.* The biggest beauty con game victims are non-whites, who have been demoralized by the LIE of white superiority.

Is the epidemic of self-loathing the karmic price the white collective is paying for perpetuating mass self-loathing among non-whites?

America is one of the wealthiest nations in the world YET Americans are plagued by more self-doubt, self-hatred, self-abuse, over-materialism, dysfunctional relationships, broken families, cruelty, jealousy, envy, bullying, vanity, narcissism, eating disorders, self-mutilation, drug and alcohol addiction, mental illness, depression, suicide, sexual deviancy, rape, incest, and homicide – than anywhere else – including the (so-called) Third World.

If the most privileged people on the planet are also the most miserable, they are missing the two most valuable lessons of their lives:

1. There is NO substitution for genuine self-respect and self-esteem. If we are mistreating others, we will have neither.
2. If we escape punishment for our ill deeds and crimes, ultimately, we will find a way to punish ourselves.

CHAPTER 26

STRAIGHT TALK
ABOUT NAPPY HAIR

"Don't remove the kinks from your HAIR. Remove them from your BRAIN." -- The Honorable Marcus Mosiah Garvey [1887-1940]

Baby, Let Your Hair Hang Down

Audrey was sitting across a candlelit table from Ernest, a man she met the week before on the commuter train to work. She had dressed carefully for their first date. Not too plain-jane but not too sexy. She didn't want him to think she was willing to trade her body for a glass of wine and a plate of blackened tilapia.

The conversation had been decent but nothing special. Audrey had been hoping for some kind of spark then warned herself to relax and just enjoy the man's company. That was the problem with single women like herself; they expected an instant connection with a man they just met. For all she knew, Ernest was having the same doubts about her.

"This fish is delicious," Audrey said, letting him know she appreciated the meal he was paying for.

"Not as delicious as you," Ernest said, bold brown eyes staring over his raised cocktail glass.

"You know what they say. Appearances can be deceiving," Audrey teased, refusing to take his comment seriously. She was a little flattered by his constant staring, but also a little unnerved. Finally, she asked, "Is something wrong?"

"Wrong?"

"You keep staring."

"Just wondering..." His voice trailed off, a wistful look on his face.

"About what?" Audrey mentally crossed her fingers. *Please don't let this man say something stupid.*

"I was wondering what you'd look like if you let your hair down."

"Let my what down?" She sat back, frowning.

"It's sexy," Ernest continued. "When a woman lets her hair down." He tilted his head back and rolled his shoulders to demonstrate.

"Uh-huh," Audrey said, a self-conscious hand straying to the French roll she'd plastered with hair goo to keep the short, stray hairs lying flat.

"If I was your man, would you let your hair down for me?"

"But, you're not my man, so I don't have to answer that," Audrey said firmly.

"I might be one day."

Now, why was he going there on their first date? And why was this fool talking about letting her hair down when it barely reached her shoulders?

Unfortunately, Audrey knew exactly what Ernest meant. If she had seen the tired scene once, she had seen it a hundred times:

The prim and proper, plain-Jane white female, hair in a tight bun, glasses, white blouse buttoned up to her chin, who hadn't had sex since the Great Depression. The handsome male hero walks in the door. Bam! Instant attraction! The top buttons of her blouse pop loose. She reaches up and pulls out that one strategically placed hairpin, shakes her head, and her long hair tumbles around her face, transforming her from a frigid librarian into a raging sex kitten!

When Audrey was younger, she wanted long hair like that, but now, just a few days short of her 40th birthday, she was no longer impressed with Hollywood's idea of sexy. She thought it fake, silly, and too contrived. In fact, spending so much time and money fretting, fixing, and worrying about her hair was wearing on her last nerve.

She was sick of waiting for hours at the beauty salon, sick of hair relaxers, hair straighteners, and hair rollers. She was sick of trying to stretch, pull, and shape her short hair into a decent style every morning.

Audrey had decided that this would be the year to throw away the relaxers and curling irons, and start wearing her hair natural. And now this clown wanted to turn her into a piss-poor imitation of a white female?

Ten years ago, Ernest's careless comment would have made her feel inadequate – or it might have driven her to the nearest hair weave salon to accommodate his inappropriate, and frankly, rude expectations. Ernest had no idea how much he had turned her off, or that this would be their last date, because he was still smiling and waiting for her response.

"Ernie," Audrey cooed, giving him a seductive smile. "I'll let my hair down on one condition."

"What?" Ernest leaned forward, an eager look on his face.

"You let your hair grow long and silky, so I can run my fingers through it." Then Audrey's eyes traveled slowly and deliberately up to the balding spot on top of his thinning, close-cropped, nappy fade.

THE END

The "Joy" Of Nappy Humor

Don Imus and his "crew" take aim at the hair and sexual morality of eight black teenaged girls on the Rutgers basketball team (April 4, 2007).

IMUS (host): So, I watched the basketball game last night between -- a little bit of Rutgers and Tennessee, the women's final.
ROSENBERG (former Imus sports announcer): Yeah, Tennessee won last night -- seventh championship for Pat Summitt, I-Man. They beat Rutgers by 13 points.
IMUS: That's some rough girls from Rutgers. Man, they got tattoos --

McGUIRK (producer): Some hard-core hos.
IMUS: That's some nappy-headed hos there. I'm gonna tell you that
now, man, that's some -- woo. And the girls from Tennessee, they all
look cute...
McGUIRK: A Spike Lee thing.
IMUS: Yeah.
McGUIRK: The Jigaboos vs. the Wannabes -- that movie he had.
IMUS: Yeah, it was a tough --
McCORD (newsman): Do The Right Thing.
IMUS: I don't know if I'd have wanted to beat Rutgers or not, but they did, right?
ROSENBERG: It was a tough watch. The more I look at Rutgers, they
look exactly like the Toronto Raptors.
RUFFINO (engineer): Only tougher.
McGUIRK: The [Memphis] Grizzlies would be more appropriate.

Nappy hair has been a frequent target of white ridicule. There is a tremendous amount of pressure for black women to imitate a beauty standard that was designed for white women. This makes hair a sensitive topic for many black females. Even though black males are not pressured to have long hair, straight hair, "good hair," or any hair at all, they are just as obsessive (and conflicted) about "black hair." One only has to turn the clock back 40 years to recall the "conk" hairstyles that were once popular among black males.

A Short Walk Down Memory Lane...

"The "conk" was a popular hairstyle for black men from the 1920s to the 1960s. The naturally "kinky" hair was chemically straightened using lye, and styled into pompadours that resembled white hairstyles. Some men chose to simply slick their straightened hair back to lie flat on their heads (like white males). At home, a "do-rag" (head scarf) had to be worn to prevent sweat or weather to from making the "conked" hair revert back to its natural (nappy) state. Relaxers had to be constantly reapplied as new hair grew in.

Malcolm X On The "Conk" Hairstyle

"This was the first really big step toward self-degradation: when I endured all of that pain, literally burning my flesh, to have it look like a white man's hair. I had joined that multitude of Negro men and women in America who are brainwashed into believing that the black people are 'inferior' and the white people 'superior' - that they will even violate and mutilate their God-created bodies to try to look 'pretty' by white standards.

Look around today, in every small town and big city, from two-bit catfish and soda-pop joints into the 'integrated' lobby of the Waldorf-Astoria, and you'll see conks on black men, and black women wearing these green and pink and purple and red and platinum blonde wigs. They're all more ridiculous than a slapstick comedy. It makes you wonder if the Negro has completely lost his sense of identity, lost touch with himself."

If the conk was a form of self-degradation for the black male, are hair straighteners, perms, and hair weaves inflicting the same kind of self-esteem damage on the unsuspecting black female?

A Classic Case Of The Pot Calling The Kettle "Nappy"

Despite the black male's own history of hair obsession, he is quick to belittle black women for all the time and money they spend on their hair, forgetting that HE is the one who rewards black females who come the closest to the white beauty standard. The black male's hypocritical and contradictory "pride" in his own blackness is seldom extended to black women who refuse to straighten their hair (imitate white beauty), and proudly and defiantly wear their natural hair short, braided, locked or dreadlocked.

Black females who wear their naturally nappy hair often run the risk of being labeled as less feminine and less attractive by black males than their long and permed-hair female peers. When black women try to live up (or down) to the unreasonable standards FORCED upon them by white society and black males (who often openly admire "white features"), they are ridiculed for wearing hair weaves, wigs, and "horse hair."

Some black male comedians -- who wear their OWN hair in locks as a sign of so-called "racial pride" -- often use black women's hair as the butt of their "unbe-weavable" and "nappy hair" humor.

> *"Now they aren't 'hos,' but there were some nappy-headed women on that team. Those are some of the ugliest women I've ever seen in my whole life." -- black comic D.L. Hughley on Jay Leno's "Tonight Show" (May 7, 2007), "joking" about the black girls on the Rutgers University Basketball team.*

Three FACTS (some) black males conveniently ignore: (1) the black female's hair is the SAME HAIR THAT GROWS OUT OF THEIR OWN SCALPS, (2) their GENES are *50 percent responsible for the hair of the black female*, and (3) their ridicule of (and contempt for) the black female's hair is **an ANNOUNCEMENT of their contempt for themselves, their genetics, and the hair on their own heads**

Men Set the Beauty Standards For Every Culture

In male-dominated cultures (like America) men, NOT women, set the standards for feminine beauty. Once this "beauty standard" is established, the women fall in line by conforming (or trying to conform) to these standards.

The most powerful males in a male-dominated society use the most desirable females to enhance their status in the eyes of other males. The women strike a similar bargain, trading their youth (fertility), and beauty (high status) for financial security (marriage).

Do not confuse 'status" with validation. In a male-dominated society, women CANNOT validate men; *only men can validate other men.*

The same is true for women in a male-dominated society. Women **do not validate** women; they COMPETE with other women. Only men can validate women.

Make no mistake. The black community is a male-dominated society. It does not matter that black females head up almost 70% of black households. That is an economic and political reality (tragedy), NOT a cultural choice. Like all males in a male-dominated society (like America) most males, in general, reject female leadership.

However, most women -- and black women are no exception -- actually welcome male leadership. In other words, most black men will not follow black women, but most black women will follow black men. The proof:

1. the preacher
2. the politician
3. the pimp

Whether it is the church, the meeting hall, or the street corner, black men usually lead; black women usually follow. With a few exceptions, black women are the foot soldiers and seldom the generals in most black organizations.

When it comes to female beauty standards, black males -- like all males in a male-dominated society -- decide what is desirable and what is not. In nearly every culture in the world, women look to the men in their culture to **validate** their self-worth and value as women.

Why is this so important to understand? **Because males collectively have the power to psychologically devastate females collectively if they do not validate their worth AS females.**

For example, the white male supremacist elevates the thin, blonde, blue-eyed, and pale-skinned female because she has the highest genetic value in a society that prizes "whiteness" and "lightness."

White females are programmed from childhood to accept this narrowly defined beauty standard, and will judge their own beauty (value) as females by this standard.

To attract men (a desirable mate), millions of white females imitate (or try to imitate) the beauty standard set by white males so they can be **validated** (and socially, financially, and romantically rewarded) by white males.

We know this is true from the astronomical number of white females (of all ages and incomes) who dye their hair blond and starve themselves to be thin.

The black(?) beauty standard for black females -- light skin, long hair, and European features -- is based on the same white supremacy standards. Black females learn the painful lesson at an early age that the most powerful and influential black males – as well as many average and ordinary black males -- "reward" black females who are closer in appearance to the white standard of beauty. The proof:

The light-skinned, Asian, or white wives and girlfriends of the most influential and successful (status-seeking) black men.

Black Male Invalidation Of Black Females

Detroit headline: A local DJ and club promoter cancels party that would let "light-skinned" black women into the club for free (2007)

In their attempt to gain status, some black males seek validation from the male with the highest status in a white supremacy society -- **the powerful white male.** When the black male deliberately chooses the female with the highest status (the white or white-appearing female) -- he is **unconsciously reinforcing his own inferiority** as a non-white person.

Even if she does not articulate it, the black female knows **instinctively** that the black male's (foolish) choice of (white) status over honoring his female mirror image is **unjust**, and is the greatest possible betrayal that a man can commit against the women of his race. This unspoken (but obvious) resentment accounts for a great deal of the black woman's anger toward black men. If the black female cannot depend on the black male to validate her worth as a female, who then can she turn to for protection?

If the black male refuses to validate (and value) the black woman (the black womb), how can he validate and value himself? Perhaps this explains his callous disregard for the black female and why black males slaughter each other without hesitation.

In 2007, when Beyonce appeared on the cover of Sports Illustrated's annual "Swimsuit Issue," angry white readers demanded subscription cancellations. One reason given by a white male subscriber: *"My daughters grew up identifying with the models in the Swimsuit Issue, and wanting to be like them. How is my daughter supposed to see herself in Beyonce?"*

The white male -- collectively -- understands the potentially devastating effect on the white female psyche when a non-white female is elevated above the white female -- even for something as trivial as a magazine cover. White males understand, collectively, that in order to validate themselves, they must validate (and uplift) the white female (the white womb). Together, this reinforces the VALUE of white life. The black male is encouraged to do just the opposite -- uplift white females and degrade black females -- yet the black male does not understand why **black life -- including his -- is so cheap.**

If black males took a page out of the white male's book, flipped their tragic (and self-genocidal) black scripts, and collectively embraced their female mirror images in all shades of brown and black, wearing a crown of natural hair, the companies that profit from hair weaves, wigs, permed-hair, and skin-bleaching products **would go out of business**.

Black males would then reap the rich psychological and spiritual rewards of LOVING THEMSELVES by elevating and honoring the (black) womb that delivered them into the world.

Bottom line: black males must accept some of the blame for the time, attention, anxiety, and insanity displayed by (some) black women about their hair.

How The Beauty Con Game Penalizes Black Males

"It is a gross contradiction (LIE) for a black male to say he loves himself yet desires to have children who look nothing like himself." -- Umoja

The black male's secret shame (of looking and being too black) explains his collective disrespect toward black females, and it explains why so many successful, status-seeking black males deliberately choose non-black females.

This has less to do with non-black women being more desirable and more to do with what non-black women represent to the self-esteem-starved black male who measures his success by white (male) standards.

Where Have All The Shampoo Girls Gone?

Recently, a black male blogger from Chicago asked: *"Where are all the white girls with the long, shiny hair I see in those TV shampoo commercials? I never seen them on the bus or the subway. They don't work downtown (like I do), or party in the suburbs. I have never once seen hair like that on a white female's head."*

The glorious manes seen on TV require hair additions, weaves, falls, wigs, sophisticated lighting techniques, film and photo retouching, and artificial substances and devices to add volume, curl, density, color, and sheen to hair. These media-manufactured (false) television images are the primary reason so many females (of all races) are so dissatisfied with the hair growing out of their scalps, and why so many women (of all races) chemically process, lengthen, straighten, thicken, curl, wave, kink, and color their hair to enhance it.

Different Is Beautiful

Black hair is unique when compared to the hair of many other races. It is only through the lens of white supremacy/ black inferiority that this difference becomes a demoralizing focal point for many blacks.

Mother Nature – the physical manifestation of God – made us perfect in God's sight. Our hair serves a sacred purpose in its natural state, growing up toward the sun, like a spiritual antenna that connects us to our Creator.

The self-loving black male and female embraces the softness, texture, durability, and versatility of black hair. They know "hair" can't cook, clean, make love, comfort us, earn a living, save a life, nurse us back to health, fix a flat tire or a leaky faucet, or raise a healthy, happy child.

They know that hair – be it long, short, curly, wavy, kinky or straight -- is only a small part of what makes a man or woman desirable. The self-loving black male and black female know from experience that a long head of hair shrinks in importance if what lies beneath the scalp is wholly unappealing.

"A person obsessed with the exterior is already inferior -- in his or her own mind." -- Umoja

"Hi everyone, I've never posted anything, but I had to get this off my chest.......

Let me start by saying that I'm 20, and I'm a dark-skinned sista. Up until my current relationship, nobody I have dated ever made any reference to my skin tone (I am not ashamed of my color, I just don't think it should be an issue in whether or not a person wants to talk to me).

On Sunday, while I was chilling in my boyfriend's room, his homeboy comes in and they start talking about girls. His boy looks at me and tells me that I'm pretty for a dark-skinned girl. My boyfriend jumps in and starts talking about how light-skinned women are so beautiful, how dark women are ugly, and how he should have gone to Southern (which is known for its light-skinned girls; we both go to Grambling).

He's been doing this a lot lately. It's confusing, as this is something he never did when we first started going out together. I've read about things like this happening to other people, but nothing compares to being face-to-face with it.

What I want to know is, has something like this ever happened to anybody else, and if so, what did you do? Give me some advice on what I should do; all help is welcome. Please, no light- or dark-skinned people bashing, as this is not the purpose of this post.

-- posted on black website (2009)

CHAPTER 27

HOW THE LANGUAGE OF WHITE SUPREMACY PENALIZES BLACK FEMALES

The white supremacy culture defines "beauty" by what is normal and desirable for white people: pale skin, hair, and eyes. This combination is considered the most beautiful -- especially for white females.

This color bias can be found in the commonly known phrases -- *"she was the fairest (lightest) in all the land"* and *"the fairer sex"* -- where *"fair"* is equivalent to *"white"* and "fairest in the land" is equivalent to "white beauty" meaning white females are the most "feminine" and the most beautiful.

The lightest (fairest) female who is blond, blue-eyed, and pale-skinned occupies the top rung of the beauty pedestal because she helps to maintain the illusion of white superiority. She is always assumed to be beautiful, regardless of how attractive or unattractive; or extraordinary or ordinary that particular pale-skinned, blue-eyed blonde may be.

The irony (and gross contradiction) of this FALSE beauty standard is the most beautiful blondes in Hollywood history -- Jean Harlow, Jayne Mansfield, Marilyn Monroe, Loni Anderson, and Pamela Sue Anderson – **were born brunettes.**

The reverse is true for the most masculine, sexually desirable male in a white supremacy society, who is often described as *"...tall, dark, and handsome."*

This definition of "male beauty," may give the dark-skinned black male an advantage in the proverbial bedroom BUT it puts him at a distinct disadvantage in the social and corporate arena. It also serves to connect the word "dark" with the word "masculine," and illustrates how the language of white supremacy PENALIZES the dark-skinned black female.

The Triple Demons Of Racism, Sexism, and Colorism

The black female in a white supremacy system is victimized by the triple demons of RACISM, SEXISM, and COLORISM, and faces more discrimination than any other person on the planet.

The black female is confronted on a daily basis by a hostile white and black world that systematically degrades AND denies her natural beauty. Starting as young as four or five, little black girls are taught that dark skin is unattractive and black hair is "bad hair," and must be straightened or permed so she will look "presentable" (less black). This destructive message follows black females well into their adult years.

The black female seldom sees her own unique, NATURAL beauty positively reflected on the TV screen, in magazine ads, music videos, or as the romantic female lead in a motion picture because *dark, feminine, and beautiful contradicts the lie of white (female) supremacy.*

Because of her consistently cruel treatment at the hands of blacks and whites, the black female has a sometimes well-deserved reputation for having a "bad attitude."

This "bad attitude" is largely a reaction AND a defense mechanism against a black-hating, female-hating, and black-female-hating world that is often perceived (correctly) by the black female as hostile and threatening to her self-esteem, physical safety, and psychological survival.

Do not misinterpret anything said here as pity for the black woman. This is not an attempt to make excuses for bad behavior, or an attempt to speak for black women. *The black female is not to be pitied; she is to be admired.*

Despite her cruel treatment over the last 500 years, the black female's style, language, innovation, creativity, courage, dancing and musical talents, intellectual brilliance, dignity, AND physical features *are imitated AND duplicated all over the world by NON-BLACK FEMALES.*

An (Unconscious) Black Celebration Of Self-Hatred

"It's like when you have coffee and it's too Black, it's too strong. So you have to add milk to it. You add enough milk you completely weaken it. If you add too much milk you won't even know you had coffee anymore." – Malcolm X

In the black community the light-skinned female OR black female with a white parent is uplifted as the ultimate sex symbol (because she looks more white) while the brown and dark-skinned female is seen as sexual chattel, or the butt of ignorant, self-hating "black" humor.

In Toni Morrison's novel, The Bluest Eye, Pecola Breedlove, a little black girl, believed that if she were white, the world would be hers. In Morrison's novel, The Color Purple, Celie was told (by another black person) that she would never be anything because she is *"poor, black, ugly, and a woman."*

When the black female is disrespected because SHE IS NOT WHITE ENOUGH, we are UNCONSCIOUSLY worshipping (ad submitting to) white supremacy AND *advertising our own self-hatred.*

Instead of celebrating the PURITY of heritage and RICHNESS of melanin the black female's beautiful dark skin represents, in our IGNORANCE, we celebrate the infusion of white blood into our genetic pool even when it was a result of *400 years of rape.*

When black people openly (or secretly) uplift lighter-skinned blacks over darker-skinned blacks, we are not only celebrating slave traditions, *we are celebrating SLAVE-OWNER TRADITIONS.*

Stolen Black Beauty

According to the 2009 American Society of Plastic Surgeons report, females accounted for 91 PERCENT of all cosmetic procedures. The most popular include breast augmentation, lip augmentation, facelifts, skin laser treatments, and butt implants.

European beauty standards have always associated full lips with beauty, youth, and sexuality -- which explains why the western medical/beauty industry is FRANTIC to create methods to duplicate them.

For example, around 1900, surgeons injected paraffin (wax) into the lips of white females *without success.* Liquid silicone was used in the 1960s to enhance lips until the fears about silicone stopped the practice. Currently, cosmetic surgeons are working on a procedure that allows them to use segments of neck muscle as lip grafts to "plump" them up.

Obviously, cost is no deterrent when it comes to MIMICKING THE BEAUTY OF BLACK FEMALES since *a single collagen lip treatment can cost $400 per injection*, and "lip enhancement" procedures can range anywhere from $500 to $5,000.

It is UNDENIABLE that the black female's round buttocks, full breasts, voluptuous lips, and age-resistant (melanated) skin are among the most prized and coveted physical features among the white female collective. The proof: the mass-production and mass-implementation of *the black female's uniquely beautiful racial characteristics* gross millions of dollars for plastic surgeons every year.

In light of the above FACTS, how can the black female still be the MOST DEGRADED FEMALE on the planet? One logical answer:

Black Females Must Be Inferior In A White Supremacy System

Openly acknowledging the beauty of the dark-skinned black female breaks the fundamental rule of the White Supremacy Beauty Con Game: *A non-white female cannot be equal OR superior to the white female.*

This explains why the black female's most coveted features -- full lips, breasts, and buttocks -- had to be DISCONNECTED from the black female and RECONNECTED to a white (or a near white) female using the awesome power (propaganda) of the white media.

However, the *illusion* of the superior white female flies in the face of the REALITY of butt implants, breast implants, face-lifts, liposuction, chin implants, curly perms, collagen lip injections, nose jobs, hair weaves, and colorful skin and eye makeup, cancer-causing suntans, and tanning salons to add COLOR to pale skin.

This blatant IMITATION and DUPLICATION of the "inferior" black female explains why the white media feverishly promotes the "round buttocks" of (a white-looking) Jennifer Lopez and the "big lips" of Angelina Jolie: *to CLAIM and RE-NAME "black beauty" in the name of "whiteness."*

The 'Hottentot Venus' (1810)

Several figures bend straining for a better look, while a male figure at the far right of the image even holds his seeing-eye glass up to better behold the woman's body. The European observers remark on the woman's body: *"Oh! God Damn what roast beef!"* and *"Ah! how comical is nature."*

***

In 1810, Saartjie Baartman, known as the **Hottentot Venus**, was lured from her South African village with promises of becoming wealthy and famous. She was exhibited (like a circus act), exploited, ridiculed due to her unique anatomy (by white standards), and forced to entertain white spectators by shaking her buttocks.

She died in 1815, penniless and heartbroken. Even death offered no relief from humiliation and exploitation. Her brain and genitals were put on display in Paris until 1974.

Several prints dating from the early nineteenth century illustrate the sensation generated by the spectacle of "The Hottentot Venus." A French print entitled "La Belle Hottentot," for example, depicts the Khosian woman standing with her buttocks exposed on a box-like pedestal.

Decades after her death, the Hottentot Venus inspired white females from America to Europe to adopt fashions that gave them the appearance of having protruding buttocks (like the "inferior" black female's).

Polanaise costume, 1883

'The Parisian' by Pierre-Auguste Renoir (1874)

The uniquely beautiful features of the black female are STILL the targets of ridicule by the white media, clearly ignoring the hundreds of thousands of white females who pay thousands of dollars, risking their health, and in some cases their lives, to undergo risky plastic surgery and skin-tanning -- **to look LESS white.**

Which brings to mind a CRITICAL (and revealing) question:

If the black female is the least attractive female in a white supremacy society, why are her unique physical characteristics the most sought-after cosmetic and surgical procedures by the MOST attractive (white) female?

IMITATION always exposes the LIE and reveals the TRUTH.

Tyra Banks Swears Off Fake Hair For Her Show (August 23rd, 2009)

Tyra Banks will be keeping it real on her talk show this fall -- it being her hair. The host announced Monday that she's swearing off extensions on the New season, starting Sept. 8. "No fake hair at all!" she tweeted. "Will be the hair coming out of my scalp! For all to see!" In a press statement, she said the show aims to help women "own and rock what they've got and be...

Months After Her Announcement...

Tyra Banks Announces Her Show Will End After Current Season (December 28, 2009)

Wrapping at the end of its fifth season in the spring of 2010, it will be lights out for the show that brought viewers memorable weave-exposing, cellulite-revealing and tear-jerking moments. Banks will focus on the launch of Bankable Studios, a N.Y.-based film production company currently reviewing possible projects.

CHAPTER 28

WHY BLACK FEMALE ENTERTAINERS MUST WEAR WEAVES THAT LOOK LIKE WEAVES

"If your hair is relaxed, white people are relaxed. If your hair is nappy, they're not happy." -- Comedian Paul Mooney

In the spring of 2010, black filmmaker, Tyler Perry, hosted an hour-long show on the TV Guide channel to promote his new movie, "Why Did I Get Married, Too?" When the first cast member, Jill Scott, a talented singer and actress, joined Perry on the stage, she looked like a beautiful black queen in her curve-hugging black dress, and perfectly groomed afro.

However, as one of her scenes in the movie played across the screen, it was hard not to wonder (with dismay) why Ms. Scott had to wear such an unflattering weave instead wearing her own beautifully natural hair?

Miss Scott is not alone. It is extremely rare to see a black female entertainer wearing her own unprocessed hair that hasn't been bleached or isn't hidden underneath an expensive wig or a unrealistic-looking weave.

This is NOT intended to ridicule black females OR their hairstyles. It's true, white females enhance their natural hair with chemicals, weaves, hairpieces, and extensions, however they're ENHANCING -- NOT DISGUISING -- the ethnic characteristics of their natural hair.

The opposite is true for today's black female entertainers, who wear weaves that do NOT match their natural hair texture, length, or color. Another difference between black females and white females who wear weaves is the vast majority of weaves REINFORCE white -- NOT black -- beauty standards.

Is "Weave-Wearing" By Choice Or By Demand?

We propose it is the latter – that black female entertainers MUST WEAR UNBELIEVABLE WEAVES THAT LOOK LIKE WEAVES -- if they want to "make it" in the entertainment industry. How do unbelievable weaves **PROMOTE** white supremacy? There are seven obvious benefits:

BENEFIT #1 -- No matter how sexy, talented or beautiful a black female entertainer is, her UNBELIEVABLE WEAVE subtracts major beauty points and GUARANTEES that the beautiful black female will **never be seen as competition or as a threat** to the throne of white female supremacy.

Malcolm X On The "Conk" Hairstyle

"This was the first really big step toward self-degradation: when I endured all of that pain, literally burning my flesh, to have it look like a white man's hair.

I had joined that multitude of Negro men and women in America who are brainwashed into believing that the black people are 'inferior' and the white people 'superior' - that they will even violate and mutilate their God-created bodies to try to look 'pretty' by white standards.

Look around today, in every small town and big city, from two-bit catfish and soda-pop joints into the 'integrated' lobby of the Waldorf-Astoria, and you'll see conks on black men, and black women wearing these green and pink and purple and red and platinum blonde wigs.

They're all more ridiculous than a slapstick comedy. It makes you wonder if the Negro has completely lost his sense of identity, lost touch with himself."

BENEFIT #2 -- UNBELIEVABLE WEAVES make it appear that black females are imitating and envying the (superior) white female. Imitation may be the sincerest form of flattery BUT NOT when it DEGRADES the imitators.

BENEFIT #3 -- UNBELIEVABLE WEAVE-WEARING black females are the best advertising white supremacy can buy, and help maintain the illusion of the superior white female by promoting white supremacy beauty standards.

BENEFIT #4 -- The rich and famous UNBELIEVABLE WEAVE-WEARING black female celebrity is the MOST VISIBLE "role model" for young (and not so young), impressionable black females, which is easily observed by the distressing number of black females who wear unflattering, easily detectable, and unnatural-looking hair weaves.

BENEFIT #5 -- Wearing UNBELIEVABLE WEAVES destroys the self-esteem of the unsuspecting black female who knows (subconsciously) that the enhanced image in her mirror is based on something that is NOT REAL. This confirms in her own SUBCONSCIOUS MIND that her own beauty is NONEXISTENT.

BENEFIT #6 -- UNBELIEVABLE WEAVES program black boys AND black men to see black females as "fakes," frauds, second-rate, and wanna-be white females who do NOT like, respect, or value themselves.

The MAIN one who benefits from UNBELIEVABLE WEAVES is the white female who NOW looks like genuine article to black males. This reinforces her superiority, and the inferiority of the black female, and has a disastrous effect on black male/black female relationships.

BENEFIT #7 -- Black females make up the largest share of the *$2-billion dollar hair-care industry, largely due to the explosion of hair weaves.*

According to the 16th annual report on "The Buying Power of Black America" by Target Marketing, a black consumer research firm, blacks spent almost the same amount **($7.4 billion)** on hair-care and personal products that we spent on education **($7.5 billion)**.

The same white-owned hair care companies that shunned black consumers in the past, are dominating the black haircare market -- to the delight of some misguided black females, who may get a psychological boost from using haircare products that are DESIGNED for the white female's hair because it makes them feel more acceptable (and more beautiful) by white standards.

The black female hair-care market is the beauty industry's biggest (and most disrespected) CASH COW. This may explain why there are NO nationally advertised products designed for the NATURAL HAIR OF BLACK FEMALES.

Is 'Natural Hair' A No-No For Black Females?

Was Paul Mooney right when he said our natural hair makes whites unhappy? After reading the evidence below, the reader can judge for him or herself.

The "Evidence"

(1987) Woman Fired For Cornrows Sues Hyatt Hotel in Virginia" - Cheryl Tatum, a cashier, was fired from the Hyatt Regency Hotel in Crystal City, VA, for her refusal to change her "extreme" cornrow hairstyle. Tatum, a black female, filed a lawsuit against the hotel, charging race discrimination and seeking back pay, punitive damages, and attorney's fees.

(2000) FedEx fired several black employees in New York for wearing dreadlocks. Six years later, FedEx reached a settlement agreeing that dreadlocks could be worn for "religious reasons."

(2006) Claire Anderson, a Marietta, GA teacher is planning to file a lawsuit after she was fired over her hairstyle, because her "hairstyle did not fit the image of the school." Just after she began to wear her hair combed out in a full afro, she was called to the office and fired.

(2006) Fox-TV's Divorce Court Judge, Mablean Ephriam, was fired after failing to reach an "agreement" over pay and her hairstyle. According to Ephriam, Fox demanded that she wear a wig to "expedite" the hair styling process. Since she was unwilling to agree to the terms, she stepped down after seven years of hosting the successful court show.

(2007) Donna Tate-Allison, a guard at Haynesville Correctional Center, was fired for violating the Department of Corrections' grooming policy, which forbids "extreme and eccentric haircuts." Tate-Allison, a 46-year-old black female, wore her short dreadlocks pinned underneath a hat.

Another black female corrections officer, Juanita Hudson, who wears her hair in cornrows, was informed that "cornrows, dreadlocks, and braids would not be allowed." After a two-day suspension, one day after receiving a favorable performance review – Hudson took her braids out.

(2010) ABC-TV reported a story about two black women who were denied employment at the Six Flags amusement park in Largo, MD, because their locks hairstyle was considered "offensive" by Six Flags management, which does not permit "any hairstyle that detracts or takes away from Six Flags' theme."

One black female job applicant was informed by a supervisor that management was adhering strictly that year to their "grooming policy," DESPITE the fact that Largo, MD area is 93 percent black.

Why Do (Some) Whites Find 'Natural Hair' On Black Females So Threatening? One Answer:

Once the black female embraces her natural beauty, her self-respect will skyrocket. The day she stops imitating "white beauty" (white supremacy) and embraces her own GOD-GIVEN natural beauty (black normalcy), she will ask herself, "What other lies have I been taught about myself?"

The black mother is the FIRST TEACHER of the next black generation. Once she sheds her former (degraded) self, her NEW EYES will help her daughters and sons to SEE what has been there all along, right in front of their eyes:

The majesty of their African ancestors

Her sons will embrace her natural beauty and stop looking elsewhere for the beauty within themselves.

The black male will take her cue, and will see the black female with NEW EYES, and will see his own reflection in her beauty. His self-respect, self-esteem, and sanity will skyrocket as he stops believing the lie, looking outside himself for what is right INSIDE himself.

And that is NOT an acceptable outcome for the black male, female, and child in a white supremacy society."

-- Umoja

Complexions

An essay by Mark Twain

(white male author of 'The Adventures of Tom Sawyer')

Nearly all black and brown skins are beautiful, but a beautiful white skin is rare. Where dark complexions are massed, they make the whites look bleached-out, unwholesome, and sometimes frankly ghastly. I could notice this as a boy, down South in the slavery days before the war. The splendid black satin skin of the South African Zulus of Durban seemed to me to come very close to perfection...

The white man's complexion makes no concealments. It can't. It seemed to have been designed as a catch-all for everything that can damage it. Ladies have to paint it, and powder it, and cosmetic it, and diet it with arsenic, and enamel it, and be always enticing it, and persuading it, and pestering it, and fussing at it, to make it beautiful; and they do not succeed.

But these efforts show what they think of the natural complexion, as distributed. As distributed it needs these helps. The complexion which they try to counterfeit is one which nature restricts to the few--to the very few. To ninety-nine persons she gives a bad complexion, to the hundredth a good one. The hundredth can keep it--how long? Ten years, perhaps.

The advantage is with the Zulu, I think. He starts with a beautiful complexion, and it will last him through. And as for the Indian brown--firm, smooth, blemishless, pleasant, and restful to the eye, afraid of no color, harmonizing with all colors and adding a grace to them all--I think there is no sort of chance for the average white complexion against that rich and perfect tint.

CHAPTER 29

STRAIGHT TALK
ABOUT BEAUTY

"Civilized" VS Primitive Beauty Standards

Americans (and other technologically advanced societies) spend billions of dollars to artificially enhance what nature did -- or did not -- give them. Body and face paint, artificially produced suntans, hair weaves, wigs, hairpieces, toupees, hair transplants, makeup, lipstick, eye shadow, hair color, tattoos, piercings, and plastic surgery are used by millions of "civilized" people to make themselves more appealing to the opposite (or the same) sex.

What, then, is the real difference between a woman from the Central African Sara tribe with lip plates and a white woman in Hollywood, California with breast implants (breast plates)?

How is the New Zealand Maori warrior with facial tattoos and body markings more "primitive-looking" than the white male college student in Paris, France with body piercings and tattoos?

The westernized Beauty Con Game is a multi-billion-dollar industry that has claimed billions of victims -- of all races -- by creating a false standard of beauty for whites and non-whites.

In order to keep the billions pouring in, the industry must set the bar for "beauty" (normalcy) impossibly high to keep the white and non-white populations insecure. Then, the industry can sell cosmetic "solutions" for imaginary imperfections.

The World's Biggest Beauty Secret

The biggest beauty secret on the planet cannot be found in a $300 vial of skin cream or in a pair of skilled plastic surgeon's hands. What is this secret?

Could it be the infusion of African genes into the European gene pool that gives pale skin more color (and a deeper tan), makes hair thicker, wavy, or curly, and adds more sensuousness (fullness) to lips, noses, and other facial features?

If one studies the history of Africans (Moors), who traveled the ancient world and conquered Europe long before Christopher Columbus sailed to America, one might imagine that "swarthy" (dark) and "olive" complexions, dark, curly, wavy, and wavy-kinky hair; dark hair, dark eyes, and full lips in *some* parts of Europe may be visible evidence of African genetic influences.

While this cannot be stated as scientific fact; it is certainly not an unreasonable theory. If, as scientists have claimed, ALL human life began in Africa -- every man, woman and child is a **modification of the original African man and woman.** (Links & sources available on website).

True Beauty Is Not For Sale At The Cosmetic Counter

True beauty is NOT a small, pointy nose, long blond hair, or a bone-thin, pale body. Beauty is the look in a lover's eyes, the curve of a woman's cheek, or a man's broad, strong back. It is a smile that lights up a face, or a laugh that makes us smile. It's the graceful way someone moves or dances. Beauty is eloquence; intelligence; wisdom; kindness; and determination.

God gave all of us something special; a special quality or gift that no one else in the world possesses in the same way we do. God's greatest gifts can be found in a pair of eyes that sparkle, in the hands of a doctor who delivers a new life into the world, or a powerful voice that makes the angels weep. Or it might be the greatest gift of all: a kind, intelligent, loving human being.

Mother Nature Gets The Last Word

Is there a beauty standard that is objective, logical, and can be applied to all human beings, regardless of race? *Absolutely.* Who is qualified to set this standard? The most powerful force on earth: **Mother Nature.** Mother Nature is the **visible, physical, and tangible manifestation of God**. The final judge of all that is good and perfect in this world.

Mother Nature does not acknowledge beauty or ugliness based on artificial, man-made standards. Mother Nature does not put more value on an eye because it is blue than she does on a brown eye. Only man and woman, in their endless foolishness, put more value on superficial, useless differences than they do on the value of a human life.

The shape of a nose, the color of an eye, the length of hair, or a jutting chin is a matter of taste, NOT proof of racial superiority. There is NO functional purpose straight blond hair has that is not also present in dark nappy hair.

Is a blind blue eye superior to a brown eye with 20-20 vision?

What does Mother Nature consider beautiful? A strong body, limbs without deformities; healthy skin, teeth, vitality, good vision, hearing, and speech are beautiful to nature. But the **most important trait in every species** is invisible to the human eye: **THE ABILITY TO REPRODUCE.** Yet, the most fertile woman on the planet – THE BLACK WOMAN – is the most demeaned woman on the planet. Again, the question is:

Could the TRUE emotion that fuels so much contempt for the fertile, full-lipped, full-hipped, curvaceous black female be ENVY?

Mother Nature may have already answered that question.

CHAPTER 30

LEGEND OF THE PURPLE PEOPLE

In a distant place and time on planet Earth, there were two races of people in a tiny country called PURPLE LAND. The PURPLE PEOPLE had bright purple skin, purple eyes, green lips, and thick, green rope hair. The white minority in PURPLE LAND had white skin, blond hair, and blue eyes.

The PURPLE PEOPLE owned and controlled all the banks (and the money), the schools and universities, the businesses, the criminal justice system, and the government.

Despite being in a supremely superior position, the PURPLE PEOPLE never missed an opportunity to tell the white people how inferior white people were. The PURPLE PEOPLE even had white statues on their lawns with exaggerated white features, like bulging blue eyes and thin lips that stretched from ear to ear.

PURPLE PEOPLE claimed the white people were too stupid to learn, but just to make sure they stayed stupid, the PURPLE PEOPLE created a separate and unequal school system that was inferior to the PURPLE schools. The white schools were in horrible condition; with leaking roofs, lead paint, broken desks, and the outdated schoolbooks discarded by the better-educated PURPLE CHILDREN.

The teachers who couldn't cut it in the PURPLE schools were sent to the white schools where no one would know the difference. Since the PURPLE PEOPLE had a superior education, naturally they got most of good jobs, while the whites took the menial jobs, or had no jobs at all.

It was a depressing sight to travel through the white neighborhoods. The sidewalks were cracked, the city street sweepers skipped weekly cleanings and the street lamps stayed broken. On every third corner, there were liquor stores that stayed open 24 hours a day – some within blocks of white grammar schools. Young white males openly sold crack, heroin, and reefer on the street corners but the police seemed oblivious to their criminal activity.

In the morning, the commuter trains from the PURPLE suburbs would pass through the white neighborhoods. The PURPLE PEOPLE on the train would shake their heads and say, it didn't make sense for people to live like animals. Of course, PURPLE PEOPLE never said it when white people were around. The white women were horrible and overweight from eating cheap junk food since fresh fruits and vegetables were too expensive.

The men were worse, always standing on street corners and drinking out of paper bags, and blaming the PURPLE MAN for all their problems. Even the movies and television were depressing because white people were always playing fools or criminals.

White people never saw white people kissing, hugging, or making love on TV. Secretly, some whites believed that love and romance were reserved for PURPLE PEOPLE. Some whites resented the PURPLE-PEOPLE-ONLY images, and started a white civil rights organization to fight PURPLE racism. Some complained to their church leaders, and were told to stay on their knees, pray, and to stop worrying about this life because they would be rewarded in the next one.

This confused the white people because no one told PURPLE PEOPLE, who read the same Bible, to stay on their knees. After a while, the white people were too confused and demoralized to fight the powers-that-be. They figured, if they couldn't beat the PURPLE PEOPLE, maybe they better join them.

They hung framed pictures of their savior, a PURPLE MAN with green hair, on their living room walls. They didn't understand why so many young white people were turning their backs on religion and on the PURPLE MAN.

If only, white parents lamented aloud, they hadn't been born with such ugly white skin, blond hair, and blue eyes, their lives, and their children's lives would have been much easier.

White women began using green dye on their blonde hair so they would look more PURPLE and less white. They bought makeup that would turn their pale pink skin a deep purple and green lipstick to wear on their lips. They wore purple contacts to hide their blue eyes then swore they weren't wearing any.

Upon seeing the white people strutting proudly in their new get-ups, the PURPLE PEOPLE would chuckle, shake their heads, and say under their breath, *"Isn't it sad to be white? No matter how hard they try, they'll never be as good as PURPLE PEOPLE."*

The white women suffered the most because white men thought PURPLE WOMEN were the absolute sex bomb. The PURPLE WOMEN loved to sneak into the white community to get some of that big, white, you-know-what that the white men were more than happy to give them.

The white man's self-esteem was so battered and bruised, he didn't feel much like a man, so he decided the easiest (and safest) way to be equal to the PURPLE MAN was to find *any* PURPLE WOMAN who would have him, so he could be less white and be more acceptable (more purple).

Unfortunately, the ones who suffered most were the white women who had to pick up the pieces and raise their children alone, while the demoralized and frightened white man sought validation in a pair of PURPLE arms. The poor white woman hid her hurt and bewilderment behind a wall of hostility because she was too proud to admit her own men thought she was inferior.

White women didn't know what to do or where to turn. They had tried looking as PURPLE as they could, but the white men wanted the REAL THING. More and more white women turned to religion. They prayed every night to the framed picture of the PURPLE SAVIOR above their empty beds and asked Him to wake the white man up and tell him to come back home where he belonged.

THE END

"When you teach a man to hate his lips, the lips that God gave him, the shape of the nose that God gave him, the texture of the hair that God gave him, the color of the skin that God gave him, you've committed the worst crime that a race of people can commit."

– Malcolm X

Recipe #10

DEGRÂDE the Black Female

A 1991 survey commissioned by the American Association of University Women, discovered that little girls lose their self-esteem by adolescence. The study also found that black girls were still self-confident in high school compared to white and Hispanic girls.

Researchers concluded that black parents may be teaching their children that there is nothing wrong with them, only with the way the world treated them.

"This should encourage white people to look with admiration at the black community," said Dr. Linda Kerber, a history professor at the University of Iowa.

AFTER the study that claimed black girls had higher self-esteem than white girls, the mainstream media launched a FULL-ON ASSAULT against the black female image.

A coincidence OR by design?

CHAPTER 31

SIX REASONS BLACK FEMALES ARE DEGRADED (IN A WHITE SUPREMACY SOCIETY)

Why are black females degraded in America?

REASON #1: MISOGYNY – HATRED OF WOMEN

Despite Sigmund Freud's claims of female "penis envy," it is more common for men in a sexist, male-dominated society to envy women. Men who seek absolute power over the lives of others often envy (and fear) women for their genetic power (the ability to create life) – something NO man, regardless of wealth or status -- can do.

Men who harbor secret homosexual urges may envy and resent women for the freedom to have sex with men without fear of exposure or disgrace. It is interesting that the word *misogyny* is derived from ancient Greek word, *misogunia*, a culture where male homosexuality was common.

If the female is envied for her SEXUAL NORMALCY and her GENETIC POWER, then the black female – the most fertile female on earth who can create life under the most adverse conditions (starvation, famine, disease) – must, logically speaking, be the most envied of all females.

This may explain one reason the black female is viciously targeted and degraded in a white male-dominated society that is founded on misogyny, sexism, racism, white supremacy, and closet male homosexuality.

Her superior genetics contradict the LIE of white supremacy. As the creator of all AUTHENTICALLY BLACK LIFE in a black-hating, white supremacy GLOBAL system, she will be attacked without mercy until she is medically, sexually, biologically, psychologically, and spiritually DESTROYED.

REASON #2: TO DISGUISE THE TRUTH ABOUT THE MASS RAPE OF AFRICAN FEMALE SLAVES

To retain a sense of their (imaginary) moral AND racial superiority, white slave-owners PROJECTED THE BLAME for their own horrific crimes BY TRANSFORMING the African female slave from a Victim into an "immoral and sexually loose" Villain. This (false) image of the black female persists to this day.

A Short History Of Rape In America

Prior to 1972, rape was a capital crime that was punishable by death. More than 90% of the executions for rape involved black males who had allegedly raped a white female BUT statistics showed the vast majority of rapes in the U.S. involved white males raping black and white females.

About 5% of executions for rape involved a black male who had allegedly raped a black female, and approximately 2% of executions for rape involved a white male who had allegedly raped a white female.

A white male has never been executed for raping a black female because raping black females was not a crime.

Was It The Evidence Or The System (Of White Supremacy)?

(1987) Tawana Bradley, a 15-year old black female, accused six white men, some police officers, of raping her. After missing for four days, she was found unresponsive in a garbage bag near an apartment where she had once resided. Her torn clothing was burned and her body had been smeared with feces. After hearing the evidence, a grand jury ruled that Brawley had NOT been the victim of a sexual assault, and that she had lied.

It was later rumored that one of the accused men had committed suicide after the story became public (the authors were unable to confirm this). Tawana Bradley, her parents, and supporters still maintain to this day that she told the truth. Alton H. Maddox, Jr., Bradley's black lawyer, lost his law license "indefinitely" due to his "conduct" in the Brawley case – an unusual and excessively harsh decision against a criminal lawyer for defending his client.

(2006) Crystal Mangum, 27, a black female student at North Carolina Central University, accused three white Duke University students, members of the Duke Blue Devils men's lacrosse team, of raping her at a party held where she had been hired as an exotic dancer.

Prosecutor Mike Nifong mounted a vigorous case against the white males from prominent white families after the case made national headlines. The defense attorneys for the white male students reported that a private DNA lab had found DNA from multiple males in Mangum's body – but allegedly none that belonged to the accused players. Based on further "investigation," the rape charges were dropped. Nifong was disbarred, making Nifong *the first prosecutor in North Carolina history to lose his law license for prosecuting a case.*

(2007) Megan Williams, 23, held captive for a week by six white males and females, who allegedly raped and stabbed her, and forced her to eat animal feces. Two years later, after a series of "encounters" with law enforcement, she Williams "recanted" her story, despite credible evidence and photos taken at the time that indicated she had been severely injured and traumatized as claimed. Did Williams tell a bald-faced lie? Or was this poor, young black female pressured by the legal system to recant her story? Unfortunately, we will never know the truth.

The Black Female AKA The "Willing Whore"

IF the black female is a "willing whore" by nature, every sexual encounter she has must be voluntary because a "willing whore" CANNOT BE RAPED. If a "willing whore" cannot be raped then it is IMPOSSIBLE for a white male to rape a black female whether during slavery, or even in the 21st century.

There is ONE indisputable FACT: Blacks do not control the criminal justice process, the evidence collectors, the DNA labs, the prosecutors, the criminal court judges, the way law is interpreted, or the way the media defines who is a victim and who is not. Nor do blacks control the hidden hands that mete out the usual kind of American "justice" that awaits most black defendants AND black victims in a white supremacist criminal (just us) justice system

Based on historical evidence, we can (logically) draw the following conclusion:

If evidence can be falsified by police and district attorneys to CONVICT black defendants, it is logical to assume evidence can be falsified to ACQUIT white defendants.

Any black female, criminal lawyer, or prosecutor who DARES to accuse a white male in a white supremacy society – especially a white male authority figure or a white male from a prominent white family -- of raping her will face the full wrath of the law.

These highly publicized false rape allegations demonstrate that black female rape victims will NEVER receive the kind of media attention or public support or empathy that white female victims regularly receive from the police, the courts, the media, and from society in general.

Black females are MORE likely to be raped than any other group in the U.S. but are LESS likely to be believed or to have their victimizers caught and convicted. Why? *Because ignoring, covering up, and BLAMING black female rape victims is an AMERICAN TRADITION.*

AXIOM #6: The "Black Victim = A Victimless Crime" Theory. A black person in a conflict with a white person (or white system) cannot BE the victim in a White Supremacy society. The black individual is ALWAYS at fault, regardless of who initiated the conflict, or what facts or evidence are present.

It is critical that the SOILED SEXUAL REPUTATION of the black female be preserved at all costs to reinforce the myth (LIE) that female slaves were WILLING WHORES – NOT RAPE VICTIMS of the most notorious rapists in the history of the known world.

How many black females have been raped by white males but are afraid to report the crimes and risk the same fate of a Tawana Bradley or Megan Williams? Unfortunately, we will never know the answer to that question.

Is there a mass-media conspiracy against black females?

On August 9, 2006, the MTV network broadcast a new cartoon portraying two bikini-wearing black women, squatting on all fours, with leashes around their necks, and defecating (using the bathroom) on the floor. Supposedly, the show was lampooning Snoop Dogg, who had no involvement in the show.

The show aired at 12:30pm on Saturday when thousands of children, teens, and young adults were watching. The cable TV station, owned by Viacom, Inc., a media giant, defended the episode, calling it "social satire."

Would MTV have created a cartoon showing two bikini-clad WHITE FEMALES, defecating on the floor with leases around their neck held by a Snoop Dogg lookalike?

The answer should be OBVIOUS....

REASON #3: TO PROMOTE WHITE FEMALE SUPERIORITY AND BLACK FEMALE INFERIORITY VIA 'THE ENTERTAINMENT' INDUSTRY

"Is there a mass-media conspiracy against the black female?" This question was recently asked in an article on a popular black website – and with good reason. The mounting evidence presented here should leave no doubt that someone is waging OPEN WARFARE against the black female.

Popular TV Shows Aimed At Black Youth

Talk Shows: an almost daily line-up of poor, promiscuous black female "baby-mommas" who don't know "who the baby daddy is." The darker the female, the more degraded she will be on the show.

Rap Songs & Rap Videos: songs about insulting, degrading, torturing, and killing black females. Young and beautiful black females are stereotyped as booty-shaking, scantily-dressed video "hos" to **neutralize the beauty (and humanity) of young, beautiful black females.**

> *"I call women bitches and hos because all the women I've met since I've been out here are bitches and hos."* Bushwick Bill (Richard Shaw) a member of the hip group 'Geto Boys'. *When asked at the National Association of Black Journalists convention what he calls his mother, he replied, "I call her a woman but I am not fucking my mother. If I was fucking you, you'd be a bitch."*

Black Reality Shows: Whenever black males are "looking for love" on reality TV, the white female is almost ALWAYS chosen over the black female. Even when competing for a black male's love, **the black female is almost ALWAYS the least desirable (inferior) choice.**

In REALITY, these reality shows are scripted by white writers, directors, and producers – regardless of any black figurehead who appears on the rolling credits as "executive producer."

Once the cameras are turned off, the "loving" interracial reality-show couple go their separate ways with paychecks in hand. In contrast, in white reality shows the white contestants ALWAYS CHOOSE a white person, and the sole black contestant is usually eliminated by the first or second episode.

TV Commercials

The dark-skinned black female has become an endangered species in most TV commercials, replaced by the racially ambiguous, non-white female with a white parent (a so-called bi-racial female).

According to one black mother of a child actor, white (female) casting directors prefer to cast the non-white children of white females over the brown and dark-skinned children of black men and women in television commercials and print advertising.

"Some black actors have to almost threaten to quit a show or movie in order to get a black actress cast as their love interest.

(Eriq LaSalle, Russell Hornsby, etc.) Otherwise, white women are usually the first and only choice by white men who really hate black men, but envy the alleged sexual prowess of black men.

Although latinas are second choice many times, white men (and white women) prefer to see white women with black men. I think they hate the fact that they enjoy watching black men and white women together and exact revenge against black men because of this sexual fetish.

Unless they have a little bit of clout, a black writer/producer takes a risk to suggest casting a black actress darker than Halle Berry who isn't Gabrielle Union or Sanaa Lathan. I'm relaying what I know to be true from my own personal experiences." -- L.R., television writer (name withheld by request)

Black Females On TV Fifty Years After Amos And Andy

NBC's "ER" (1994-2009), a medical drama, where black actor, Eriq LaSalle, and his white female co-star, Elizabeth Corday, engage in an on-again, off-again interracial romance.

LaSalle's was uncomfortable with his character's affair with a white woman and felt it was an insult to black women because his character had unsuccessful relationships with black women in the past. LaSalle "requested" that the show's writers end the affair because *"it sends a message I'm not comfortable with, a message that this relationship could be a happy one."*

Ally McBeal (1997-2002), a comedy-drama featuring a single white female lawyer in an all-white law firm. Ally's best friend, a single black female, could not get OR keep a man. To add insult to injury, the first black actor cast in a recurring role on the show only had eyes for white Ally McBeal, who eventually dumped him.

Desperate Housewives (2004-present), a comedy-drama focused around the lives of several white females and their love lives. The first black female cast member, actress Alfre Woodard, portrayed an older, dark-skinned, overweight female wearing an unkempt, multi-colored wig. Of course, she was manless (except for the man she kept chained in her basement).

HBO's Sopranos TV Series (1999-2007), a drama about Italian mobsters, cast the following handful of black actresses during its eight-season run:

- A dark-skinned homeless female who defecates on a public sidewalk then wipes her (brown) behind with a piece of newspaper
- A dark-skinned, toothless prostitute who sexually propositions Tony Soprano's demented, elderly uncle
- An overweight, dark-skinned female who gets into an argument with Tony Soprano's sister during an anger management session
- An attractive, light-skinned undercover FBI agent (a potential white man's whore) who flirts with Tony Soprano at a doctor's office
- A prostitute (a white man's whore) in a Jewish-owned whorehouse who boasts she can make the Hasidic Jew's "bennie' (penis) spin."
- The dark-skinned girlfriend of Tony Soprano's elderly Jewish friend, who is NEVER seen with her in public. She dies in his bed without a wedding ring, any fanfare, or even a funeral in a television series OBSESSED with funerals. (a typically bad ending for a white man's whore).

Grey's Anatomy (2005-present), a medical drama featuring a passionate, interracial relationship between black actor, Isaiah Washington, and Asian actress, Sandra Oh. *It is very revealing (and anti-black-female) that the most VIRILE black male on the show is paired with a non-black female.*

1899 sheet music cover published by Saxx Music Co.,Boston

"I'm calling you ugly, I could push your face in some dough and make gorilla cookies." -- Fred Sanford speaking to Aunt Esther, a dark-skinned black female. (from the hit TV series "Sanford and Son" (1972 -1977)

The Top Seven Roles For Black Actresses In Hollywood Movies (With A Few Exceptions)

1. The light-skinned or non-white female with a white parent who lusts after white men (aka a "white man's whore"). The "provocative mulatto wench" stereotype is a carryover from the early 1900s minstrel shows). Some examples of the tragic mulatto/white man's whore are black actresses Lisa Bonet in *'Angel Heart'* and Halle Berry in *'Monster Ball.'*
2. The long-haired, light-skinned, and/or so-called 'bi-racial' black female who plays the love interest of the main black male character (if he is not romantically involved with a non-black female).
3. The brown-or-dark-skinned, hostile, immoral, tough, ghetto, black female who can't get or keep a man.
4. The brown- or dark-skinned monster mother.
5. The brown-or-dark-skinned female prostitute
6. The dark-skinned obese, single, and desperate black female, mammy figure, or demonic character.
7. A black actress who does not fit any of the above six categories automatically defaults to the largest category of black actresses: *the UNEMPLOYED.* It is the NORM to see one black actor in a commercial, TV show, or movie without a single black actress in sight.

The 'Defective, Undesirable Black Female' Theme

District 9 (2009), science fiction movie portraying (dark-skinned) Nigerian women as savage cannibals/prostitutes who have sex with insect-aliens.

Hollywood Wives: The New Generation: (2003), made-for-TV movie. Robin Givens plays the single black female friend of romantically involved white females. True to Hollywood's racist form, Givens was the only female who did not have a man. (aka the defective, unlovable black female).

Lord of War: (2005): an arms dealers (Nicolas Cage) is propositioned by two beautiful, dark-skinned African prostitutes but finds out that both women are HIV-infected. By linking the sexually attractive black female with immorality, low character, and disease, this effectively NEUTRALIZES the beauty of the black female: A NECESSITY in a system of white supremacy.

Norbit (2007), Big Momma's House 1 & 2 (2000-2006), and Tyler Perry's Madea comedies: revolve around black males wearing wigs, dresses, and pantyhose to portray dark-skinned, obese, crude, violent, and romantically undesirable black females.

To the authors' knowledge, there are NO WHITE ACTORS who have built an entire movie career stereotyping obese white females by wearing dresses, wigs, and stockings. In fact, it is rare to see an obese white female in a Hollywood film or television show DESPITE the significant number or real-life obese white females in America.

REASON #4: TO HUMILIATE (DEMORALIZE) BLACK FEMALES

The most infamous example of public black female degradation occurred on April 4, 2007 when shock-jock Don Imus called the black females on the Rutgers University Basketball Team, *"...nappy-headed hos..."* In a previous, lesser-known incident, Don Imus attacked Gwen Ifill, the black female moderator of the highly acclaimed television political news show, "Washington Week: *Isn't the Times wonderful? It lets the cleaning lady cover the White House."*

XM Shock Jocks Opie and Anthony "joked" about an unidentified homeless man raping the first black female Secretary of State, Condelezza Rice: *"I just imagined the horror on Condelezza Rice's face as you were just, like, holding her down and fucking her."*

Even the 7.0 Magnitude earthquake in Haiti in 2010 where 200,000 people were feared dead was seen as a golden opportunity for Florida shock jock, Bubba the Love Sponge, to take a nasty shot at black women: *"I would have to say that Haitian hookers are probably infected with a whole bunch of stuff, you might have to, you know what, maybe this is actually a good thing."*

"A lot of talk shows appeal to the angry white guy. The shock jock gives voices to the really ugly thoughts: 'Minorities have gotten too much. I'm not doing as well as I used to." -- Jane Hall, an assistant professor in American University's School of Communication.

Black Male Entertainers And White Supremacy

Black male entertainers are often rewarded by the white supremacy system for participating in the PUBLIC degradation of black females.

"Now, they aren't 'hos,' but there were some nappy-headed women on that team. Those are some of the ugliest women I've ever seen in my whole life." –D.L. Hughley on Jay Leno's "Tonight Show" (May 7, 2007), "joking" about the black girls on the Rutgers University Basketball Team.

Six months after his comment on the Tonight Show, D.L. Hughley hosted:

- The 13th Annual Critics Choice Awards on VH1 (Nov 2007)
- The 39TH NAACP Image Awards (Feb 2008)
- The BET Awards (June 2008)
- A short-lived CNN comedy/news show, 'D.L. Hughely Breaks the News' (Oct 2008), which featured chitling jokes during the presidential election campaign of Barack Obama. Shortly after the election ended, so did the show.

What could be more DEMORALIZING for a group of women than being publicly degraded before the entire world by the same men they gave birth to?

Apparently, the magic elixir for reviving a stagnant career is degrading black females. Six months after fellow comic, D.L. Hughley hit the entertainer payload, actor/comedian Damon Wayans appeared on the daytime show, 'The View:

"Freedom of speech, what happened to that? What happened to expressing yourself? At least I know where he stands. And you know what? When he called them nappy-headed ho's, I went, 'Wow, he's right!' "Black people at home are laughing right now." -- Damon Wayans on the Don Imus controversy on "The View" TV show. (Nov 2007)

As of this writing, Wayans hasn't hosted any CNN talk shows OR star-studded awards show. However, he is planning to write a book.

What a shame.

REASON #5: TO DEMONIZE THE BLACK MOTHER FIGURE -- THE WOMB THAT PRODUCES ALL AUTHENTICALLY BLACK LIFE

Black (Monster) Mothers

Losing Isaiah (1995) – A black baby boy, abandoned by his (black) crack-addicted mother (Halle Berry), is adopted by a "caring" white (female) social worker and her husband. Once the baby's mother finds out her son is not dead (like she was told), she goes to court to get him back.

The Day the Earth Stood Still (2008), a remake of the science-fiction classic. White female scientist (Jennifer Connelly) risks life and limb to save earth, and still finds time to raise her black stepson from a previous marriage to a conveniently deceased black husband. The black birth mother is never mentioned, and at the end of the movie, the black boy calls the white female "momma."

Precious (2009): an obese dark-skinned black female (Gabourey Sidibe) is tortured by a horribly cruel, sexually perverted evil black mother (Mo'Nique), her rapist black father, and a random assortment of good (mulatto) blacks, and bad (dark-skinned) blacks.

The Blind Side (2009) A "caring" white female (Sandra Bullock) rescues a homeless black boy -- taking another shot at "defective black mothers."

(To the authors' knowledge no movie has been made about the white children of a defective white mother who are rescued by a black female.)

Thanks to white Hollywood and their well-paid black puppets, black mothers have become synonomous with crackheads, welfare cheats, and sexual degenerates, a not so different image found in early white American society.

"They are the greatest menace possible to the moral life of any community where they live. And they are evidently the chief instruments of the degradation of the men of their own race. When a man's mother, wife, and daughters are all immoral women, there is no room in his fallen nature for the aspirations of honor and virtue...I cannot imagine such a creation as a virtuous black woman." -- from a 1904 pamphlet "Experiences of the Race Problem. By a Southern White Woman"

Black females -- the VICTIMS OF MASS RAPE BY WHITE MALES -- were labeled "immoral" by a "moral" white female who blamed them for being raped.

What happened to the black mother/mammy images that nurtured Black and White America? And what are the long-term consequences for black boys who are being programmed to see white females as the most loving mother figures for black boys?

The Double Oppression of Black Women in America

"Dat man ober dar say dat woman needs to be lifted ober ditches, and to have de best place every whar. Nobody eber helped me into carriages, or ober mud puddles, or gives me any best place and ar'n't I a woman?

"Look at me! Look at my arm! I have plowed, and planted, and gathered into barns, and no man could head me -- and ar'n't I a woman? I could work as much and eat as much as a man (when I could get it), and bear de lash as well-and ar'n't I a woman?

"I have born 13 chilern and seen em mos all sold off into slavery, and when I cried out with a mother's grief, none but Jesus heard-and ar'n't I a woman?"

-- Sojourner Truth, at the women's rights convention of 1851 in Akron, Ohio, after being greeted with boos and hisses (from white females).

"Why are American white women so anxious to adopt a "dusky little heathen" child from the Third World? It's the latest fad of the White Woman Savior, and it carries high status.

A white American woman must adopt a Third World child (preferably a non-white) to really keep up the savior image. It's a grand American tradition, dating back to the early 19th century Christian missions.

Only today, you don't have to be Christian at all. You just have to be white, female, (and preferably) single."

(from 'American White Women Adopting Dark, Foreign Children' by David Yeagley, www.badeagle. com/2010/04/14/american-white-wome-adopt-ing-dark-foreign-children/)

FOR SALE: BLACK BABIES — TO THE HIGHEST BIDDER
The Myth Of The White Female Savior "Saving" Black Babies

Some Common Characteristics Of The White Female Savior:

- She is rich and famous, and usually works in the entertainment field
- She is single or divorced
- She dates and marries white males exclusively
- She has few to NO blacks in her social or professional circle
- Her PREFERRED adoption "choice" is a dark-skinned black male baby

In light of all the above, what is the TRUE motivation of the **White Female Savior**? Is it a fad or competition between white celebrity rivals? Is it a desire to help a child in need? Is it a hidden desire to have a black (melanated) child without the scandal (and professional fall-out) from being impregnated by a black male? Or is it a HIDDEN COMPETITION with the black female?

It is an interesting coincidence that these trendy **White Female Savior** adoptions of black babies (usually black males) are occurring around the same time white females are experiencing a FERTILITY CRISIS, and Hollywood is producing "black monster mother" movies for the black and white masses.

Are these adoptions an attempt to replace the black female as the authentic mother figure for the next generation of black men? Or is it the increasingly infertile white female's desperate attempt to be EQUAL to the genetically superior, highly fertile black female by TAKING the black female's babies and making them her OWN?

Interracial Adoptions Are A One-Way Street

Whites are allowed to adopt black babies with ease, but it is highly unlikely that whites would approve (or permit) a single black female -- even a rich and famous one -- to adopt a white baby.

Whites know their OFFSPRING are their most valuable resource and the future foot soldiers for white supremacy. They know it is NOT in the white collective's best interests for non-whites (their enemies) to raise (and program) white children who might resist the idea of maintaining the system of white supremacy.

In fact, black couples usually face MORE hurdles than white couples when adopting black children because white institutions are still deciding the fate of black children -- **over 140 years AFTER slavery.** Sadly, some blacks are thrilled whenever whites "adopt" (buy) black babies, and may be secretly relieved to be relieved of the "burden" of caring for our OWN.

BUYING BLACK BABIES is simply an updated version of an old AMERICAN SLAVE TRADITION during a time when black men, women, and babies were sold to the highest WHITE bidder.

Stolen Generation

"Between 1910 and 1970 up to 100,000 Aboriginal children were taken forcibly or under duress from their families by police or welfare officers.

Most were under five years old. There was rarely any judicial process. To be Aboriginal was enough. They are known as the 'Stolen Generations.'

Most were raised in church or state institutions. Some were fostered or adopted by white parents. Many suffered physical and sexual abuse. Food and living conditions were poor. Most grew up in a hostile environment without family ties or cultural identity.

They received little education, and were expected to go into low-grade domestic and farming work."

As adults, many suffered insecurity, lack of self-esteem, feelings of worthlessness, depression, suicide, violence, delinquency, abuse of alcohol and drugs and inability to trust.

(SOURCE: www.enjar.org/stolengenerations.html)

Aboriginal cricket team at MCG in 1867

What Is the TRUE Motive Behind White Adoptions (THEFT) Of Non-White Chidren?

"Imagine everything that you know and love gone and you never get to see it again," Helen Moran said. "I thought I hadn't been good enough, I must have done something wrong, I must be a bad person."

Helen Moran was 23 months old when she was one of the thousands of Aboriginal children stolen from their parents by (white) Australian officials. Even though her family was extremely poor, she was loved and cared for, but a court ruled her parents unfit and her parents lost all six of their children. She never saw her parents again.

Tragically, similar tales were told by other Aboriginal children, like Avis Gale, who was taken from her mother's breast when she was seven days old, and Bob Randall, who was adbucted by a strange white man on a horse at the age of five and never saw his family again.

What was the END RESULT of these forced "adoptions" by whites? The deliberate and systematic destruction of an entire NON-WHITE race.

Aborigines make up about 2% of Australia's population but they suffer disproportionately high rates of imprisonment and ill-health." (SOURCE: 'Aboriginal children 'starving,' welfare workers say' by Phil Mercer, BBC News, August 4, 2010).

The Bottom Line

If the **White Female Savior** TRULY wanted to help black babies, she would speak out AGAINST the white racism in her own industry, and refuse to star in movies that demonize black men and women -- the NATURAL PARENTS of the same black babies she claims to "love."

She would use her "star power" to speak out against the white racism that creates black poverty and black family dysfunction -- the same circumstances that made black adoptions necessary in the first place.

She would use her financial muscle to support black organizations that are fighting the closure of black public schools, and would join the protest lines outside police stations after a white policeman murders the full-sized version of the black baby boys she so "lovingly" adopted.

She would help fight a criminal justice system that imprisons black fathers and mothers for 5-10 years for having a drug addictions, and she would fight against the white imperialists who deliberately bankrupt, LOOT, and PILLAGE African nations under the banner of white supremacy, robbing poor Africans of their ability to feed their own children

And if that was too big a job and too big a sacrifice, she could help the same VILLAGE or community instead of LOOTING another black family or African village of their most valuable resource: *their children.*

For the price of a diamond bracelet or a Birkenstock handbag, the White Female Savior could educate and feed an entire African village for an entire year. She could help MOST by helping an African village take care of its OWN children, rather than bringing that black or African child into a strange, white, hostile environment where to be black is to *be abnormal and undesirable -- even for blacks born in the states.*

The Dark Side Of Interracial Adoptions

Blacks who are adopted by whites and raised in all-white communities, often speak of being alienated, having an identity crisis, being extremely lonely, and even suicidal. They have been victims of racial slurs and comments, often by their own adopted "family" members, schoolmates, and neighbors. Understandably, they often wished they were white like their adopted family, and experienced difficulty in being accepted by either race.

While single black mothers are DEMONIZED for raising their OWN black sons without a black father, the **SINGLE White Female Savior** is PRAISED for adopting black boys who will NEVER have a black male ROLE MODEL, and are UNLIKELY to have any intimate contact with blacks at all.

A white female – be she rich or poor; ordinary or famous – CANNOT BE A MALE OR FEMALE ROLE MODEL FOR A BLACK BOY OR GIRL. Money may buy material comforts *but it CANNOT take the place of the kind of role modeling black children desperately need in a black-hating society.* That is the bottom line when it comes to the so-called "benefits" of black children and their **White Female Savior Mothers.**

REASON #6: DEGRADING THE BLACK FEMALE DEGRADES ALL BLACK LIFE -- MALE AND FEMALE -- AND CREATES AN INFERIORITY COMPLEX THAT CAN LAST A LIFETIME.

The Long-Term Dangers of Degrading the Black Female

The "social position" of a race is determined by the social position of the female. In EVERY culture, the mother is sacred. She is the "civilizer" of her culture, community, children, and society.

As the FIRST TEACHER, her primary responsibility is to "civilize" the children by passing along the values and traditions of her culture to the next generation. The way the female sees herself will determine the way that ethnic group ultimately SEES, VALUES, and RESPECTS ITSELF.

What kind of values will today's young, degraded black mothers pass along to their already endangered children?

Once the BLACK MOTHER (the black female) is so degraded she becomes "uncivilized," she will not be able to civilize anyone else. As a result, the children, the men, the community, and the ENTIRE NATION become demoralized, self-hating, self-disrespecting, and UNCIVILIZED.

By creating the image of the female mother as that of a "whore," the male AND female child will be psychologically devastated, which partly explains the despair, anger, and hopelessness that so many black children are experiencing today.

Since the black female is the CREATOR of all **authentically black life,** the more damaged she is, the more likely she will bear damaged crops that will be NO THREAT TO THE SYSTEM OF WHITE SUPREMACY.

What Is The Collective Response Of Black Males To The Mass Media Degradation Of Black Females?

SILENCE

One black male's explanation: *"The black man is always getting dogged out, it's a relief to see somebody else getting it for a change."*
> *– Reggie, 38, refinery worker*

The problem with that logic, Reggie, is that "somebody else" is your mother, sisters, and daughters. That "somebody else" is the **mother of the next black generation**, and the first female role model for black children.

If we do NOT stand up COLLECTIVELY -- as men and women -- and oppose the degradation of the black mothers of our Black Nation, we will reap the bitter harvest of MORE damaged black children, and the eventual destruction of the Black Nation.

"No nation can rise higher than it's woman."

-- the Most Honorable Elijah Muhammad (1897 - 1975)

The Honorable Elijah Muhammad addresses
followers including Muhammed Ali

During a 1969 interview by Sammy Davis, Jr (on the Mike Douglas show):

Sammy asked Ali: "What does black power mean to you?"

*Ali: Well, to me, black power means, number one, black men respecting
and protecting -- with their lives, if necessary -- their women. Because
we are taught by our leader that a man's woman is the field which
produces his nation. If he doesn't protect his field, he'll produce a bad
nation...she's the field that produces our sons and our daughters..."*

"Is not your woman more valuable than that crop of corn, that crop of cotton, that crop of cabbage, potatoes, beans, tomatoes? How much more valuable is your woman than these crops that you should keep the enemies from destroying the crops?

Yet you are not careful about your women. You don't love them. Why? It is because you have allowed visitors to run in and out of your house, thus they have destroyed your love for your woman and your woman has not the love for you that she should.

Until we learn to love and protect our woman, we will never be a fit and recognized people on the earth. The white people here among you will never recognize you until you protect your woman.

The brown man will never recognize you until you protect your woman. The yellow man will never recognize you until you protect your woman. The white man will never recognize you until you protect your woman."

-- "Message to the Black Man in America" by the Honorable Elijah Muhammad

A Partial List of what "black female"
signifies in a white supremacist society:

Mammy, defective, ugly, ghetto, mean, monster
momma, crazy, violent, can't-get-or-keep-a-man
or find a husband, nappy headed, weave-wearing,
ho, whore, sexually promiscuous, Jezebel, a "white
man's whore," illiterate, Sapphire, emasculating,
sexually-disease-carrying, siddity, baby momma,
uppity, big-lipped, wide-nosed, gorilla-faced, big-
booty, gangsta video ho, too evil, too-educated-
for-her-own-good, money-hungry, gold-digger,
stuck-up, materialistic, money-hungry, mannish,
mentally unstable, violent, criminal, welfare-
cheating, obese, fat, government-cheese-eating
bitch.

CHAPTER 32

THE TYRANNY OF MEN

"I told you I was defending myself, if I gotta do this anger counseling shit, her ass should be sitting right here with me." The young woman punctuated the sentence by punching her fist into an open palm. She was barely twenty, thick-bodied, with a pecan-brown complexion.

Karen King, an anger-management specialist for the Morrow County court system, sat, stoic-faced, in a chair a few feet away. It was going to take more than four sessions to crack through her client's tough, defensive shell and get her to take responsibility for breaking her ex-lover's arm.

That wasn't surprising, considering the counseling had not been voluntary. The domestic violence judge had sentenced Leslie to ten weeks of anger management after her female partner declined to press assault charges.

Karen was well aware of the difficulty in dealing with a reluctant client, especially one who was extremely angry from what Karen suspected was childhood sexual abuse. The first thing she usually established during their first session was the obvious: that sitting in her office for an hour twice a week was preferable to sitting in a jail cell.

When Karen glanced at her watch, Leslie jumped to her feet. "We finished?" Her tone was hopeful.

"Next week, same time, and Leslie --" Karen put a little steel in her voice, making Leslie pause at the door. "Same time means *be* on time." Karen shook her head as the door slammed then scribbled some notes in an open file.

She just didn't get it. It was a phenomenon as alarming and puzzling as the AIDS epidemic in the black community. Over the last several years, Karen had noticed a stark increase in the number of bisexual and homosexual black women, especially under the age of forty.

Karen didn't buy the "bisexual" label. In her experience, it was rare to find a man or woman who was equally attracted to both sexes and didn't have a preference. She believed some had adopted the "bisexual" label because of the stigma of being a full-out homosexual.

Then there were people like a client, Nina, a 34-year-old black pharmacist, who said she knew she was gay by the age of nine, but had married out of peer pressure from her family.

Karen believed the new generation of lesbians were not lesbians at all, but were "acting out" sexually because they perceived men as a threat to their emotional or physical well-being. With the rise of HIV infections in the black community, some black women felt safer sexually with other women.

Some wanted to reject men as they had been rejected, especially if they didn't fit the stereotype of black beauty. The black male shortage forced others to seek love wherever they could find it. Whatever their reasons, the emotional and sexual disconnect from men often represented a significant power play on their part.

Over drinks at a psychiatric symposium last year, Karen met Phyllis, a 46-year-old black physician who, after taking her first female lover four years ago, admitted she felt free for the first time in her life from the crippling beauty standards forced on her by society -- and by black men.

Phyllis said her black female lover wasn't threatened by a successful black woman since she was one herself. After she stopped beating herself up for not having longer hair or lighter skin, her attitude toward black women -- especially the vanilla crème, long-haired girls she'd once envied -- greatly improved because she wasn't competing for the attention or approval of men.

Phyllis's story mirrored what another female client, a 32-year-old single mother, told Karen. She turned to women for her emotional needs after she ended an abusive relationship with the father of her two children. She said, being with women freed her *"from the tyranny of men."*

In the privacy of Karen's office, more and more black female clients echoed similar sentiments: that dealing with men offered more risks than rewards, because they never felt valued in those relationships. The handful who dated white males exclusively admitted they still felt undermined if they were -- as one black female surgeon said – "too uppity."

The feelings of alienation were even more profound among her darker complexioned clients, like Francine, a beautiful, forty-something lawyer, who had recently divorced her husband of eighteen years after discovering he'd had a series of affairs with white women.

Her ex-husband's parting shot was his bizarre confession that he started sleeping with white women because dark-skinned women weren't "sexy." Francine said she could have forgiven him for almost anything but that since he knew about her issues growing up as the darkest one in her family.

Just a few hours after his "confession," Francine committed her first act of violence against another human being. While her soon-to-be ex-husband dozed on the living room sofa, Francine poured an entire bottle of scotch on the cushions and set them on fire. Luckily, only the sofa was damaged. Francine was charged with domestic violence and court-ordered to do 12 weeks of anger management -- at her expense -- or lose her law license.

Karen patiently explained to Francine that her husband said what he said to hurt her after she refused to call off the divorce. *Obviously,* he found dark-skinned women attractive enough to marry since no one put a gun to his head and forced him to walk down the aisle. After two months of counseling, Francine was still a work in progress.

Karen understood firsthand the pain and anger that ran deep in many black women's psyches despite their accomplishments and sophisticated polish. The daily assault on their self-esteem was seldom acknowledged, so most suffered in silence until their rage was too great to keep inside.

Even though the background details differed, some of Karen's white female clients echoed a similar desire to disconnect emotionally from men. Some had stopped dating men, or dated men of color exclusively and were unapologetic about it.

They claimed that black and Hispanic men were less judgmental about their physical imperfections and didn't expect a woman to look like something out of a Playboy centerfold. It was fascinating -- and extremely frustrating -- to hear her white female clients say they felt validated by black men versus her black female clients who often felt the opposite.

In spite of that, her female clients had more in common than not. Most had come from a dysfunctional family background. Some were victims of rape, physical abuse, or incest. More than half were single or divorced mothers, and had an emotionally distant or physically abusive father, while a third hadn't known their fathers at all.

What ultimately brought them all to Karen's office was their inability to cope with their own pain and rage without resorting to self-destructive behaviors, or their personal relationships escalated into violent confrontations that landed them in court and mandatory anger management counseling. The biggest thing that separated her lesbian clients from the heterosexual ones was their unwillingness to be sexually involved with men.

While Karen fully understood their disenchantment with the opposite sex, the rising trend of disconnect between black men and women greatly concerned her. How would the black community survive if black men and women stopped turning to each other and started turning to the same sex or to another race? What would happen to their children? What *was* happening to black children?

She already had part of the answer: the luckier ones sat in an office like hers, where a trained professional would give them half a fighting chance at dealing with their pain. The less fortunate ones either wound up in jail or in the graveyard.

After eighteen years in the mental health field, Karen understood why some of her colleagues were actively pursuing second careers. The professional term was "burn-out" but, in reality, they were fed up.

It was stressful enough dealing with your own baggage without carrying someone else's, knowing in the end you couldn't relieve their load. The last and sometimes only recourse was prescribing medication. Karen considered drug therapy for emotional issues an absolute admission of failure on the part of the therapist, cloaked in impressive-sounding medical jargon.

As she finished up some paperwork, she kept thinking about Francine, the divorced lawyer, who had broken down in her office earlier that afternoon. Francine had asked, through tears, how black men could say the same ugly things about black women that white racists said?

It was the question of the decade, as far as Karen was concerned. One she didn't try to answer. Absently, she opened a small, mirrored compact and dabbed a bit of powder on her chocolate-brown nose, chin, and forehead. Still single, still looking, but a lot less hopeful. She frowned at her reflection. How long had it been since a man found her attractive?

After shoving some papers into a leather briefcase, she turned out the lights, and locked the office door behind her. Thank God, the work day was done.

Recipe #11

~~DEMONIZE~~ the Black Male

A scene from the movie 'Birth of a Nation' (1915)

The movie, directed by D.W. Griffith, premiered with the title, 'The Clansman,' and was the highest-grossing film of the silent-picture era. The controversial and inflammatory film portrayed the Ku Klux Klan as heroes, and protectors of (pure) "white womanhood,"and portrayed black males as animalistic rapists who lusted after white females, and blacks in general as violating the rights of whites.

CHAPTER 33

SIX REASONS BLACK
MALES ARE DEMONIZED
(IN A WHITE SUPREMACY SOCIETY)

Why are black males degraded in America?

REASON #1: TO TRANSFORM 500 YEARS OF BRUTALITY, RAPE, AND MURDER OF BLACK MALES INTO "WHITE FEAR AND INNOCENCE"

"It is illogical to believe that white people, who control every institution in America, including education, employment, and law enforcement, would be "afraid" of any black male who is powerless to stop even one civil servant armed with a badge and gun from snuffing out his life. The men who should be the most afraid are the ones whose lives have no value." -- Umoja

It is indisputable that the black male is the most brutalized and dehumanized man in American history. He has been enslaved, raped, lynched, burned alive, whipped, branded with hot irons, dismembered, castrated, exploited, slaughtered, and robbed of his language, history, land, inventions, music, dance, resources, culture, religion, freedom -- even the right to protect or claim his women and children.

The black male has been denied the right to earn a living wage, or any living at all, and deprived of an equal education and equal justice under the law. He has been unjustly accused, imprisoned, and executed in the same nation he built with his sweat, blood, and tears.

The black male is the most likely person to be beaten, sodomized, or murdered by law enforcement; to be underemployed or unemployed (regardless of experience or education); and to be stripped of his constitutional (God-given) right to own a firearm to protect himself and his family than any other man or woman in America.

After 500 years of documented abuse, rape, exploitation, and murder, how has the most POWERLESS MAN in America (the black male) been cast as the most feared and dangerous? There is ONLY one possible answer: ***the mainstream media.***

The black male has been transformed from a VICTIM of white supremacy into a living, breathing, walking, and talking stereotype of a rapist, criminal, monster, boogeyman, super predator, sex-crazed Mandingo; the King Kong of all deadbeat fathers -- and a convenient BLACK SCAPEGOAT for all of America's social, political, and economic ills.

Public Enemy Number One: The Black Male

A common fear among the white collective is being raped or murdered by a black male. However, this (false) "white fear" flies in the face of reality -- and US government statistics:

> *"According to a government report, 85% of white murder victims were slain by whites. The remaining 15% included blacks, Hispanics, and other minorities."*
> *(http://www.splcenter.org/intel/intelreport/article.jsp?aid=255)*

> *"Rapes of white women by black men represent less than **10 percent of all rapes**, according to the Justice Department."*

Where incest, rape, and murder are concerned, white females have MORE to fear from white males -- their fathers, uncles, teachers, neighbors, husbands, and boyfriends -- than they do from black males.

False White Innocence And The MUBM
(The Mysterious, Unidentified Black Male)

The "black boogey-male did it" has become the standard excuse by white male and female criminals who are trying to escape responsibility and punishment for their own heinous crimes:

(1969) Charles Manson sent "Manson Family" members to the home of actress Sharon Tate, where five people were murdered in cold blood, Manson Family killers wrote the word "pig" in Sharon Tate's blood on the front door of the residence, possibly to infer that the Black Panthers had committed the crime. According to prosecutors, Charles Manson hoped his murder spree would provoke a race war between blacks and whites.

(1989) Charles "Chuck" Stuart, a white male, murdered his pregnant wife, Carol, then told police that a black gunman forced his way into their car, robbed them and murdered his wife. Stuart's brother, Matthew, admitted he saw his brother shoot his wife and then shoot himself to support his false story. On January 4, 1990, Stuart jumped from the Tobin Bridge to his death.

(1994) Susan Smith, a white female, murdered her two boys by driving her auto into a lake while the children slept in their car seats, initially reporting to police that she had been carjacked by a black man. Nine days later, after an intensive, heavily publicized investigation and nationwide search, Smith confessed to drowning her children.

(2003) Brian Wells, a white male pizza deliveryman, told police that a group of black men had taken him hostage, locked a bomb around his neck, and forced him to rob a bank. He was killed when the bomb exploded. Later, police discovered that Wells and a few of his white friends had cooked up the entire scheme.

(2007) Amanda Knox, a white female American exchange student living in Italy, was convicted in the 2007 stabbing death of her British roommate, Meredith Kercher. Knox initially tried to pin the blame on a black man, Patrick L., the owner of the Le Chic bar. The Reggae musician was locked up on murder charges, but released after 10 days when his alibi checked out.

(2007) DNA Test Clears Man After 27 Years. A man enjoyed freedom Tuesday for the first time in nearly three decades after a DNA test proved he did not commit a 1979 rape. According to the Justice Department, rapes of white women by black men, represent *less than 10 percent of all rapes*, Half of all rape exonerations were black men who were falsely convicted of raping white women. (SOURCE: ATLANTA (AP) – 2007)

(2008) Ashley Todd, a white female Republican, claimed that was assaulted by a black male "Obama supporter" who carved a backwards "B" on her face. She later admitted she had fabricated (LIED) and had assaulted herself.

(2009) Bonnie Sweeten, a white female, claimed two black men had abducted her and her nine-year-old daughter, after a fender-bender, and stuffed them into the trunk of a black Cadillac. It was later discovered that the "abduction" was a hoax and that Sweeten had fled to Disney World with her daughter. Sweeten was later indicted for allegedly stealing $700,000 from her employer, a Bucks County law firm.

(2010) Robert Ralston, a white male Philadelphia police sergeant, claimed he was shot by an unidentified black man, but police later discovered that he had shot himself and had fabricated the entire story (LIED) to look like a "hero."

(2010) Conrad Zdzierak, a white male, robbed four banks and a CVS pharmacy wearing a 'black man mask.'

Central Park Jogger Rape Convictions Tossed: Five Men Cleared After DNA Implicates Another Man For 1989 Attack

Thirteen years after the brutal rape and beating of a Central Park jogger, a judge on Thursday dismissed the convictions of all five men who served prison time for the attack. (2002) (SOURCE: http://www.cbsnews.com/ stories/2002/10/02/national/main523996.shtml)

After spending nearly 15 years in prison for a rape-murder they didn't commit, three young (black) men were given gilt-edge plaques etched with today's date and a simple message, "The first day of the rest of your life."

A massive insult on top of a massive injury.

News Media/Entertainment Industry

When it comes to the evening news, black males are more likely to be seen wearing handcuffs than a tailored suit or surgeon scrubs. The majority of images portray black males as natural-born criminals, clowns, TV court jesters, thugs, pimps, bullies, drug dealers, hustlers, deadbeat baby daddies, fools, and animalistic brutes.

When it comes to Hollywood and TV roles, black males are usually limited to one of four roles: the crooked (or straight) cop, the criminal, the clown, or the sexual predator.

The images of successful black males are usually limited to entertainers: actors, athletes, comedians, sitcom buffoons, dancers, AND politicians. With a few exceptions, black males are usually portrayed as more BRAWN (muscle) than BRAINS. In contrast, white males are usually shown as having more BRAINS than BRAWN, and often have an impressive amount of BOTH.

Domestic Terrorism Of Black Males By Law Enforcement

The stereotype of black males as violent criminals is used to JUSTIFY abuse and murder of black males by law enforcement -- regardless of the facts or ANY videotaped evidence (of the Rodney King beating).

Documented Torture Methods By Chicago Police:

From 1972 to 1991, over 200 black men were tortured by Chicago Police Commander Jon G. Burge and other Chicago detectives to obtain confessions. In 2008, Burge, who was living in Florida on a Chicago police pension, was arrested for lying in court during a civil lawsuit -- NOT for torturing black males!

- Suffocation with the plastic cover of a typewriter
- Being battered with telephone books
- Burned with cigarettes and radiators
- Threatened with handguns
- Electrically shocked with a telephone generator
- Cattle prod applied to men's nipples, genitals, and rectal interiors

Jeremiah Mearday VS Chicago Police

"I didn't know my son," Jeremiah's father said when he went to the hospital on September 26, 1997. "He was a bloody mess. He had two holes knocked in the top of his head, his five front upper teeth along with the gum, severed, and a broken jaw. They stomped him in his stomach and there was trauma to his back." -- Revolutionary Worker newspaper #934, November 30, 1997.

(1997) Jeremiah Mearday – an unarmed 18-year-old black male was kicked and beaten with flashlights by two white Chicago police officers for no apparent reason. After the beating, Mearday was hospitalized with a broken jaw and head injuries.

On November 7, nearly 200 white police officers forced Jeremiah Mearday and his attorneys to walk a gauntlet of intimidation in a Chicago courtroom. This Gestapo display -- which was tolerated by the presiding judge -- was met by protest and outrage by Mearday's supporters.

Five years later, the city of Chicago agreed to pay Jeremiah Mearday $1.75 million to settle the police brutality case if he dropped his lawsuit.

Driving While Black (DWB)

"Driving while black should be called driving while white people are being white." -- Dr. Kamau Kambon

"Racial profiling" refers to a police officer or a person of authority who harasses or arrests non-whites because they are NOT white. In many cases, racial profiling is encouraged by (white) city officials to send a message that blacks -- especially black males -- are not welcome to live, work, shop, or even drive through certain white areas.

It is a psychological tool of intimidation (and demoralization) used against black males to remind them that they are inferior, unequal, and will not receive the same courtesy and rights that whites take for granted.

"Rogue Cops Caught on Videotape" Is Psychological Terrorism

Why would the same mainstream media that portrays black males as natural-born criminals ALSO broadcast the VIDEOTAPED evidence that PROVE that black males are the VICTIMS of law enforcement?

One (Possible) Reason:

To remind (terrorize) black males that at ANY time, ANY place, and for NO reason whatsoever their rights can be violated by law enforcement. This psychological tool of terror is a CONTINUATION of the same process that began during slavery to **instill FEAR in the black male so he will not rebel against the very (white) systems that oppress him.**

***

AXIOM #6: The "Black Victim = A Victimless Crime" Theory. A black person in a conflict with a white person (or white system) cannot BE the victim in a White Supremacy society. The black individual is ALWAYS at fault, regardless of who initiated the conflict or what facts or evidence are present.

REASON #2: TO DESTROY BLACK MALE INTELLECTUAL POTENTIAL

"Only 12% of African-American males are proficient in reading by 8th grade. If a boy is not on grade level of reading by the end of first grade, they only have a 20% chance of reaching grade level by 12th grade." -- Dr Jawanza Kunjufu, author of 'The Conspiracy to Destroy Black Boys'

In America's Public Schools Black Boys Are More Likely To Be:

- Tracked into special education, remedial, and vocational classes
- Excluded from gifted programs and college preparatory classes
- Given the drug Ritalin for "behavior" problems
- Labeled as "mentally disabled" (when they are not)
- Suspended/expelled more often than white students for same offenses
- Score lower on standardized tests
- Drop out before completing high school

What happens to the INTELLECTUAL POTENTIAL of black boys in a school system that is DESIGNED to provide an inferior education? What happens to their intellectual ambition if the most influential adults in their lives – the teachers, school administrators, politicians, the media, and sometimes, even their own parents -- think they're incapable of learning? Can the answer be found in the lower test scores and higher dropout rates for black boys?

Brawn Versus Brains

"I'm gonna be a rapper or play pro ball. Why should I go to college? College won't make me rich." – Jamal, 23-year-old black male.

Why are black boys being PROGRAMMED to think being black, male, and book smart do not go together -- and their BEST and (only) chance for success is to become an entertainer or a pro-ball-player?

So they won't pursue the mental and occupational skills necessary to build an independent, self-sustaining society: doctors, scholars, authors, lawyers, engineers, chemists, scientists, physicists, programmers, accountants, mathematicians, builders, inventors, and manufacturers.

Derailing the educational potential in black boys GUARANTEES a population of black males (slaves) who will always be dependent on other men for their basic needs, and will remain an easily exploited and easily enslaved population.

We cannot afford to ignore the facts: There is a national agenda to destroy the intellectual potential of black boys. While white boys (of privilege) are trained to be masters of the universe, black boys are trained to be future candidates for the prison-industrial complex.

232

CHAPTER 34

FLIPPING THE EDUCATIONAL SCRIPT

SCENE: A giant meteor explodes in space, and showers cosmic dust over every square mile of the United States. By morning, black people have traded places with white people in all areas of human activity, and both think it has always been that way...

SETTING: A small town in the heartland of America.

From kindergarten to high school, white children are taught history from a made-up, SUPER-AFROCENTRIC viewpoint – meaning black people created, discovered, and invented everything of any importance.

The white students are secretly ashamed because their history books "prove" whites contributed nothing to art, history, medicine, science, or civilization. All they have is February – the shortest month of the year – to learn the same tidbits of "white history." Most stopped caring years ago.

The teachers are harder on the white students even though the black students goof off and can't answer the teacher's questions, either. By grammar school, 25% of white boys are in special educational classes because the teachers say they don't read and write as well as the other (black) students.

The little white girls prefer black dolls because they are "prettier" and love reading about the adventures of (black) Nancy Drew, wishing they were black, too. Little white boys play with (black) army men and read comic books about black superheroes (since there are no white ones).

On Saturday afternoons, the little white boys and girls in town line up to see the latest (black) Harry Potter movie, and cheer when good (black) triumphs over evil (white). In the evening, after supper, they watch their favorite TV shows. Most of the faces are black, sprinkled with a few white faces and a handful of white women who are mostly fat and unattractive.

By the age of six, the little girls and boys believe that the prettiest women are black because that's what they see on TV, in movies, and magazines. Once in a while, there are one or two pretty white women, but they look more black than white. The children never question this because they believe this is "normal.

In the integrated high school, most of the white students are tracked into the vocational courses while most of the black students take college-bound courses. There was a cheating scandal about the placement tests that got their previous principal fired last year but it was swept under the rug by the powerful school board made up of mostly black parents.

As a gesture of good will, the girls' athletic coach chooses a white girl to be a cheerleader even though most of the football and basketball players are white.

When the black parents discover one of the history teachers -- the only white teacher -- created a "White History" course to motivate the white students, the black parents threaten to boycott the school.

At the local school board meeting, one of the black parents explains her opposition to teaching "white history" by saying, "I don't think any one group should be studied. Plus, it makes whites feel really bad about their race when they actually did not have anything to do with it."

A black father adds, "Isn't white history already taught in history class? As far as I know, my kids learned about Tom Sawyer and Frank Sinatra, so what's the problem?"

To appease the black parents, the school board suspends the white teacher for a week. The white parents retreat in angry silence, hesitant to push the issue because some of the black parents in the room are their employers and bosses.

Upon learning of the white teacher's suspension, the white students become even more demoralized than before. A month after the school board meeting, a white boy and a black boy get into a fight. Neither one was hurt but the principal calls the police anyway.

The white boy was arrested and permanently expelled but the black boy only got a week in detention. The white kids are angered, scared, and shocked that a simple schoolyard fight could result in a felony conviction and a permanent criminal record for their 17-year-old white classmate.

After their schoolmate was expelled, the "slow" white boys, who had been in the special education classes since grammar school and were permanently labeled as "educationally challenged," start dropping out of high school.

The white boys said they were "tired of being put down" in front of the other kids. Besides, what was the point of staying in school when everyone said white boys had no future?

THE END

Can you imagine white parents tolerating this kind of abuse against their children from their school system?

THEN WHY THE HELL ARE WE?

Tragically, it appears the "WAR" against the intellectual potential of black boys has been largely successful.

According to the Schott 50 State Report on Public Education, only 47% of black males graduate from high school.

In cities, like Dade County, Florida; Cleveland, Ohio; and Detroit, Michigan, the graduation rate is as low as 27%.

According to a 2010 report by the "Council of the Great City Schools," black boys drop out of high school at twice the rate of white boys, and that black men represented only 5% of college students in 2008.

"Fear of jail is the beginning of wisdom."
-- seen on a brightly painted chamber pot in Nigeria

REASON #3: TO PROGRAM YOUNG BLACK MALES TO BELIEVE GOING TO PRISON IS A "RITE OF PASSAGE" TO BLACK MANHOOD

It is obvious the mainstream media is GLAMORIZING black male hip-hop celebrities who have been charged with and/or convicted of crimes OR who have served time in prison. The list is too long for this book but includes: *Tupac Shakur, Chris Brown, Beanie Siael, Flesh N Bone, T.I., Steady B, Mac, Lil Boosie, Cassidy, Sadat X, Royce Da 5'9, Maino, Styles P, Cool C, Lil' Wayne, Black Rob, Mystikal, Gucci Mane, John Forte, DMX, Chil Ali, Prodigy, C-Murder, Da Brat, Shyne, and Pimp C.*

The revolving prison door for young black male celebrities appears to be part of a bigger scheme to PROMOTE the PRISON "lifestyle" to impressionable young black males -- especially poor black males -- **as the ONLY TRUE "rite of passage" into black manhood**.

Are these jail-prone and criminally-inclined black male celebrities innocent stooges (and victims) OR have they been promised MORE fame and money in exchange for making their mostly poor, black male fans a PSYCHOLOGICAL AND SOCIAL BLOOD SACRIFICE to the system of white supremacy? This is NOT an unreasonable assumption since there is AMPLE EVIDENCE that the white supremacy system is grooming young black males as FUTURE PRISON INMATES -- instead of doctors, lawyers, and engineers.

According to an article entitled, *T.I. -- "The Longer I Sit, The Smarter I Get,"* rapper T.I., in a letter to his fans after being jailed for drug possession, claims he is: *"...doing better locked up..."*

T.I. also adds, *"It doesn't matter how long it'll be before the next time you see me. What matters is that I'll be a better man before that time comes. The longer I sit, the smarter I get." (SOURCE: The Urban Daily).*

The responses from T.I.'s "fans" confirms our suspicions:

"T.I. is one of the best rappers in the world! He is only human, everybody makes mistakes. I support him 100%. He still sells albums. He is making money while he is in jail. When he gets out he is not only going to be smarter but being a better person as a father and a celebrity."

"If y'all don't realize when you in jail all you do is write so I would not be surprised if made 2 or 3 albums while he is locked up. Look at 2PAC he is the greatest rapper ever and most of his stuff he wrote in jail."

"And there it is. He kept it G, and still gon sell a hit. DO WORK, T.I."

"T.I. ain't no Joke, God sent a Strong Black Positive Young Man that is giving back to the community and they can't stand that so they tries to sit you down."

In just ONE generation, a felony conviction has more status for some young black males than a college degree.

If "Sagging Pants" Could Talk, They Might Say:

"Look at him, white people. He's no threat to anyone (but himself). He is not that strong black man you fear, hate, and want to destroy.

In fact, he's not a man at all, and he will spend every waking moment proving he's as harmless as a child, so you won't harm or kill him the way he has seen you destroy strong, masculine black men.

Even though he lives in some of the nation's most dangerous neighborhoods, he can't run from danger; he can hardly walk. He is a harmless, almost comical nuisance in his sagging pants, and an eyesore to anyone who lays eyes on him.

By wearing me, he has submitted to his own black male inferiority, and has waved the white flag of heterosexual black male surrender with just a few yards of fabric. If I could talk, I'd say, "A job well done!"

(FYI, "saggin" spelled backwards is "niggas")

Sagging Pants (Hanging Off The Ass)

Where did the "sagging pants" style come from? There are two explanations floating around. One explanation is homosexual inmates in New York state often wore sagging pants for EASY SEXUAL ACCESS, a signal that they were sexually available to other male inmates.

A second explanation is prisoners were forced to wear pants without belts, because their belts could be used as weapons or to commit suicide by hanging, so their beltless pants "sagged."

Some black males claim wearing sagging pants is no different than wearing baggy pants. However, they have overlooked one big difference between the two. Baggy pants were created by professional clothing designers whose profits allow them to buy cars, homes, and stock portfolios.

Sagging pants were created by inmates who own nothing, **including the right to own a belt.** There is a more troubling imagery associated with sagging pants: *The sight of young black males walking (shuffling) like slaves who have their ankles shackled together.*

Slave Tradition OR Future Rape Victim?

Why are some young black males so eager to belong to the modern-day SLAVE PLANTATION (aka the PRISON INDUSTRIAL COMPLEX) that they mimic the prison chic of MODERN-DAY BLACK MALE SLAVES?

Sagging pants may be a SYMPTOM of the collective low self-esteem that plagues young black males in America, and a subconscious way of using "fashion" as CAMOUFLAGE against the relentless attacks against the masculine black male in American society.

For the young black male who has witnessed the wanton destruction and murder of black males by white authority figures, he may be terrified of being seen as a BLACK MAN (a threat), and wants nothing more than blend into the background, stay in the dark, and stay in his place. Putting on a pair of "sagging pants" may be the least expensive and easiest way to do it.

There is a different risk associated with wearing sagging pants:

Fleece Johnson is a long-term inmate at Kentucky State Penitentiary who was profiled during an episode of "Lock-Up." He shamelessly admitted to raping other male inmates, and delivered a dire warning to the new generation of inmates that they asking for trouble from old-timers like himself:

"You know, they got this thang where they sags they pants past their butt...you know, it's sexy to us, right. So, you sag your pants in here man, somebody will be up in your butt. It's just that simple." (Source: MSNBC "Lock-Up" prison show).

In 2008, just two weeks before the November election of America's first black president, Barack Obama, two noteworthy events occurred:

On October 15, 2008 Comedy Central created a "fake news" show, which was hosted by black comic David Alan Grier, replete with stereotypes of black males as criminals, gangbangers, and transvestites.

Not to be outdone -- or perhaps by mutual agreement -- on October 25, 2008 Cable news giant, CNN, hosted its first comedy-news show; the first show hosted by a black male -- 'D.L. Hughley Breaks the News' -- which featured "hilarious" skits that included pimp and porkchop jokes.

In March 2009, just two months after Obama was inaugurated as president, both shows were abruptly cancelled. One can only assume that black comics Grier and Hughley had "outlived their usefulness."

The images of two black male "entertainers" promoting black buffoonery balanced the image of the articulate, educated black male, Barack Obama.

The degraded black male image had been restored.

REASON #4: TO IMPOVERISH THE BLACK MALE

"What is the definition of a "man?" The most basic definition is a provider and a protector of his women and children. What happens to the morale of a man who is relentlessly and persistently denied that God-given right? The answer to that question can be found in the 500-year history of the black man in America." -- Umoja

Shiftless Or Short-Changed? A Short History Lesson

After slavery, Jim Crow laws were created in the South to prevent blacks from achieving educational and economic equality with whites. Many blacks migrated north, hoping for a better life, only to discover they faced rampant discrimination in employment and housing.

Unable to find work that paid a living wage, some black families were forced to seek government assistance to survive. As more blacks became dependent on welfare, the rules changed, forcing the black man to leave home if his family received benefits.

Many black men were faced with two gut-wrenching choices: (1) stay with their family and let their children go hungry, OR (2) leave, so their children would have adequate food and shelter.

There was a third, more humane and moral option: give black men the SAME opportunity to earn a living wage that would allow them to support their families.

Historically, black males were barred from most high-paying occupations even when they had the educational requirements. Prior to the 1970s, the American Medical Association barred black physicians from membership, professional support, and advancement. Many U.S. school districts excluded black professionals and teachers from working as public high school teachers until the 1950s.

If a black man found a job, it seldom paid a living wage, and usually involved menial labor with no opportunity for advancement or higher pay, regardless of his education and experience. In many instances, the black male was either unable to secure adequate employment or settled for being financially exploited by racist bosses and coworkers.

The black man was stripped of the ONE thing every man needs to feel like a (real) man: ***the ability to ADEQUATELY provide for and protect his women and children as the head of his household.***

2010 AND Black Men (Still) Not Working

"It's more difficult for a black man with no criminal record to get a job than a white man with a criminal record. Being black in America today is basically the equivalent to having a felony conviction."– CNN, 2008

Wage inequality and employment discrimination still persists to this day. Black men earn 78 cents for every dollar white men earn, even when education is comparable. College-educated black males fared no better, and are twice as likely to be unemployed as similarly educated whites.

Affirmative Action = A Lose-Lose For Black Males

While affirmative action opened a few doors for a limited number of black males, it created a wall of white resentment. If black males strive for higher education, and take a coveted university seat, some whites cry, "reverse discrimination!"

Once they graduate from college and land a good-paying job, they're accused of using affirmative action to cheat whites. Behind closed doors, their hard-earned credentials are routinely dismissed as "dumbed-down affirmative action degrees." When it comes to corporate "downsizing," black males are usually the first to get a pink slip.

If black males attempt to join the skilled construction trades, they're confronted by abrupt rule changes and impossible hurdles. If they attempt to join the police or fire department they're accused of practicing "reverse racism."

If they don't pursue higher education, a trade, a profession, or find adequate employment that pays a living wage, they're labeled as shiftless parasites who feed off the labor of hard-working (white) taxpayers.

Clearly, it's a case of damned if black males do anything, and damned if they don't do any damn thing at all.

***

"The hardest hit group of workers – African-American men – were hit hardest again. Their unemployment rate is 17.3 percent, up from 16.7 percent, nearly double the 8.9 percent unemployment rate for white men. Women of both races fared better – 7.1 percent unemployment for whites, 13.2 percent unemployment for African Americans." -- (Source: The St. Louis American, September 3, 2010).

***

A recent study in New York found one out of four black males between the ages of 16 and 24 has a job, which is the equivalent of a 75% unemployment rate.

"About 35 years ago, I applied for a job at this Wall Street firm. I had a college degree, and graduated in the top 10 percent of my class. I was 23 years old and naive as hell about the ways of the white world.

They tested me and then set me up for an interview. The white man who gave me the first interview told me I had scored higher than anyone he ever tested. He acted like he was impressed and set me up for a second interview.

While I was waiting, I was scoping out the place, thinking, I got this job. I was asking the receptionist, a young white female about my age, about the company.

As soon as the second white man saw that young white female smiling at me, I knew I wasn't getting that job.

We went through the charade, but instead of asking about my qualifications, he talked about sports! I never heard from that company again. My biggest regret is they got away with it. I should have sued -- even if I didn't win."

-- Harry S., 60, retired government employee

BILLY KERSANDS.
CALLENDER'S (GEORGIA) MINSTRELS.

Billy Kersands, the most popular black comedian and dancer of his day, was well known for playing in minstrel shows as a moronic black male who entertained the white crowds by putting billiard balls and saucers into his "wide" mouth. (1842-1915)

REASON #5: TO DEMORALIZE THE BLACK MALE

The Demoralized, White-Identified, Self-Hating Black Male

Some black males have become so demoralized AND fearful that they deliberately seek out the "safety" of white friendships, relationships, and environments, hoping to escape the fate of other, less fortunate black males.

They may (desperately) mimic the attitudes, tastes, and lifestyles of the whites they wish to emulate, and may go as far as to avoid other blacks completely except for family -- for fear of being "too black by association." Some males will degrade other blacks around whites to separate themselves from the despised black masses and their OWN despised black selves.

At a highly publicized 2006 Cape Cod murder trial of a black male accused of the rape and murder of a white female, the sole black male juror told a white female juror that all his brothers' wives were white, that he had always been around white people, and that he did not like blacks because, "look at what they are capable of."

How (Fearful) Black Males Submit To White Supremacy

1. **Excessive grinning, smiling, joking, playing, clowning, acting a fool,** and adopting a foolish or clown-like persona in the presence of whites, hoping to be safe from attack by whites who see the strong-minded, self-respecting, black-identified Black Man as a threat.

2. **Adopting effeminate (feminine) behaviors,** personality, language, walk, and wearing female clothing and makeup; being docile and non-assertive with whites, shunning facial hair, wearing dangling earrings (like a female), and excessive jewelry (like a vain, effeminate peacock).

3. **Rejecting black females romantically and dating white females (or non-blacks) exclusively:** *"I have neutralized myself by choice, and have NO INTEREST WHATSOEVER in black unity; in creating more black babies (that look like me); or in challenging the system of white supremacy/black inferiority. The best evidence is the (non-black) female I am with."*

4. **Negatively stereotyping other blacks to impress, appease, or reassure whites**: *"How can I be a threat to white supremacy? I'm black and even I don't like blacks (or myself)! Please exclude me even while you're mistreating other black people."*

5. **Raping, robbing, and murdering other black people** is THE MOST PROFOUND ACT OF SUBMISSION TO WHITE SUPREMACY THAT A BLACK PERSON CAN COMMIT. It is an expression of extreme self-hatred, and an unconscious desire to return to SLAVERY, and the modern day plantation -- *the Prison Industrial Complex (PIC).*

Is there a mass-media conspiracy to Homosexualize black men?

"Many of us who are alarmed over this growing sexual confusion are mostly reacting to what is being done to our sons.

And, because of this, we are unable to effectively arrest the European psychosexual assault on them. We do not see ourselves as powerful enough to stop others from turning our sons into their daughters.

In the Western cultural context, men fear men, not women. And European men fear Afrikan men for many good reasons."

-- Mwalimu K. Bomani Baruti, African scholar, and co-founder of Akoben Institute

REASON #6: TO DESTROY BLACK MALE HETEROSEXUALITY (AND BLACK GENETIC POWER) BY FEMINIZING BLACK MALES

Promoting More Contempt For Black Females Guarantees An Increase In Homosexual Black Males

The (racist) mainstream media almost ALWAYS portrays the black female as untrustworthy, unstable, undesirable, and naturally antagonistic toward black males -- in sharp contrast to the white female, who is almost ALWAYS cast *as a loving friend or soulmate of the black male,* and a MORE nurturing mother figure for the black male child than the monster or missing-in-action black mother.

If the black male has been PROGRAMMED from a young age to despise the black female, he will NOT BE ABLE to love her, respect her, or desire her romantically, and will be more prone to abuse and abandon her, turn to another race of females -- *or to another male.*

How can a man have a loving, respectful, and sexually satisfying relationship with someone he has been taught to despise? And if the black male believes he came from the most DESPISED female in America -- his BLACK MOTHER -- how will he ever love and respect HIMSELF?

This may ALSO explain the reason the mass-media entertainment industry promotes AND rewards black-male entertainers who demean black females for profit and take their "blood money" to enrich white and non-black females.

Is there a link between the degradation of black females in the media and the increase in homosexuality and suicide among young black males over the last fifteen years? We believe there is.

Black Men In Dresses: Comedy Or Conquest?

- Flip Wilson (as Geraldine – the original cross-dressing female)
- Jamie Foxx (as Wanda on 'In Living Color')
- Damon Wayans & David Alan Grier (as homosexuals on 'In Living Color')
- Tyler Perry (Madea Movies)
- Tracy Morgan
- Howard Rollins (deceased, appeared in a dress on a talk show)
- Chris Tucker
- Will Smith
- Eddie Murphy (As Rasputia)
- Kenan Thompson (as Virginiaca)
- Martin Lawrence (As Sheneneh, Big Momma's House I & II)
- Arsenio Hall (In Coming To America)
- Rupaul's reality show (a famous BM drag queen)
- Wayan Brothers (In White Chicks)
- Wesley Snipes (In To Wong Foo With Love)
- Little Richard (who explained his "girlish" persona was designed to keep whites from assaulting him whenever he performed in the South).

Why Does (White) Hollywood Love Black Males Who Wear Dresses?

It's a question comedian Dave Chappelle pondered when he appeared on the Oprah Show in February 2006, shortly after he turned down a $50 million Comedy Central deal, and an offer to wear a dress in a film with black actor, Martin Lawrence:

> "I'm a conspiracy theorist to a degree. I connect dots that maybe shouldn't be connected. Certain dots like when I see they put every black man in the movies in a dress at some point in their career. Why all these brothers got to wear a dress?

> This happened to me. I'm doing a movie with Martin, the movie's going good, so I walk in the trailer, and I'm like, man, this must be the wrong trailer, cause there's a dress in here. The writer comes in, and like "Dave, listen, we got this hilarious scene where Martin's sneaking out of jail so he disguises you as a prostitute, and you put this dress on. Naw, I'm not doing that, I don't feel comfortable with that."

As of this writing, Chappelle hasn't appeared on film or TV since 2006. Is this his "punishment" for not allowing himself to be "feminized" and for NOT selling himself (and his soul) for $50 million?

White Men Versus Black Men In Dresses

Some blacks dismiss this predominantly black male OCCUPATION as harmless entertainment, but if it is so "harmless" why are black males the MAIN ONES doing it?

A handful of white actors have ventured into the sacred territory of panty girdles and high heels, BUT they ALWAYS play a MAN who ONLY puts on a dress to accomplish his goal then TAKES IT OFF before the end of the movie. The authors were unable to find even one white actor who built an entire movie career *dressing up as an ignorant, obese white female.*

In fact, it is rare to see an obese white female in a Hollywood film DESPITE the significant number of real-life, obese white females in America. For example, in the movie, 'Mrs. Doubtfire,' Robin Williams puts on a dress to accomplish the *manly goal* of spending time with his children.

The movie character, Mrs. Doubtfire, was a very likeable, well-mannered, and admirable character, unlike the females portrayed by most black actors. When the dress no longer served Mrs. Doubtfire's purpose, Robin Williams *took the dress OFF -- and reclaimed his manhood and fatherhood.*

A fourth difference is the *lack of balance* for black actors, who generally fall into one of five categories: (1) a crooked (or straight) cop; (2) a criminal; (3) a clown; (4) a drag queen (female), or (5) a human sacrifice who risks his life to save a white female, white female child, or white civilization.

Black Males In Drag Throw Black Females "Under The Bus"

Black men in "drag" usually promote the most unappealing AND cruelest stereotypes of black females. It is easy to dismiss the degrading images of black females as the business of show business, but EVERY BLACK MALE needs to realize that *whenever black males throw black females under the bus, they are going along for the ride.*

Why White Males In Drag Never Stereotype White Women

All the black millionaires and billionaires COMBINED would NOT have the money or the juice (power) to persuade white males to produce, promote, or perform in a movie that *degraded white women for being white.*

Not because the white male loves and respects the white female. It is due to his UNDERSTANDING that the white female is the TRUEST REFLECTION of the kind of man he is, which is why the white male puts the white female on a pedestal -- *and rewards the black male for doing the exact opposite to the black female.*

The lower the black female goes, the lower the black male FALLS, which is reflected in the condition of black males collectively, while the rest of the non-black people on the planet wonder:

"What nature of men enjoys and profits from degrading their own mothers, sisters, and daughters?"

Why Does (White) Hollywood Love Black Males Who Degrade Other Blacks?

Comedian Dave Chappelle during an a 2006 appearance on the Oprah Winfrey show explained his reasons for turning down the $50 million Comedy Central deal. He recalled a particular sketch, where a white crew member laughed, and was struck by the thought that this white person was laughing at him, not with him.

He confessed that some of his sketches made him feel "socially irresponsible," making him question the kind of messages his comedy was sending to the millions of viewers who tuned in each week.

Later, on "Inside the Actor's Studio" he admitted he walked away because the show's spirit was changing:

> "I would go to work on the show and I felt awful every day, that's not the way it was...I felt like some kind of prostitute or something. If I feel so bad, why keep on showing up to this place? I'm going to Africa. The hardest thing to do is to be true to yourself, especially when everybody is watching."

Chappelle appears to be the exception to the majority rule of black male actor/comedians who profit from perpetuating the same negative stereotypes that demonize their own mothers, sisters, and daughters.

Punishing Black Males Who Refuse To Embrace Homosexuality

"Well, you know I hate gay people. So I let it be known. I don't like gay people and I don't like to be around gay people. I am homophobic. I don't like it." -- Tim Hardaway, black former NBA player, was permanently banished from All-Star Weekend and stripped of all product endorsements. (2007)

"No, I did not call T.R. a faggot. It never happened." -- black actor Isaiah Washington from the hit TV show 'Grey's Anatomy' after he allegedly called white castmate, T.R. Knight, a *"faggot"* on the set of the TV show.

Under the relentless pressure of negative publicity, Washington formally apologized in the Golden Globes press room. "I apologize to T.R., my colleagues, the fans of the show and especially the lesbian and gay community for using a word that is unacceptable in any context or circumstance." (Jan 2007). A few months later, Washington was fired.

What are the long-term ramifications for black boys who learn it is more profitable (and safer) to be a "feminine" black MALE than a strong, masculine BLACK MAN?

Is It A Fear Of Black Males Or A White Obsession With The Black Penis?

The black male and his legendary penis have long been the object of envy, fascination, lust, and hatred, beginning with slavery. Ironically, while white males mercilessly raped black male and female slaves for over 400 years, the black male was somehow transformed into a savage black rapist.

This myth of the black rapist and his "huge black penis" is so powerful within the white collective mentality, that just the mere thought of a black male raping (or having sex with) a white female has provoked white males into murderous rages throughout history.

A key scene in D.W. Griffith's 1915 film, "Birth of a Nation" depicted a psychotic black male rapist assaulting a white female. This scene so inflamed white audiences that race riots broke out in Boston, Chicago, Denver, and in other major cities.

The 1933 movie, King Kong, where a gigantic (black) gorilla (nigger male) abducts a blonde white female (Fay Wray), was symbolic as the "monster black male lusting after the white female."

The fascination with and degradation of black male genitalia has made a fortune for the porn industry, by producing videos showing dark-skinned, black male performers with large penises "ravaging" petite white and Asian females.

Sexual Voyeurism OR Hidden Homosexuality?

There are numerous "private" clubs in the U.S. where white males pay black males (Mandingos) to have sex with (rape and ravage) their white wives. Some black males have reported being approached by white strangers who offer money in exchange for having sex with their white wives.

"I like seeing Amber (my wife) get off. It excites the hell out of me. And it's better if they're black. All Amber wants is sex. Black guys get that. And I know that Amber would never date a black man." -- Jeff, a 40-yr-old white male, and a member of a private sex club where "dates" are arranged at the homes of white couples between black males and married white females. (SOURCE: "Meet the Mandingos" http://www. details.com/sex-relationships/sex-and-other-releases/200703/meet-the-mandingos?currentPage=1)

OUR TRANSLATION: *"I like seeing Amber get off, but I'm really not interested in my wife. All my focus is on that black male and imagining it is ME who is having sex with a black man. This is the only way I can satisfy my secret homosexual desire to experience AND possess a BIG, BLACK PENIS."*

The authors could not find a single sex club where black males paid white males to have sex with their black wives.

The widespread fear and fascination with black male sexuality is evident in the black male stereotypes in TV and films:

- the cowardly black male, popular in early films (symbolic castration)
- the super-hero black male (the virile, masculine, sexually dominate male)
- the dangerous, violent, animalistic (rapist of white female) black male aka King Kong who must be destroyed
- The sexless, neutered black male friend or rescuer (symbolic castration)
- The black male in dresses, high heels, and earrings (symbolic castration)
- The foolish/ignorant black male buffoon (self-castration)

The obsession with black male sexuality (genitalia) is MOST evident among law enforcement:

(1992) **Stacy Koon** (white male), the Los Angeles police sergeant acquitted in the Rodney King beating, gave this description in his unpublished "memoirs," of how Mr. King acted when Officer Melanie Singer (a white female) of the California Highway Patrol approached King with a gun:

"He grabbed his butt with both hands and began to shake and gyrate his fanny in a sexually suggestive fashion. As King sexually gyrated, a mixture of fear and offense overcame Melanie. The fear was of a Mandingo sexual encounter."

In a *Los Angeles Times* interview, Koon defended his "memoirs" by saying he was trying re-create the antebellum image of a *"large black man"* and a *"defenseless white woman."*

"In society," Koon said, "there's this sexual prowess of blacks on the old plantation of the South and intercourse between blacks and whites on the plantation. And that's where the fear comes in, because he's black."

Koon dismisses the MASS RAPE of African slave women by white males by describing it as "intercourse," to PROJECT THE WHITE MALE'S HISTORY OF RAPE onto black males by pretending (LYING) that black males have a history of raping "defenseless white females."

As was true then and is STILL true today -- at least according to FBI statistics -- MOST white female rape victims were raped by white males.

Even in police custody, black male genitalia are NOT safe:

"White cops are scared of black men. The bigger or darker the man, the more frightened the white cop. I can't shake that; it's a belief I will take to the grave." -- Norm Stamper, white former Chief of Police of Seattle, WA.

(1977) Documented torture methods used against black males during "interrogations" in Philadelphia (PA) police headquarters included twisting or kicking testicles, and stabbing one suspect in the groin with a sword-like instrument.

(1972-1991) Chicago Police Commander Jon G. Burge and Chicago detectives tortured over 200 black men to coerce confessions. Some documented torture methods: applying a cattle prod to nipples, genitals, and rectal interiors.

(1997) Abner Louima, a Haitian immigrant, was sodomized with a broomstick handle inside a New York (70th Precinct) police station by two white police officers. While officer Schwarz (white male) held him down, officer Volpe shoved a wooden stick into his rectum (sodomized him).

(2007) Coprez Coffie -- an unarmed black male sodomized by white police officers with a screwdriver in an alley after being pulled over by Chicago police officers. Doctors reported tears to Coffie's rectum and a screwdriver was found in the police car's glove compartment with fecal matter on it.

(1993) Seven African immigrant van drivers accused a white male Queens, New York police officer of raping and sodomizing them in separate incidents. The District Attorney Richard A. Brown dismissed the charges. (1993)

Are these depraved sexual assaults by white males a desperate attempt to turn the black male into a non-threatening female?

Fear Of Black Males OR A Fear Of Forbidden Desires?

(2007) Florida Representative Bob Allen (a white male Republican) was arrested for soliciting sex from an undercover black male cop. The reason he gave to the police? He was afraid of becoming another "crime statistic."

> *"...this was a pretty stocky black guy, and there were a lot of other black guys around in the park, and, you know..."*

It is illogical to believe Rep. Allen was so *"afraid of becoming another crime statistic,"* that he VOLUNTEERED to perform oral sex on a black male (undercover officer) in the men's room at a public park.

Perhaps, this "fear" has LESS to do with being a victim of crime -- and MORE to do with the secret, sociopathic, and homosexual obsession about the black male's PENIS -- and his GENETIC DOMINANCE.

Is the homosexual longing for black males so powerful (and so unacceptable) that it leads to unprovoked violence against black males -- and black male genitalia?

Fear Of Black Males OR Fear Of A Strong Black Man Planet?

The Strong, Heterosexual, Self-Respecting, Black-Loving, Black-Identified Black Man REFUSES to hide behind the false facade of femininity, bisexuality, or homosexuality to appease those who are threatened by STRONG BLACK MASCULINITY because his women and children *need him.*

The Strong, Heterosexual, Self-Respecting, Black-Loving, Black-Identified Black Man has NO DESIRE to breed himself out of existence by fathering children who do not resemble him OR his ancestors, because this destroys his powerfully melanated African genetics.

The Strong, Heterosexual, Self-Respecting, Black-Loving, Black-Identified Black Man does NOT define himself by a white supremacist, materialistic, non-spiritual definition of what a man should be. He REFUSES to degrade black people for profit. He REFUSES to be used against his own people for personal gain because at the end of the day, he knows the collective condition of his black community, his black women, and black children *depends on what he does AND who he is.*

The Strong, Heterosexual, Self-Respecting, Black-Loving, Black-Identified Black Man is white supremacy's BIGGEST FEAR because he is a **WEAPON OF MASS INJUSTICE DESTRUCTION.**

On the day the BLACK MAN makes the fateful decision to die on his feet fighting for justice than live on his knees as a slave is the day the world will rejoice because the sleeping giant, the BLACK MAN -- the first man God made -- will reclaim his rightful throne.

CHAPTER 35

TALES OF THE BACKSIDE: FLIPPING THE HOLLYWOOD SCRIPT

Disclaimer: The following is entertainment satire and a work of fiction. All names, characters, places, and incidents are the product of the authors' imagination and used fictitiously. Any resemblance to actual persons, living or dead, business establishments, events, or locales is entirely coincidental.

SCENE: Rufus Smurf, the black superstar singer/entertainer/actor, walked into the oak-paneled boardroom where studio execs were waiting to hear his latest brainstorm.

"How about this?" Rufus said, wide-eyed with excitement. "A sequel to 'Great Big Whale of a Black Momma,' called -- 'Great Big Whale of a White Momma!"

The icy silence that followed made big balls of sweat pop out on Rufus's brown forehead. "Don't you get it?" Rufus continued hastily. "Instead of a fat, nasty, ignorant black momma, she'll be a big, fat, nasty, ignorant white momma!"

"Mr. Smurf." The silver-haired Chairman of the Board fixed his steely blue gaze on the quivering black man standing before him.

"Yassuh?"

"Do you want to work in this town again?"

"Oh, yassuh!" Rufus's lips stretched as wide as the white-toothed grin on the black statue of Rastus that the Chairman kept on his desk.

He felt like kicking his own black butt! He shoulda known better than to mess with white women when he got one of his brainstorms! He'd better stick with the nigga females from now on!

"Then stick to the program," the Chairman ordered, sliding a fat white envelope across the desk. "And do the job you were hired to do."

"Sho nuff, boss!" Rufus glanced inside the envelope stuffed with large-denomination bills.

"Just a little bonus for your 'Great Big Whale of a Black Momma,'" the Chairman said. "And we're submitting your name to the Academy for your portrayal of nigg -- black women."

"Yippee!" Rufus flashed a big white grin as he jumped up and clicked his heels in the air to punctuate his glee.

The white men in the room chuckled and shook their heads. One murmured low to another, "Niggers sure can jump."

"Can I go now, boss?" Rufus giggled, pretending not to hear.

"What's your hurry, boy?" The Chairman asked sternly.

Rufus cocked his head to one side and hunched his shoulders, like a puppy caught peeing on the new rug. "Got a court date with my new baby's momma," he said, feigning embarrassment, but secretly proud that these white men knew he was a baby-making stud.

"You colored boys sure love the pootang."

"Yassum, we sho do!"

The Chairman waved an imperial hand. "Go ahead. Don't spend all that cheddar on too much black booty, boy."

"I won't, nassum," Rufus said, as he backed out of the room.

After the door closed, the Chairman's cold smile evaporated. He reached under the table and opened a cardboard box filled with white robes and pointy white hoods. "Time to get rid of these damn things once and for all," he said. "The blacks are doing all our dirty work for us."

"The nerve of that nigger, thinking we'd demean our white race with a movie like that," The redheaded VP of programming finally spoke.

"My grandfather, bless his dear, departed soul, used to talk fondly about the good old days," the Chairman said, with a nostalgic smile. "He loved those old minstrel shows with darkies singing, dancing, and making fools of themselves."

"What good old days?" the redheaded man sneered. "What's changed?" His question was met with derisive laughter from the men in the room.

"Blacks are animals. They respect nothing, not their own women, mothers, churches, or themselves," said a blond man, shaking his head in disgust.

"Of course, they're animals. That's their nature. Personally, I thank God every day for making niggers." The Chairman patted the backs of the men as they filed out the door. "That 'Great Big Whale of a Black Momma' just paid for my new 80-foot yacht."

Why (White) Hollywood Loves Black Men In Dresses

"To defeat my enemy, I must destroy his manhood. I will turn the black male into my conquered male/female (she-male) and pay him millions of dollars to wear a dress, two earrings, stockings, and high heels in front of the TV and movie camera.

I will make this conquered black male (she-male) the role model for millions of black men and boys all over the world, so the entire world can see that no matter how rich or famous or talented or successful the black man becomes, he is still "a white man's bitch."

Recipe #12

Interracial relationships

Tales From the (White) Relationship Battlefield

"Have you seen what single women have to pick from as partners? I am tired of dating losers, and unemployed, little whiny, mommas-boys." -- Genny, Jacksonville, FL

"A lot of women avoid marriage because they have to take care of the children and the housework, work a 9-5, and wait hand and foot on a husband. Why should they do it? It's a life sentence, and I'm on my 23rd year." Susan, San Antonio, TX

"Why get married, get loaded down with debt, bratty, ungrateful kids, and a wife who nags, complains, every day. Stay single, you keep control of your time, money, sex, without worrying that one day, some judge is going to take everything you earned away from you." -- Lloyd, Westbury, New York

"Women have figured out they don't need a man to have a successful, happy, peaceful life. Life lasts too long to put up with an annoying man, or woman, for that matter." Jan, Corvallis, Oregon

(video responses from white viewers on a TV poll on being single VS being married)

CHAPTER 36

THE INTERRACIAL CON GAME

From CNN specials, sensationalized "relationship" books, degrading movies, and Internet articles by black authors seeking fame and fortune at any cost, blacks are BOMBARDED by a barrage of negative (and false) information about black-on-black love. On the heels of all this "bad news" comes the media-manufactured cure: *interracial relationships.*

What the mainstream media DOES NOT EXPLAIN is how whites -- with a 50% divorce rate – can be the CURE for what ails the romantically frustrated black male and female?

Americans – regardless of ethnicity, class, income – are plagued by divorce, broken homes, missing and murdered spouses, domestic abuse, emotionally traumatized children, incest, cheating spouses, closet homosexuality, and babies born outside of a two-parent, committed marriage.

Married-with-children white senators and governors are stepping down in disgrace after their homosexual affairs are publicly exposed. More than half of white American women and men are single or divorced, and the men MOST LIKELY to seek a mail order bride from China and Russia are white males.

The explosion of dating ads, websites, and professional "match-making" services aimed at the romantically frustrated single WHITE population reveals the cleverly disguised TRUTH (revealed from the poll on the previous page):

Blacks aren't the ONLY ones having relationship problems.

In spite of this TRUTH, **black-on-black love** is relentlessly demonized by the mainstream media, while interracial (white/black) relationships are promoted as the superior alternative for blacks. Some blacks see the blatant promotion of interracial dating for blacks as a sign of "racial progress" but the message "interracial is better" *is NEVER aimed at the white population*, nor are whites encouraged to uplift blacks as a "superior alternative" to whites.

Contrary to popular belief -- especially among the black collective -- **the LEAST COMMON interracial marriage in America is between blacks and whites.** The MAJORITY of the tiny minority (less than 9%) of whites who marry non-whites marry Asians and Hispanics.

Despite these facts, **black/white interracial dating** has caused MORE bitterness between black males and black females than any other relationship issue, including adultery, divorce, child support, and domestic violence, which leads to a crucial – and self-respecting -- question:

Why are black males and black females fighting so bitterly over the TINY NUMBER of whites who are interested in marrying us?

(Note: the following "White Female Supremacist" excerpts were taken from an article (supposedly) written by a white female white supremacist. The authors could not verify the identity or existence of this particular white female, but found the excerpts useful in exposing the mindset and motivations of the racist white female who has sexual intercourse with black males.

* * *

"White Supremacy must embrace Interracial Sex. The fatal flaw of past white supremacy was segregation and Apartheid. By outlawing and preventing Interracial Sex, it led to more pure blacks being bred.

Sex is the second most powerful tool after political/social repression of non-whites. Britain, France, Spain and Portugal conquered non-white colonies first with deception, second with military force, and finally through Interracial Sex."

-- White Female Supremacist (Der Kosmonaut, 1972)

What is the real agenda behind the INTERRACIAL CON GAME? The 'Top Ten Interracial Myths' should provide some answers -- and some long overdue food for thought.

THE CON

Debunking The Top Ten Interracial Relationship Myths

NOTE: For the purposes of this chapter, "interracial" refers to the most divisive interracial combination in Black America: blacks and whites.

MYTH #1: Black male/black female relationships are more dysfunctional than white male/white female relationships.

Comparing black relationships to white relationships in a white supremacy society – as if all things were equal -- is as logical as comparing black poverty to white poverty; black schools to white schools; or apples to elephants.

FACT: The black family (and the black male/black female relationship) was systematically DESTROYED by over 500 years of institutionalized slavery, racism, and racist media stereotypes. **The white family was not.**

FACT: Black couples have the SAME pressures white couples have **in addition** to the social, psychological, and economic pressures of being black in a racist society. **Whites are NOT penalized for being white; they are rewarded at the expense of non-whites.**

FACT: Blacks are continually bombarded with propaganda about the (superior) benefits of interracial relationships. **Whites are NOT.**

FACT: Black males and females are pitted against each other by the white supremacy system via the economic, educational, social, political, legal, and law enforcement systems that penalize ALL non-whites. *White males and females are NOT.*

FACT: After African traditions were destroyed during slavery, the ONLY relationship role model for former slaves was the white male/white female relationship.

What TRUTH does the above reveal about the quality of white male/white female relationships?

"Some people say they date people from another race because they don't see color, and that's the way it is for me.

I also think it's refreshing for a white woman to be with a black man; that adds something to the relationship...

There's more openness, more of a feeling that you don't have to conform to everything society tells you... If I were white, I thought I could be a little happier. I wanted to be white because I was black, and black was never the right color."

-- Dennis Rodman, former NBA ballplayer

MYTH #2: Love is "color-blind."

Unless an individual is LEGALLY BLIND, it is impossible to NOT see the skin color of another individual. It is common for blacks and whites who date interracially to deliberately shun romantic partners of their OWN ethnic group. Yet, most will passionately insist they didn't "choose" to fall in love because "love is color-blind" (even if they are not).

Just because a relationship was not "planned," does not mean our choice of a partner was an accident. Most people would not "accidentally" fall in love with a 400-lb, blind paraplegic, even if that person had all the other qualities they were looking for.

Certainly, a black person who chooses one white lover after another is NOT color-blind, but is **color-obsessed**, acting out a skin color fetish where white skin represents something (superior) that black skin (including theirs) does not.

Some blacks date or marry whites exclusively even when they secretly or openly dislike whites in general. The same is true of whites who date or marry blacks exclusively even when they secretly or openly dislike blacks in general.

It is just as common for whites who date and marry blacks to have few or NO black friends, and to avoid socializing with blacks of the SAME SEX for fear their black partner will come to his or her senses, and go "back to black" (where even the white person deep down knows they belong).

Most interracial couples are so uncomfortable talking honestly about racism or facing the racial hang-ups that brought them together in the first place, that just initiating a discussion about racism/white supremacy is enough to send them scurrying into deep denial – or out of the room altogether.

They prefer to ignore the 800-lb gorilla (white supremacy) even when it is standing with one huge foot on their (and our) collective necks. If an interracial couple cannot deal honestly with their own racial issues, they will simply spread their sick confusion to their non-white children and any black person within their area of psychological contamination.

In fact, the need (to pretend) to be "color-blind" is actually an ADMISSION of *color obsession*, and a big RED FLAG that the white person making that false claim is probably practicing racism. The black person who claims to be "color-blind" -- even while they are being VICTIMIZED because of their skin color -- clearly illustrates his or her white-identified, confused mindset.

Otherwise, why deny the ability to see color unless color has some negative associations -- or provokes feelings of guilt or shame?

It is possible (but unlikely) for whites and blacks to be attracted to each other where skin color fetishes, racial and sexual stereotypes, and self-hatred issues played NO major role in their initial attraction, but eventually that interracial couple will have to face the harsh realities that are IMPOSSIBLE to ignore in a white supremacy society:

Color Always Matters.

A Bratter and King study in 2008 found White/White and Black/Black marriages have the same divorce rates;

Black husband/White wife marriages were twice as likely to divorce as White/White couples; and White husband/Black wife couples were 44% less likely to divorce than White/White couples.

(SOURCE:http://docs.google.com/viewer?a=v&q=cache:1NZ6fP5sycEJ)

MYTH #3: Interracial couples are more committed than black or white couples because they have to be.

It is difficult to prove the "commitment" argument, when the divorce rate for interracial marriages is higher than same-ethnic group marriages. According to the 'Bratter and King' Study found on the previous page, the marriages MOST LIKELY to end in divorce were black husband/white wife marriages. Assuming this study is correct, here are some possible (but unscientific) reasons:

- Many black male/white female couples marry at younger ages, based on societal and sexual stereotypes like the black male sexual prowess ("swagger"), or the perceived social status of white females. It is common for young (immature) interracial couples to rebel (get revenge) against social customs, white society, or white parents (black parents are seldom the targets). However, once reality intrudes on the fantasies that brought them together, these marriages often collapse.

- Lower-income black males are usually limited to marrying lower-income white females, since the majority of middle and upper-income white females prefer white males. These interracial marriages have the added strain of financial difficulties and pressures from family and society in general.

- The highly protected status of the white male (in a white supremacy society) makes him less likely to be penalized for his romantic choices.

- Black females who marry white males tend to be educated with equal or greater status, education, and income. These couples also tend to wait longer to get married, giving them greater financial stability and life experience.

- White males are more particular about the quality and compatibility of the black females they marry (she must be white-identified). The black female must bring more to the table since her "black-ness" is NOT seen as an asset -- UNLIKE the black male who is usually less concerned about the quality of white female he marries because her white-ness is automatically seen as an asset, and she often only needs to bring her "white-ness" to the marital table.

- Since all females and non-white males have been PROGRAMMED to submit to white male domination, it may be easier for the black female to submit to her white husband than a (powerless) black one. It does NOT matter if the black wife has a dominant personality; she is still submissive to white supremacy.

- Unless the black male is already white-identified (submissive to white supremacy), he may eventually resent (and rebel against) his more powerful AND privileged white female partner, who expects him to submit to her white reality and value system. It does NOT matter if that black male abuses that white female; at all times and in all places, she is the most powerful person, and at any given time she can pull the plug on him -- and their relationship.

"Now we come to the importance of bi-racial children for the White Supremacy Project.

First, lighter babies are produced. The children of black males and white females will be educated to hate blacks.

They will be raised in all-white settings. The children will date and sex whites. Finally, these children will marry and have kids with whites. Their offspring will turn white.

It is possible for black males to have sex with white females and have no impact on the white population. When the kids of interracial unions are raised by whites, the numbers will be regained.

The end result is the white population increases, the black population decreases. From the black male perspective, interracial sex is a form of racial suicide."

-- White Female Supremacist (Der Kosmonaut, 1972)

- If the white female's MAIN reason for marrying a black male is rebellion, curiosity, sex, money, or to enrich her genetics by having more melanated children (producing color), she is more likely to divorce the black male after her "mission" has been accomplished, or the thrill has worn off.

MYTH #4: More interracial sex and breeding -- "the browning of America" -- will eventually end racism.

This belief is anti-historical wishful thinking, and ignores the 400-year legacy of American slavery and the REALITIES of the global white supremacy system.

One only has to look at Brazil and other Latin American countries with a large population of **non-whites who have a white parent (NWWP)** to see the white minority STILL rules the black and NWWP majority who are stuck at the economic and educational bottom.

In South Africa, there were (and still are) separations between the ruling white class, the oppressed black class, and the "coloureds" **(NWWP)** who get a few more crumbs than blacks. Even in America, a small white minority controls the white AND the non-white majority.

"In the UK (United Kingdom) interracial marriage has created a lot of confused black people who think they are white -- until some white person calls them a "nigger" and then they are shocked." – Michael, 37, health care worker, UK

It is the **QUALITY**, not the quantity (of numbers) that counts the most. If the majority of the (non-white) population are (deliberately) deprived economically and educationally, the majority will lack the resources OR the will to resist oppression by the (white) minority.

The Smaller The White Minority, The Greater The Need To Oppress The Non-White Majority

When the white minority is greatly outnumbered, they will feel MORE threatened and MORE determined to do whatever they deem necessary -- no matter how cruel, wicked, unjust, or immoral -- to maintain their economic, educational, and political DOMINATION over non-whites.

More non-white children with a white parent ((NWWP) in America will NOT reduce OR eliminate racism, just like the election of the first identifiably "black" president in 2008 DID NOT reduce racism. In fact, Obama's election has INCREASED overt racism and resentment from the white collective.

The non-white person with a white parent **(NWWP)** *historically* has been used by the white minority as a "buffer" between privileged whites and oppressed non-whites because he or she is MORE likely to promote white supremacy than OPPOSE it since their "white side" offers more privileges.

The black person with a white parent, is more likely to have a white mother; to be raised by a white mother; and to grow up without their black birth father. They are more likely to be white-identified (since most children are more sympathetic to their mother's side); are more likely to distance themselves from their "black side;" and are more likely to marry and breed with whites.

The same is true for the black person with a white father and a white-identified black mother. Since MOST white-identified blacks with a white parent usually prefer white lovers and spouses, the so-called "browning" soon becomes more beige, then whiter by the 2nd or 3rd generation.

Contrary to the "melting pot myth," MORE interracial breeding between blacks and whites actually LENGTHENS and STRENGTHENS the reign of white supremacy, destroys black genetics, and reduces the overall black population – which are the main reasons the (white) entertainment industry promotes INTERRACIAL SEX for blacks.

"The melting pot of the races began around the northern perimeter. The end result was always the same: The Blacks were pushed to the bottom of the social, economic and political ladder whenever the Asians (meaning whites) and their mulatto offspring gained control.

This scheme of weakening the Blacks by turning their half-white brothers against them cannot be overemphasized because it began in the early times and it became the universal practice of whites, and is still one of the cornerstones in the edifice of white power..." -- Chancellor Williams, "Destruction of Black Civilization -- Chapter II: Ethiopia's Oldest Daughter: Egypt. pg. 61."

No Son To Carry On His Name

After two years of living together, Bernard's white girlfriend, Becky, becomes pregnant. When he finds out they are having a boy, he is thrilled because he will finally have a son to carry on his name.

The first time Bernard lays eyes on his son, he is shocked by the pale skin and gray eyes. It never occurred to him that their baby would look more like the mother than the father. As his son grows older, the pale skin and the straight brown hair never gets any darker (or kinkier) like he secretly hoped it would.

Two years later, he and Becky separate. Bernard sees his son, Seth, who is three years old, only a few times a month instead of every night. Whenever he brings his son around his family, everyone makes a fuss over him, but Bernard just can't shake the disconnect he feels toward the gray-eyed boy with straight brown hair. He tells himself that it shouldn't matter what his son looks like. It's still his blood. So, Bernard resigns himself to do right by his son.

The years pass quickly. To Bernard's dismay, Seth shuns the black kids at his grammar school in favor of the white kids. Bernard tells Becky that it's important that Seth knows his "black culture" but after a heated argument, Becky says Seth is her son, too, so why should his black culture be more important than her white one?

Bernard tries to instill some "black pride" into Seth but his son clearly isn't interested in his father's lessons. It's also clear that Seth doesn't identify with black people at all. The "pretty white baby" has turned into a white stranger who prefers white music and can't dance or keep step with the rhythm. Behind Bernard's back, his relatives shake their heads, and some privately ask, *"What kind of name is Seth for a black boy?"*

Bernard suspects that Becky and her new white husband are deliberately playing down or outright ignoring Seth's mixed heritage and prefer to pretend he is all white.

Permanently soured on interracial dating, Bernard relocates to another state, marries Aretha, a black woman, and has a daughter with her. He invites Seth – now in his 2nd year of high school – to spend the summer with him, Aretha, and his half-sister, Debra, but Seth politely declines. He says his stepfather -- who owns a speedboat -- is teaching him to water-ski. Bernard knows he can't compete with that. He never even learned to swim.

The "white" son and the "black side" of the family drift even further apart after Seth graduates from high school. Bernard's attempts to bond with his son over the years hits an impasse. Seth is nothing like the sons of his sisters and friends, who are into all that is "black." Bernard hates to admit he is envious of his nephews, with their cool fade hairstyles and fun-loving personalities, who represent the kind of son he secretly wishes he had.

The years pass. Seth graduates from college, gets a job at his stepfather's company, and a fiancée -- the daughter of a white businessman. Bernard is not surprised that he, his wife, and daughter are the only black people at the 150-plus-guest wedding. Bernard is positive that most of the guests have no idea who he is, and assume Becky's white husband is the "father" of the groom.

For his son's sake, Bernard swallows his anger and humiliation and stays in the background. He has a thought that will haunt him for years to come: *his only son's children and grandchildren -- Bernard's grandchildren AND great grandchildren -- will talk white, act white, and be white.* Since he and Becky never married, Bernard's family name, legacy, and bloodline will be wiped out by the next generation.

If the current (suicidal) trend of black males feverishly breeding with white females continues, black males will eventually accomplish what slavery, racism, sterilization, the Tuskegee Experiment, lynching, castration, crack cocaine, segregation, discrimination, malt liquor, and the Prison Industrial Complex (PIC) have failed to do: **wipe out future black generations.**

END OF STORY

"Keep your friends close; and your enemies closer."
-- *Niccolo Machiavelli (1469-1527)*

"What act brings your enemies closer than sexual intercourse?"
-- *Umoja*

Aboriginal Bathurst Island men

Interracial Sex Between Whites and Non-Whites = The Systematic Destruction Of Non-White People

Aborigines make up about 2% of Australia's population but they suffer disproportionately high rates of imprisonment and ill-health." (SOURCE: 'Aboriginal children 'starving,' welfare workers say' by Phil Mercer, BBC News)

The ORIGINAL (native) people that once populated Australia have become a micro-minority in their own nation due to European colonization and INTERRACIAL SEX with whites, which has led to the cultural, psychological, and genetic destruction of the Aboriginal people.

This dynamic has played out for hundreds of years, whenever non-whites and Europeans cross paths, from the Native Americans of North America, the Fugi people (Fugi Islands), South Africa, Latin America, Haiti, the Aboriginals (in Australia), the (original) Hawaiians (South Pacific) to millions of African slaves held in bondage.

Interracial sex between whites and non-whites ALWAYS leads to non-white educational, economic, and political oppression; the genetic destruction of non-white populations; and MORE not LESS racism. The proof: the original Australian Aborigines who once populated Australia are now less than 2% of the population.

274

Native Americans from the Cherokee, Cheyenne, Choctaw, Comanche,
Iroquois, and Muscogee tribes -- Photos date from 1868 to 1924

The Non-White Genocide Scoreboard:

- 100 million people for North American Indians (blacks)
- 18 million for the area north of Mexico
- 28 million from the African Holocaust

*"In 1910, the total population of North American Indians was about
400,000, down from about 18 -19 million in 1492." -- David Stannard in
'American Holocaust'*

*"The Indian [was thought] as less than human and worthy only of extermina-
tion. We did shoot down defenseless men, and women and children at places
like Camp Grant, Sand Creek, and Wounded Knee. We did feed strychnine
to red warriors. We did set whole villages of people out naked to freeze in
the iron cold of Montana winters. And we did confine thousands in what
amounted to concentration camps." —The Indian Wars of the West, 1934*

Native Americans And The Interracial Sex Connection

The 2009 U.S. Census estimates the Native American population -- that
once numbered in the tens of millions -- is currently **only one percent of
the 307 million people in America.**

Native Americans marry whites at a higher rate (56%) than any other
non-white population in the U.S. If this sad trend continues, the Native
American people will eventually **breed themselves out of existence.**

"I wish to be acknowledged not as Black but as white...who but a white woman could do this for me? By loving me she proves that I am worthy of white love. I am loved like a white man. I am a white man.

Her noble love takes me onto the road of self-realization – I marry white culture, white beauty, white whiteness. When my restless hands grasp those white breasts, they grasp white civilization and dignity and make them mine." – 'Black Skin, White Masks,' Frantz Fanon (1952)

Frantz Fanon, a trained black psychiatrist, wrote about the feelings of dependency and inadequacy that Black people experience in a White world.

As a result of the inferiority complex programmed into the minds of the black male, he will try to appropriate and imitate the cultural code of the colonizer (and his oppressors).

(Unfortunately, Fanon fell prey to his own diagnosed disease: he married a white female).

MYTH #5: Black males are "forced" to date/marry white females because black females are defective (inferior).

This is the MOST divisive (and hurtful) myth because it automatically implies that black females are so INFERIOR in character and appearance, that a black male seeking an attractive, quality mate is FORCED to date outside his race. Since the majority of black males marry black females, this racist myth -- like all interracial myths -- fails the ultimate test of LOGIC.

"The (defective) black female made me date outside my race."

A popular black radio talk program was debating the pros and cons of interracial dating. A 30-something black male caller, Bill, admitted he only dated white women. When the host asked him why, Bill said, *"Black girls rejected me in high school because I was too dark."*

Tom, a white male, told a similar tale when he was interviewed by a computer industry publication. He recalled being shunned and ridiculed by the pretty, popular girls in his high school because, *"I was a short, skinny nerd."*

Tom's best friend, John, was Asian-American, and just as unpopular with the handful of Asian girls at their high school who preferred white males. *"Instead of dating, John and I spent most evenings and weekends on our passion: writing and debugging computer programs."*

In their freshmen year of college, they wrote a program that was purchased by a major software firm. After graduation, Tom and John started their own software company, and today, both men are millionaires. Both men are also married, with children.

Tom married the same blonde, cheerleader-type that rejected him in high school. John married an Asian beauty contest winner. Do Tom and John remember being the two most unpopular "nerds" in high school? Absolutely. Did that experience make them want to 'get even' by rejecting all the women in their race? *Absolutely NOT.*

Bill's reasons for having a 'Jim Crow' (whites-only) dating policy was NOT caused by any TEENAGED black girls who rejected him in high school; it was caused by his black inferiority complex -- which may explain why Bill is on his third interracial relationship in five years: *because he is dating white females for the wrong reasons.*

Bill's need to blame black females for his OWN behavior is PROOF he knows his behavior is incorrect. Otherwise, there would be NO need for Bill to blame black females OR anyone else.

Unlike Bill, Tom and John had not been programmed to dislike themselves or their own ethnic group -- so they had no need to condemn OR reject their female mirror images.

"Now, you integration-minded Negroes are trying to force yourselves on your former slave master, trying to make him accept you in his drawing room; you want to hang out with his women rather than the women of your own kind....

Because only a man who is ashamed of what he is will marry out of his race. There has to be something wrong when a man or woman leaves his own people and marries somebody of another kind. Men who are proud of being black marry black women; women who are proud of being black marry black men.

This is particularly true when you realize that these Negroes who go for integration and intermarriage are linking up with the very people who lynched their fathers, raped their mothers, and put their kid sisters in the kitchen to scrub floors."

-- Malcolm X being interviewed by Louis Lomax
(1963)

Black Male Homosexuals NOT Immune to "Jungle Fever"

The same (self-hating) dynamic is at work for the homosexual black male who PREFERS homosexual relationships with white males -- **despite the rampant racism within the white homosexual community.**

According to Keith Boykin, a "homosexual rights" advocate/columnist who frequently writes about the black homosexual community, some black male homosexuals refuse to date black males.

Referring to a black male acquaintance, Boykin writes: *"He did not want to date a black man. He wanted a white man instead. To catch his eye, a black man would have to be twice as gorgeous and twice as successful as an average white man."*

Ironically, the self-hating homosexual black male who discriminates against other black males, is often reluctant to talk about his sexual encounters with white males. He may realize on some level that he is just a sexual object to the racist white male, and later may feel he was degraded by the sexual contact.

This "realization" may not deter the most self-hating homosexual black male from seeking white partners because they represent the ONLY source of the white validation he so desperately needs. This is typical of the irrational, self-destructive mental illness among blacks infected with "jungle fever."

Revisiting Dennis Rodman's "explanation" for dating interracially:

"Some people say they date people from another race because they don't see color, and that's the way it is for me. I also think it's refreshing for a white woman to be with a black man; that adds something to the relationship...there's more openness, more of a feeling that you don't have to conform to everything society tells you...if I were white, I thought I could be a little happier. I wanted to be white because I was black, and black was never the right color."

***

If we flipped Rodman's contradictory script to explain why some black male homosexuals only "date" white males, it might read something like this:

"Some people say they date people from another race because they don't see color, and that's the way it is for me. I also think it's refreshing for a white man to be with a black man; that adds something to the relationship...there's more openness, more of a feeling that you don't have to conform to everything society tells you...if I were white, I thought I could be a little happier. I wanted to be white because I was black, and black was never the right color."

Perhaps, "the (defective) black female" excuse should be expanded to include "the (defective) black male homosexual made me date a white male" excuse.

"White females engaging in Interracial Sex is White Supremacy with a Human Face. The white female has the psychological and sexual advantages over black males that white males could never have...the white female has more trust and credibility among black males than the white male does.

The black male loves, lusts after, and desires the white female. The white female can get away with racism and racial oppression against the black male, without arousing the anger and bitterness in black males that white males do.

The white female is in the last stages in her war with the white male. She is better educated than white males. While the white female finishes off the white male, she is in no way ready to give up her white supremacy.

The sexual and political rise of the white female over white males must happen through her conquest and dominance of black males. To fend off any threat to white female hegemony, we must dominate N*ggers sexually."

-- White Female Supremacist (Der Kosmonaut, 1972)

MYTH #6: White females are "more supportive" than black females.

"White women treat they man like a king and black women feel like they ain't gotta do that shit." – rapper "Slim Thug" in a Vibe magazine interview (2010)

"It's like a white woman told me once....black women treat their men like property; white women treat their men like people even if they don't always agree." – BiggLoc, black male poster on black website

These comments are not nearly as surprising as the impressive number of black males who CLAIM they have first-hand knowledge of how white females treat white males -- like kings -- **behind closed doors.**

However, just for argument's sake, if we assume Slim Thug is correct when he says, *"white women treat they men like a king...,"* why is the white husband/white wife divorce rate over 50%? How would Slim explain the even higher black husband/white wife divorce rate, which is TWICE as high as the black husband/black wife divorce rate? (see Bratter and King study, page 268).

If the white female is MORE supportive than the black female, and black husband/white wife couples have a HIGHER divorce rate than black husband/black wife couples, there can be ONLY be one logical conclusion: **the black male must be the least supportive.** It is this kind of (false) logic that illustrates the dangers of blacks stereotyping other blacks.

Black Males Who Sing The Praises Of White Females

Certainly, any black male who has DEPENDED on a **("supportive")** black mother, sister, aunt, or grandmother for the **first eighteen (or more) years of his life** -- but dares to uplifts white females above black females is suffering from terminal memory LOSS at best -- or is at the very worst, **a dishonest, dishonorable, and ungrateful individual.**

Black Males Who Use Interracial Relationships As A Weapon

The threat of having an interracial relationship has become the weapon of choice for the (powerless) black male to control (or punish) the "uppity" black female. He is powerless to limit her educational or economic opportunities. He is powerless to imprison her OR make her a social outcast, but he can REJECT her romantically and make a public spectacle of himself while doing it.

Some black males resent black females for their independence and achievements, and for making black males feel they are the only men in America who are NOT in a superior position over their women. Some black males resent the black female's unwillingness to "submit" to him as an "inferior" person, because they naively believe the white female willingly submits to the white male.

However -- if white females WILLINGLY SUBMITTED to white male domination, there would be NO (white) women's liberation and feminist movements against white male sexism, and there would definitely be no white females having sex with black males.

Since the "white females are more supportive" myth is one of the most DIVISIVE (and false) interracial myths, it is time to DEFINE what a "supportive" female is VERSUS one who is not.

Is "Supportive" Sharing White Wealth With Black Males? Rich White Females Do Not Marry Rich OR Poor Black Males

With a few exceptions, wealthy white females DO NOT date OR marry black males. Since most marriages occur between people of the same ethnic and socioeconomic background, this is not surprising. *However, there is ONE glaring exception: rich and famous black males.*

Rich and famous black males are the MOST LIKELY GROUP in America to marry DOWN. Some well-known examples are the stripper and flight attendant wives of Montel Williams; the nanny wife of Tiger Woods; the waitress wife of OJ Simpson; and the receptionist wife of the late Michael Jackson.

What is NOT surprising is once the former working-class white wives divorce their rich black husbands, they usually take their newfound wealth back to the white community and into the arms of a white male.

When the authors attempted to flip that particular script, we failed to turn up a single example of a rich white female who married the black male equivalent of a stripper, nanny, waitress, or receptionist; or a rich white male who married a black female stripper, waitress, babysitter, or receptionist.

We were also unable to find an example of a rich black female who married the white male equivalent of a stripper, nanny, waitress, or receptionist.

To add insult to financial injury, rich black male celebrities are almost always excluded from the dating and marriage pool of rich white females, who overwhelmingly date and marry white males.

Perhaps, these affluent white ladies feel that marrying a black male of any economic, educational, or professional status is still "marrying down." Unlike their poorer white sisters, rich white females have no financial incentive to trade their "whiteness" for the wealth of a white-status-seeking black male.

Is "Supportive" Transforming A Black Actor (Like Denzel) Into A Tom Cruise, Richard Gere, or Brad Pitt?

While white females, individually, might occasionally admire a black male actor (like Denzel), they overwhelmingly **PREFER** white males as their **sex symbols. Even popular black actors (like Denzel) are NEVER chosen as the sex symbols of the white female collective.**

Every black actor who has become a "sex symbol" owes his success to his first and ONLY real fan base: *black females.* Sadly, all too many black male "sex symbols" show their GRATITUDE by dating and marrying anyone BUT a black female.

Is "Supportive" Seeing Black Males As The Social And Romantic Equals Of White Males?

A 20/20 Survey On Interracial Dating

In 2006, on ABC's 20/20 TV program, host John Stossel did a special on the book, 'Freakonomics,' which revealed the following about interracial dating:

White women overwhelmingly preferred white males while dating online (97% of the time). To get the same responses from a white female that a white male would receive:

- A Hispanic male had to make $77,000 more than a white male
- An unattractive male had to earn $150,000 more than an attractive male
- A Black male had to make $154,000 more than a white male
- An Asian male had to make $247,000 more than a white male

The conclusion: the VAST majority of white females (93%) prefer white males when seeking a SERIOUS partner for marriage and reproduction.

> *"They (black women) resent our taking their men. But in truth, black sisters, we're after the sex, not the ring, and these guys aren't the marrying kind anyway." – Susan C. Bakos, 'A White Woman Explains Why She Prefers Black Men.'*

Is "Supportive" Pulling A Brother Up the Corporate Ladder?

Thanks to affirmative action, white females are rocketing up the corporate ladder, while black males are falling off in record numbers. Black males – regardless of education and experience – have the highest unemployment rate in America -- even higher than illegal immigrants who do NOT SPEAK ENGLISH. In contrast, white females are the MOST LIKELY people in America to be employed even compared to white males.

According to the US Labor Department, the biggest beneficiaries of affirmative action programs were white females, who, strangely (and predictably), represent some of the most VOCAL opposition to the same policies that opened employment doors for **qualified black males**.

The number of white females holding executive positions in Corporate America with the ability (power) to hire and fire employees has skyrocketed, but few use that power to **employ or promote black males.**

Unfortunately, these cold, hard FACTS have done little to dispel the myth of the **"supportive white female"** among the black male collective who conveniently ignore one more FACT:

It's SEXISM – not RACISM – that makes the upwardly mobile white female HOT around her starched white collar.

Is "Supportive" Accusing Black Males Of Crimes They Didn't Commit?

A (very) incomplete and infamous list of white females who FALSELY accused black males of crimes they didn't commit:

(1955) Carolyn Bryant, white female, accused Emmett Till, 14, visiting relatives in Money, Mississippi, of "whistling" at her. Till was beaten, tortured, and murdered by a mob of white males, who were acquitted by an all-white jury (of males AND females) even after admitting they killed Till to *"make an example of him."*

(1994) Susan Smith, white female, drove her auto into a lake while the children slept in their car seats, initially reporting to police that she had been carjacked by a black man. Nine days later, after an intensive, heavily publicized nationwide search, Smith confessed to drowning her children.

(1996) Elise Makdessis, white female, who prosecutors alleged had conspired with her (white husband, Eddie), to file a false sexual harassment lawsuit against the Navy. Earlier, it was claimed that Elise made two videotapes in which she accused several coworkers at the Oceana Naval Air Station (Virginia). One of the accused was Quincy Brown, 37, a black male employee.

Prosecutors alleged that Elise and Eddie Makdessis lured Brown to their apartment to have sex with Elise, during which Elise asked to be tied up after the sex act. Eddie later claimed to police that he was knocked unconscious, and awakened to find Brown raping and stabbing his wife. He said he shot Brown in self-defense then called 9-11.

After a ten-year investigation, Eddie Makdessis, was arrested and charged with the murder of his wife. Prosecutors alleged at his trial that after Brown and caught Brown with his wife, shot Brown to death and stabbed his wife to death.

Prosecutors claimed that Makdessis's plot to get insurance money by first murdering Brown, killing his wife with a knife, washing the knife, than planting it in Brown's hand. On March 2006, Makdessi was convicted of two counts of first-degree murder and sentenced to life in prison. Makdessi is planning an appeal.

(2007) Amanda Knox, white female American exchange student in Italy, was convicted in the 2007 stabbing death of her British roommate, Meredith Kercher. Knox initially tried to pin the blame on a black reggae club owner, Patrick L., who was arrested for murder but released after his alibi checked out.

(2008) Ashley Todd, white female Republican, claimed that was assaulted by a black male "Obama supporter" who carved a backwards "B" on her face. She later admitted she had fabricated (LIED) and had assaulted herself.

(2009) Bonnie Sweeten, white female, claimed two black men had abducted her and her nine-year-old daughter, after a fender-bender, and stuffed them into the trunk of a black Cadillac. *"It's a terrifying thing for a community to hear that two black men in a black Cadillac grabbed a (white) woman and her daughter,"* said Bucks County District Attorney, Michelle Henry.

It was later discovered that the "abduction" was a hoax and that Sweeten had fled to Disney World with her daughter. Sweeten, was later indicted for allegedly stealing $700,000 from her employer, a Bucks County law firm.

(2010) Jill Quigg, a white female, actress, was charged with burglary, after she and a white male accomplice allegedly broke into a neighbor's apartment, and blamed the crime on a black man.

(2011) Unidentified white female, a Catholic nun, falsely reported being raped by a 6'4," 250 lb black male but later recanted her story, which she created to cover up a sexual relationship with a non-white male.

How many black males have been convicted OR executed after being falsely accused by white females? (The authors were unable to find a single case of a black female who blamed a black male for a crime she committed).

Is "Supportive" Championing the Civil Rights Of Black Males?

Since only a tiny minority of white females get involved in civil rights issues, it is safe (and accurate) to state that the main issues that negatively impact black males -- unemployment, police brutality, unjust incarceration, inferior schools, and murder-by-cop -- receive little to no support from influential white-female-headed organizations OR from powerful, high-profile white females.

White females also make up the MAJORITY of white jurors who convict black males with little or no evidence, OR acquit white policemen who are accused of beating or murdering unarmed black males.

If young white males were dying at the same rate as young black males -- that EVERY powerful white-female-headed organization in the nation would be using ALL their financial and political "muscle" to solve the problem.

Is "Supportive" Pursuing Sex with Black Males Under The Guise Of Pursuing Justice?

It is common for the anti-racism-activist white female to be sexually involved with black males, which leads to an obvious question: *What is the true agenda of the 'anti-racist' white female activist? Justice or sexual intercourse with black males?*

"Anti-racist" white female author, Dr. Tochluk, revealed a personal story during an interview on the C.O.W.S. internet radio show in August 2010. After a particular black male refused to date her because she was white, she said: "At that time I could not see why the injury to black women was important, or more correctly, I did not want to care about what this man saw and what black women would feel. I could not grasp why what someone else thought about our potential relationship made a difference." **(SOURCE:** *www.contextofwhitesupremacy.com)*

Rosa Parks (1913 – 2005), "the first lady of civil rights", and "the mother of the freedom movement." Nine months before Parks refused to give up her seat, 15-year-old Claudette Colvin refused to give up her bus seat on the same bus system. Rosa Parks' act of defiance -- and her involvement with civil rights leaders, like Dr. Martin Luther King, Jr. -- help to launch the national civil rights movement.

Is "Supportive" Opposing The Practice Of Racism?

In September 2010, the National Federation of Republican Women (NFRW) held its annual fall Board of Directors meeting in Charleston, S.C., called "The Southern Experience."

South Carolina Senate President, Glenn McConnell, dressed up as a confederate soldier, flanked by two grinning black males dressed as "slaves." Since there was no PUBLIC CONDEMNATION of the racist spectacle by this well-heeled group of professional, educated WHITE FEMALES it is reasonable AND logical to assume they NOT only found African slavery a source of entertainment, it is quote possible some actually long for a return to the "good old days."

Is "Supportive" Raising White Children Who Will Oppose The Practice Of Racism?

If white females are the mothers, civilizers, teachers, and the transferrers of values for white children, are they teaching white boys and girls to oppose white supremacy OR to continue practicing it to maintain their white privileges?

Would raising anti-racist white children be the ULTIMATE FORM OF SUPPORT by the white female?"

The "Unsupportive" Black Female"

The flip side of "the supportive white female" is "the unsupportive black female" who has raised, loved, nurtured, provided for, protected, and financed the college educations of black boys, often without the assistance of their fathers.

The *"unsupportive black female"* is the **WORKHORSE OF EVERY BLACK ORGANIZATION,** from black churches, homeless shelters, food pantries, grassroots organizations, and national foundations.

The *"unsupportive black female"* marches, protests, petitions, donates, and devotes countless BLACK-WOMAN-HOURS to assist, defend, finance, and **SUPPORT THE RIGHTS OF BLACK MALES**.

An *"unsupportive black female"* college student is credited (by some) with starting the petition that launched a national movement for the **Jena Six** – six black teenaged boys from Jena, Louisiana who were being railroaded into prison for a simple schoolyard fight in 2006.

The majority of people who descended upon Jena, a small dusty Louisiana town, arrived in cars, buses, and planes to rally around six black boys THEY DIDN'T KNOW FROM A HOLE IN THE GROUND were *BLACK -- not white, Hispanic, or Asian females.*

Black children are dying on the streets of America on a daily basis, YET the response from the "supportive white female" is SILENCE -- even from those with non-white, black children.

"I am 54 years old and I remember the luxury car commercials and the messages were always the same: buy this Cadillac, and you'll be a successful man with high status, and you'll be popular with blonde white women!

As a little boy I could never figure out why there was always a white woman with blond hair sitting in the passenger side of the car.

Naturally, when we consider that our black fathers and grandfathers watched those commercials at least ten times a day before they became grown men, we see that this "formula" for success and status was still ingrained into the black man's psyche and subconscious."

– Frank, 54, sales representative, Memphis, TN

MYTH #7: Black males prefer white females because they are more attractive than black females.

At the risk of sounding cruel, it is OBVIOUS to even the casual observer of the typical black male/white female couple that beauty (or even average attractiveness) is NOT a requirement when it comes to white females.

In the mind of a white-validation-seeking, low-self-esteemed black male, a white female will always be superior to a black female, regardless of the black female's beauty, intelligence, accomplishments, or attitude because a black female cannot give him the kind of (white) validation he so desperately craves because she has no more status than he has.

To the self-hating black male, the black female's "blackness" is a hated reminder of his own failures and secret shame as a powerless black male (victim) of the white supremacy system. Adding a black female to his romantic equation is too much black (self).

The Value Of White Females To The Low-Self-Esteemed, Status-Seeking Black Male

According to Dr. Levin (a black psychiatrist), some black males find it hard to connect with the black female because she *"serves as the symbol of his failure."*

For the white-status-seeking, low-self-esteemed, non-white male -- be he black, Hispanic, Native American, or Asian -- the white female is a highly visible human passport of acceptance into the white world and a "soothing lotion" for his wounded pride and ego.

The physical attractiveness, intelligence, or accomplishments of his white female "prize" are less important than her white status, which explains why the majority of rich black males who marry white *almost always marry down.*

There is a very long list of marriages between wealthy black males and typically unaccomplished, undistinguished, and often unattractive white female waitresses, receptionists, flight attendants, strippers, and nannies, who bring little to the marital table other than their youth (fertility) and white skin.

By "possessing" a white female, the status-seeking, low-self-esteemed black male can IMAGINE he is the equal of the most powerful and most privileged male in America: *the white male.*

"If I were white, I thought I could be a little happier. I wanted to be white because I was black, and black was never the right color."
-- Dennis Rodman, former NBA Player

If white supremacy was transformed overnight into a "system of purple supremacy," and the most privileged females had PURPLE SKIN and GREEN HAIR, they would be the most beautiful and the most sought-after females to the low-self-esteemed, status-seeking, non-purple male.

Speaking about an interview with Ms Fairy Tale, a black female who said she was "glad" she had a "relationship" with a white man, Reneathia Tate, author of "Pieces of a Puzzle (1997), writes:

"Black females will talk (or even brag) they had sex with black males to everyone, particularly other black females like myself.

But she (Ms Fairy Tale) really did not want to remember or talk about all of her experience (particularly the sex part) with this white man.

Ms. Fairy Tale, like most black females (who had sex with white men), had a vague feeling that they were either robbed or raped after these terrible experiences."

Myth #8: Black females are "too loyal" to black males to have sex with white males.

The Biggest Sex Secret In Black America: *Black Females Having Sexual Intercourse With White Males*

Black females often condemn black males who date or marry white females, but some are just as guilty of the same "crime:" *talking black and sleeping white.*

The white male's shameful history of rape, economic exploitation, and degradation of black females drives some black females to hide their sexual affairs with white males from "prying eyes."

Black females know many whites and blacks (especially black males) assume a black female who is having sexual intercourse with a white male is either prostituting herself (exchanging sex for money, favors, or material things), or is being sexually exploited by the white male (whoring for free).

The black female who sexually submits to a white male (or a series of white males) often discovers she is "involved" with a racist who has no intentions of making a serious commitment and who dislikes blacks in general. Her biggest fear is being duped into the role of a "racist white man's whore" – and in most cases, her fears are justified.

In fact, most interracial "relationships" between black females and white males are simply a CONTINUATION of the same (white supremacy) sexual exploitation/power dynamic that began during slavery: *the (inferior) black person submitting to the will (and sexual exploitation) of the (superior) white person -- which often includes verbal and physical abuse.*

For this reason, some black females often look back on sex with white males with much shame and regret, and may be EXTREMELY RELUCTANT to admit any prior sexual involvement with white males.

Many black females resent black male/white female relationships because the white female has a stronger "hand" (more power) and is treated with more respect in the black/white sexual power dynamic than the black female.

It is possible for a black female and a white male to be attracted to each other for the same reasons any man or woman is attracted to each other, but "love" is seldom the emotion that fuels the SECRET SEX RELATIONSHIPS between black females and white males (or black males and white females).

The White Male Who Has Sexual Intercourse With Black Females

Some white males keep their sexual affairs with black females a secret for fear of harming their reputation with their white peers and family members. Some white males avoid dating black females even when they are attracted to a particular black female OR black females in general for the following reasons:

- the history of rape of black females by white males
- the lower caste (status) of black females in a white supremacy society
- the fear of losing white peer approval, status, and privileges
- the fear of rejection by the "inferior" black female
- the fear of not measuring up to the "sexually dominant" black male
- his desire to maintain the racial integrity of his offspring
- he is not interested in an interracial relationship with a black female
- he is a white supremacist (a racist) who understands (consciously or subconsciously) that ignoring black female desirability is ESSENTIAL to maintaining the "superiority" of the white female and white male.

In spite of all the above, some black females still find the attention of white males flattering (and desirable), and will have sexual intercourse with a KNOWN racist white male. The white-identified black female may put white males on a pedestal -- regardless of status, physical appeal, or racist attitudes -- ignoring the odds are against white males returning the favor.

The (Inferior) Position of the Black Female in the White/ Black Interracial "Dating Game"

Logically speaking, if the lightest female is the most superior in a white supremacy system, the darkest female must be the most inferior. Following the LOGIC, the black (and non-white) male who is seeking white acceptance and status will see the black female as the last LOGICAL choice.

The white supremacy programming of black and non-white males reflects MORE on their mentality (and low self-esteem) than it does on the desirability of the black female.

Black Females Who Date White Men Exclusively

The black female, due to her (artificially created) inferior position, may seek alternative forms of validation if black males collectively do NOT validate her worth. For some black females, an interracial relationship with a white male *offers the ultimate white validation* -- which serves as proof to her bruised and battered ego that she is NOT the worthless, undesirable creature that white society (and some black males) have made her out to be.

Her uniquely beautiful racial characteristics are often seen as "exotic" by her non-black admirers, making her feel MORE APPRECIATED than she is by the males in her own community.

The dark and brown-skinned black female who does not fit the "black?" beauty standard (light skin, long hair, European features) may pursue a relationship with the white male for the same reason the DEVALUED white female -- who does not fit the white beauty standard -- seeks a relationship with a black male: *to be validated as an attractive, desirable woman.*

Their motto – *"it is better to be 'exotic' than disregarded altogether"* – should be a clear warning to the white males and black males who oppose interracial dating by the women of their race.

Black Females Who Refuse To Date Non-Black Males

Overall, black females are **LESS likely to date outside their group** than Asian, Hispanic, Native Americans, and white females. Some "detractors" claim this is due to the black female's lack of "appeal" BUT the simple and well-known FACT is: *most black females prefer black males.*

The hyper-masculine, soulful image of the black male makes it difficult for non-black males to compete in the sexual or romantic arena for the attention of black females -- something non-black males are well aware of.

A significant number of black females -- especially the black female who understands the connection between racism and interracial sex -- shun interracial relationships despite a shortage of black males to marry. They would rather live their lives as a single female than give in to the racist media's interracial PROPAGANDA that "white is better."

The less confused, black-identified black female knows that as long as white supremacy exists, having interracial sex with white males (or females) makes her PART of the problem, NOT part of the collective solution.

And the authors wholeheartedly agree.

MYTH #9: Black females are jealous of white females.

This accusation is often leveled at black females by white females and black males who are sexually involved. However, **the true emotion** is NOT jealousy; it is **resentment** -- the same resentment anyone would feel if they are unfairly stereotyped and rejected by the members of their own group.

In reality, the *"jealous black female"* is the MOST TOLERANT of white female/black male relationships, and is the MOST LIKELY to welcome a black male/white female couple to her home.

She is the LEAST likely to disown OR shun a son, grandson, father, uncle, nephew, or neighbor who dates or marries outside his race -- unlike white males and females who are the MOST LIKELY to disown or shun a son or daughter who brings a non-white (especially a black) partner home.

The *"jealous black female"* is also the MOST likely to CONTINUE supporting black male entertainers who DO NOT DATE OR MARRY black females, UNLIKE many black males who stopped "supporting" Halle Berry after her on-and-off-screen sexual relationships with white males. It is a certainty that any white entertainer who refused to date white people would lose the support of their white male AND female audience.

There is one more thing the *"jealous black female"* is LESS likely to do: covet the men and babies of another group as her own -- UNLIKE the white female who has a **well-deserved reputation** for COVETING and claiming black males AND black babies as her own.

It seems that the "jealous black female" may be the LEAST "jealous" when compared to white females, white males, and black males.

White females can sex N*ggers and still be racist. The white female knows she is superior to everyone else because she is white. She's superior to black males because she is a white female.

White females will submit sexually to black males and admits that blacks are superior to her sexually but she knows that her white skin gives her social and special privileges.

A white female can be a white supremacist and sex N*ggers at the same time. Many white females hate black males but love black c*cks.

-- White Female Supremacist
(Der Kosmonaut, 1972)

MYTH #10: A white person in an interracial relationship CANNOT be a "racist."

This myth is the most deceptive and dangerous of all **Ten Interracial Myths** because it gives the interracially-involved black person a false sense of security, making them LESS LIKELY to recognize racism and less ABLE to protect themselves even when their white partner is practicing racism against them. Overall, whites benefit MORE from interracial relationships than blacks. To understand why, let's examine the psychological benefits of being a (superior) white person in an interracial relationship with an (inferior) black person.

14 Hardcore Reasons (Some) Whites Pursue Sexual Intercourse With Blacks That Have Nothing To Do With "Love" BUT Have Everything To Do With Racism And White Supremacy

1. "THE BEAUTY AND THE BEAST" SYNDROME/RAPE FANTASY. allows the marginally unattractive white female (by white standards) her best (and often her ONLY) opportunity to feel feminine, desirable, and attractive. Regardless of her appearance OR intellect, she will ALWAYS be superior to the (black) male she is involved with, something she cannot assume with a white male.

She may see herself as the "white prize" who has "sacrificed" her "pure" white femininity to the hyper-masculine, hypersexual black male "beast" – a real life version of "King Kong." It is a common fantasy among white females AND males to imagine (or create) a situation where the white female is being "taken" (raped) by a black male (beast) -- which explains the appeal of King Kong movies for whites.

In other words, her attraction to the black male may be BASED ON A RACIST MOVIE FANTASY, and may be a form of HUMAN BESTIALITY.

The tip-off of a supposedly "color-blind" racist white female: *she is only attracted to dark-skinned black males.* The clueless black male is flattered by the white female's attention, and is unaware that the same "bestial" stereotype used to justify the murder of black males throughout American history **is a sexual "turn-on"** for the racist white female.

A 30-something black male called an Atlanta, GA black radio talk show seeking advice. He said his white female companion wanted him to play the role of a slave while she played the role of a white master (mistress). He said she wanted to beat him, mistreat him, call him a "nigger," and put him in handcuffs and shackles. She also encouraged him to look more "primitive," – exposing the racist white female companion's black sexual fetish:

"...since the winter, I kinda like grew out my beard, and she's like, cool, cool, I want you to keep it thick and nappy, and...look like, basically, like, a slave, and I'm gonna beat ya, and ride ya, and call ya all kinds of degrading stuff."

It is possible that the black male caller suspected the white female was a RACIST because he was worried about "going off" on her (for her racist behavior). Unfortunately, it is also highly possible he had already allowed her to degrade him on multiple occasions, and called the talk show for advice ONLY after he became deeply troubled by his OWN willingness to be degraded just to please a racist white female.

2. SEXUAL FREEDOM WITHOUT CONSEQUENCES. The white female is often more sexually uninhibited (more promiscuous) with black males than she would be with white males because the white male's opinion of her carries greater weight in her social circle.

The sexually aggressive white female knows the black male has NO POWER to destroy her reputation or her social standing in her white community because neither he NOR his opinion is welcome there.

She is more comfortable approaching, pursuing, and sexually experimenting (freaking) with black males because she doesn't care what the random black male thinks of her sexual or moral behavior.

Just like a rich, privileged female doesn't care what her servants think of her sexual or moral behavior, because they are NOT her social or economic equals, and are NOT fit to judge her -- in her opinion.

In the presence of her "servants" (inferiors), the rich, privileged female is literally free to be herself, no matter how low that self might go. Even if her servants gossiped about her sex life, who would they tell that mattered?

However, in the presence of her equals OR her superiors, the rich and privileged woman will put on her "company face," and be mindful of what she wears, drinks, eats, drives, and says.

The white female's burning desire to be sexually "free" has caused the white female – collectively – to have a somewhat well-deserved reputation in the black community for being promiscuous (sexually loose).

It is a common sight in nearly every black community to see random white females openly pursuing black males -- even total strangers -- for no-strings sexual encounters.

"The (white) woman who goes after black men is a...'white bitch' in heat... white women turn to black men when their sex drives kick into higher gear and their social inhibitions recede into the rearview mirror. It's a "yes, baby, now I'm ready for you" reaction." – Susan B, 40-plus, white female. A WHITE WOMAN EXPLAINS WHY SHE PREFERS BLACK MEN By Susan Crain Bakos -- Vol 18 - Issue 50 - December 14-20, 2005 http://www.nypress.com/18/49/news&columns/SusanCrainBakos.cfm

It is unheard of for black females to "cruise" white neighborhoods, bars, and parks for anonymous sex with white male strangers. Perhaps, the white female's sense of "white entitlement" (white power) emboldens her to feel welcome in non-white communities or anywhere else she chooses to roam.

Her "right" for sex-on-demand from black males is confirmed by the ever-eager black male who sees the white female's promiscuity as a character asset instead of a character flaw. In fact, a promiscuous black female is MORE likely to be condemned by black males than a promiscuous white female.

"I was talking to a black female friend and the subject of white women came up. She knew I had dated white women in the past, and asked how long it took before we had sex. I told her, usually it was their idea and happened the first night because white females were more laid back about sex. She said, if a black female had sex with me on the first date, would I call her laid back, or a ho. I had to admit, she'd be a ho." – Renaldo, 37.

Some black males praise the white female for her 'sex without strings" approach but few understand that the white female's lack of "drama" may be due to her lack of sincere interest in him as a man, and an acknowledgment of his inferior status as a non-white male.

"They (black women) resent our taking their men. But in truth, black sisters, we're after the sex, not the ring, and these guys aren't the marrying kind anyway." 'A White Woman Explains Why She Prefers Black Men' by Susan Crain Bakos -- Vol 18 - Issue 50 - December 14-20, 2005 http://www.nypress.com/18/49/news&columns/SusanCrainBakos.cfm

***

3. USING BLACK MALES TO GET REVENGE AGAINST WHITE MALES. A white female who has been emotionally or sexually abused by her father, male relatives, or white males in general, may develop a hatred for white males, and may seek revenge by flaunting her black male lovers.

Since the father is the girl's first AND most important role model, a white female who shuns all white males is a major tip-off of a dysfunctional upbringing or personality. Some white females use black males to get revenge against the white male even though she KNOWS the black male will pay the price for her "betrayal" in the form of job losses, incarceration, and in some cases, the loss of life.

4. A SHORTAGE OF HETEROSEXUAL WHITE MALES. The shortage of single, heterosexual white males has forced some white females to pursue non-white males for sex, romance, and companionship. This is especially common for white females who are past their physical "prime" where white males are concerned, or who are less attractive than their white female competition.

5. HAVING THE SUPERIOR POSITION IN THE RELATIONSHIP = CONTROL AND POWER OVER A MAN. Being in a relationship with a male she can control is very empowering and satisfying to the white female who feels oppressed in a sexist, white-male-dominated society.

She may find the white-identified (confused) black male EASIER to manipulate than a white male, or may consider him a temporary fad; a human sex toy (dildo); a sexual fetish; a possession to parade around to impress or amuse her white friends, OR to compete with black females.

The white female's expectations of the black male are often lower than her expectations of a white male -- which means she can lower her expectations for herself. For the first time in her life, she may feel superior to her male partner. The tip-off: *"Black men are more 'down to earth' than white men."*

The white female knows the black male IS NOT her equal (in a white supremacy system) regardless of all her denials. She knows his hunger for (her) white validation greatly increases the odds that he will cater to her, try to appease, impress, praise, and please her. The racist (cunning) white female often uses that knowledge to her advantage (or her amusement) by demanding the black male publicly disrespect the black female in her presence to show his loyalty.

However, the racist white female will NEVER respect the self-hating black male because he does not respect himself.

It is her LACK OF RESPECT for the self-hating black male that allows the racist white female's comfort level, sexual freedom, and feelings of superiority to be greater with a black male than with a white male.

6. ENVY AND COMPETITION WITH BLACK FEMALES. The insecure racist white female often envies AND secretly competes with black females. This is due in part to her racist upbringing that taught her that she must be superior to the (inferior) black female -- at all costs.

Her insecurity may lead her to pursue (capture) a black male and flaunt her "catch" around black females as PROOF OF HER WHITE SUPERIORITY. However, her insecurity is always just beneath the surface:

"I recall an incident that happened to me when I ran into a male friend who was dating a white woman at the time. When he spoke to me, he addressed me as 'Sista.' Later on, he told me his white woman was on him all day about calling me a 'Sista,' saying things such as, 'Why don't you call me that?' Needless to say, they broke up about a month later. She couldn't accept him being friendly toward black women." – Nichelle, 35, paralegal

The insecure racist white female will NEVER admit she is envious of black females, but is quick to accuse the black female of being jealous of her. However, whenever a black female -- who is sexually attractive or is sexually involved with a white male -- intrudes on the racist white female's sexual territory, she usually responds with hostility -- and jealousy.

"On Saturdays, after shopping, I stop for a cocktail at this really nice bar in the shopping mall. I was having a casual conversation with this affluent-looking white man when I noticed a white female sitting on the opposite side of the bar giving me a 'why is he talking to you' kind of look.

This white female was sitting with her friends, but all her attention was on us. When she couldn't take it anymore, she got up and sat on the other side of the white man I was talking to. I guess she had too much to drink, because she started talking about welfare. The white guy looked annoyed, she looked stupid, and I was bored, so I left. White females can dish it all day long, but they can't take it when their men hit on us. " -- Pamela S., 41, business owner.

The racist white female assumes her "whiteness" guarantees a superior position over the black female – when it comes to **white and black males** -- and will aggressively assert her (superior) position if given the opportunity.

"I ran into Patrice, a black female who lives in my building, at Wal-Mart. We were standing in the checkout line, talking about jazz, when this older white female in line ahead of us jumped in the conversation. She said she was from Seattle and asked if there were any good jazz clubs in the city.

I didn't think much about it until she got all up in my face, and started telling me about her man problems. After she paid for her stuff and left, Patrice gave me this nasty look, and said, 'She's from Seattle, she's used to black men kissing her ass." After I saw it with my own eyes, I couldn't argue with her." -- Ernest, 46, repairman

Using Deceit To Compete

Just like a single female pursuing a married man, a deceptive white female may use the black male's complaints about black females to TEMPORARILY TRANSFORM her behavior to make it appear she is DIFFERENT from (better than) the black female.

However, once her true personality surfaces, and the black male realizes a white female is not the ticket to a drama-free romantic life, it is likely that their relationship will bite the dust, like the majority of short-lived black male/white female relationships.

It is common for the cunning racist white female having sexual intercourse with a black male to despise -- even hate -- black females, and to try to poison him against all black females -- **a clear announcement that she is a racist:**

"It's like a white woman told me once....black women treat their men like PROPERTY; white women treat their men like PEOPLE (even if they don't always agree)." – Mark, black male poster on black website

This leads to an important, black-self-respecting question for the black male who breeds with the white female:

How can a white female who dislikes black females raise a mentally sane black daughter? This may explain why so many black girls with white birth mothers often wind up in permanent foster care -- or are raised by the black side of the family.

"One reason for my fear is my own mixed reactions to my daughter. Don't get me wrong, I love her. But when I turn to the mirror in my bedroom to admire us together, I am shocked. She seems so alien. With her long, dark eyelashes and shiny, dark brown hair, she doesn't look anything like me. I know that concentrating on how my daughter looks is shallow. But still, I can't shake off the feeling of unease... why does she feel so alien?"- Lowri Turner, a white female currently married to a non-white male.

7. "THE BRAINS AND THE BEAST" FANTASY. This is the white male version of the **"BEAUTY AND THE BEAST" RAPE FANTASY,"** which allows the "civilized" white male to indulge in his lust for the "primitive" (savage), whorish, and usually dark-skinned black female. Like the racist white female, the racist white male's attraction to the black female may be based on a racist and twisted form of HUMAN BESTIALITY.

"A luscious mulatto passing. Creamy, light-brown skin. Was she a whore?"
– from the novel, 'My Days of Anger' by James T. Farrell (1954)

Another common white male sexual fetish object is the hot-blooded, sexually immoral "mulatto" female (a black female with a white parent). She is almost always portrayed in television and film as a "white man's whore" who openly lusts after white males. The mulatto (or half-breed) female sexual object was a staple in many early Hollywood films, and more recently in movies like 'Monster's Ball' (Halle Berry), and 'Angel Heart' (Lisa Bonet).

8. SEXING BLACKS AS A SEXUAL "RITE OF PASSAGE" FOR WHITES.
During AND after slavery in the South, the "ritual" of raping a young black female was the first sexual experience for many white males to vent their lust and depravity on black female slaves to maintain the "purity" of white females.

It is common for a white male to have sex with a black female to "round out" his sexual "resume" by putting a black notch on his white belt. The naïve black female may believe the white male's interest is sincere; however, our 400-year history of rape contradicts any connection between SEX and RESPECT.

Sexing A Negro Is Not The Same As Respecting A Negro

"I can't even count how many white females I've been with, just round it down to about 40. Out of those 40, I know for a fact 30 of them had a man. It started 21 years ago in Texas, every time this chick got into a fight with her man she would come over and do me. 21 years later, this 50 year old white female got her 65 year-old white sugar daddy to pay the bills but keeps calling me late at night to give her some when she knows his old azz is in bed.

I have been let in through bedroom windows, back doors, getting a blow job at a party while her man went to the bathroom, did two cousins one night, I was going with one and in the middle of the night got up and did her friend once or twice a week on her lunch break.

Did my manager's daughter a couple of times and all her mother talked about at work was how sweet and innocent her girl was...yeah...right...lol"
– black male poster on black message board

***

"I am a white man who prefers to date black women because they are more attractive to me!" – Max, a white male who posted a comment on a black website article opposing interracial relationships.

When a black male poster asked "Max" if he defended his black girlfriends when someone white practiced racism on them, Max never responded. If Max's attraction to black females is sexual, he is one of a million-member, centuries-old, white male club that has lusted after black flesh but is UN-WILLING to oppose white supremacy OR give up the benefits of white privilege.

Why would a "superior" white person want to have sex with an "inferior" black (non-white) person? One possible answer:

If white culture associates dark skin with something primitive, savage, and animalistic, and the darkest-skinned blacks are the PREFERRED sexual objects for racist whites, then it is logical to assume this sexual "desire" is NOT based on love, respect, or admiration, but in fact, is a form of human bestiality (sex with animals = animalistic sex). How do we know this is true?

If dark-skinned black people were so highly "prized" by whites, they wouldn't be the most severely penalized people outside the bedroom.

9. OLDER WHITE MALES WHO PURSUE BLACK FEMALES. It is common to see black females over the age of 40 being pursued by older white males. Many 40-plus black females report they are more likely to be approached by an older white male than a black male of any age. Some possible reasons:

- Since he has already been married, and had his children with a white female, he is free to indulge in his attraction to (and lust for) black females that he may have hidden during his prime reproductive years because he does not want non-white offspring with a black female.
- Mature black females are more likely to have some financial stability and education; are less likely to want more children; and are more likely to have adult children who will not "intrude" on the white male's sexual activities.
- The mainstream media's stereotyping of "single, desperate black females" may lead some white males to assume most or all black females are so desperate, they will date (have sex) outside their race.
- Unless he is wealthy or has some professional status, the older white male who is past his physical and sexual prime, can get a higher quality black female than a white female simply BECAUSE he is white.

- He may feel less pressure to marry from a black female than he would feel with a white female.
- If an affluent white male marries a black female, he is UNLIKELY to leave the bulk of his estate to his black widow to keep his (white) wealth from falling into the wrong (black) hands.

10. ENVY OF AND COMPETITION WITH BLACK MALES. The insecure white male who envies and resents the black male for sexually "ravaging" the white female may pursue black females to "even the score."

He may take pleasure (revenge) in seducing a black female who is involved with OR married to a black male, or may find it flattering to be "involved" with a (confused) black female who disparages other black people, especially black males in his presence -- which leads to an important and BLACK-SELF-RESPECTING question for the black female who breeds with the white male:

How can a white male who fears or despises black males raise a mentally sane black son? Perhaps this explains why so many white males abandon their non-white children.

11. TRADING UP. It is easier for the white male or female to get a higher quality black person than it is to get a high quality white person, particularly if they are not considered a "prime catch" by other whites. In other words, the racial/ sexual dynamic in a white supremacy system usually insures that the white person gets the better deal when they choose a non-white person.

The white person often only has to bring the ability to FUNCTION as a white person to the relationship table. The black person must bring TANGIBLE assets (education, money, looks, etc) to the table to equalize the union of the "superior" white person and the "inferior" non-white person.

It is important to understand that the white person always choose the black person, not the other way around. It is also rare for the above average (in looks, education, and appearance) white female or male to date OR marry a black male or female who is below average (by those same standards).

Most black males -- even successful black males -- are usually restricted to the peripheral (or undesirable) white female population with low or no status who could NOT get the same quality "package" in a white male due to fierce competition from MORE desirable white females.

This explains why an ordinary (or substandard) white female can "catch" a Tiger Woods, Michael Jackson, Michael Jordan, or Montel Williams, but would NEVER have a shot (or a chance) at a Donald Trump, Bill Gates or Brad Pitt.

"This brother, Lee, lived down the street. He owned his own business, and wanted to date me but he was always making excuses for racist white people and that turned me off. He started dating this skinny, plain white female, which surprised me because Lee wouldn't look twice at a bony black woman. One day I ran into her at the supermarket.

I could tell she wasn't comfortable with blacks, or maybe she wasn't comfortable with an attractive black female living so close to her black man. I had a feeling she was racist and then she said something that confirmed it. Out of the blue, she says, "You know, Lee's different from other black guys." I asked her what that meant, and she said, "Well, he doesn't use slang and he's not ignorant.'

I never told Lee what she said but after I heard he married her, I wish I had. I doubt it would have made any difference. Some black men want a white female so bad, they just don't give a damn how racist she is."

12. INCREASING WHITE "SELF-ESTEEM" (FALSE EGO) AT THE EXPENSE OF THEIR BLACK PARTNERS. The white male or female who is involved with a white-identified, self-hating black male or female is well aware of their partner's self-esteem "issues."

For example, it is common for a black person in an interracial relationship to make negative comments about other blacks (clearly forgetting THEY ARE BLACK, too). Unbeknownst to the black person, their white partner may view their "self-hatred" the way one would view a handicap, a mental illness, an addiction, or a physical disfigurement, like the Elephant Man.

The personality "disfigurement" of the self-hating, white-identified black person may cause the low-self-esteemed white person to feel superior by comparison (since a "normal" white person with HEALTHY SELF-ESTEEM would be repulsed by a black person who disliked their OWN RACE).

Rather than helping their black partner put themselves in a better psychological place where they can be SELF-LOVING and SELF-RESPECTING, the white partner often ignores or exploits their mental illness because it guarantees that their black partner will remain submissive to white supremacy (and to the whims of their white partner).

13. ENRICHING WHITE GENETICS BY CREATING A "NEW RACE." It is puzzling why so many white females are deliberately breeding with black males even when they have no interest in marrying them -- until one examines the white infertility crisis. By "mixing" the stronger genetics of blacks with the increasingly fragile genetics of whites, there appears to be an attempt by whites to create a "new race" and avoid white genetic extinction.

14. MAINTAINING THE SYSTEM OF WHITE SUPREMACY. Contrary to what some blacks believe, MOST whites do not care about the tiny minority of disposable white males and females that marry blacks.

In fact, the POWERFUL white supremacists take comfort in the high number of successful blacks who take their BLACK WEALTH back to white America (instead of enriching black America).

They know these lost blacks -- despite their education, talent, and money -- will NEVER challenge the system of white supremacy because they are literally married to it.

13 Hardcore Reasons Blacks Pursue Sexual Relationships With Whites That Have Nothing To Do With "Love" AND Everything To Do With Black Self-Hatred And Black Inferiority Complexes

1. Black males who believes white females are sexually freer (freakier)
2. Self-hatred/black inferiority complex
3. To express hostility toward blacks of the opposite sex
4. White Validation (is white-identified) and to impress or fit in with whites
5. To "whiten-up" their offspring so they won't look too black (like them)
6. For financial gain (or exploitation)
7. Easier to hide homosexual "activities" from a culturally clueless partner
8. Believes whites are more "loving" than blacks (without taking into account this judgment ALSO applies to themselves)
9. To get rewards within certain professional/entertainment circles
10. To avoid responsibility for fixing the problems in the black community
11. To avoid fixing what is wrong with him or herself.
12. Has a genuine attraction to an individual white person where "whiteness" was not a major factor. HOWEVER, if a black person is ONLY attracted to whites, he or she is NOT "color-blind," they are color-obsessed, *and "whiteness" has EVERYTHING TO DO WITH IT.*
13. **BECAUSE IT IS EASIER TO "LOVE" WHITE PEOPLE.** From cradle to grave, blacks are programmed to see whites as superior, smarter, sexier; cleaner, harder-working, and just plain nicer than black people. Being with another (oppressed) black person DOUBLES the oppression in the minds of a black person looking to escape their OWN. A white partner gives them the white validation denied by the white collective, and serves as a "soothing lotion" that coats (hides) the TRUTH about his or her existence (and true status) as blacks in a white supremacy society.

"Loving" whites keeps OUR secrets safe. *For the black person who is afraid of true intimacy, a white person may be a perfect fit.* An "intimate" relationship WITHOUT honesty can only go so deep. Neither person will ever know the other because neither is being honest about the REAL differences between them. White-identified blacks hide the truth about what it means to be black in a white supremacy society, and whites *don't want to know.* If a black person cannot be honest with his or her white partner about the racism that DEFINES their quality of life from cradle to grave, *he or she is NOT being his or her TRUE SELF.*

The white person who denies racism is victimizing their black partner, and denies they are BENEFITING from white privilege *should be viewed as a racist by their black partner.*

As Mr. Neely Fuller, Jr. said about interracial relationships between blacks and whites in a white supremacy system:

"The best it gets is tacky."

CHAPTER 37

OMAR THORNTON SHOULD BE A WAKE-UP CALL FOR BLACK AMERICA

The Event:

On August 3, 2010, Omar Thornton, a 34-year-old black male, walked into his workplace, fully armed, and shot and killed eight of his white coworkers at Hartford Distributors, a beer delivery company in Hartford, Connecticut.

The reason, in the words of Omar Thornton: "...*you probably want to know the reason I shot this place up. They treat me bad over here, and they treat all the other black employees bad over here, too, so I just take it into my own hands and I handled the problem...*"

Transcript of Omar Thornton's 911 Call

(10:20 PM EDT, August 5, 2010)
Dispatcher: State Police.

Thornton: Is this 911?

Dispatcher: Yeah, can I help you?

Thornton: This is Omar Thornton, the, uh, the shooter over in Manchester.

Dispatcher: Yes, where are you, sir?

Thornton: I'm in the building. Uh, you probably want to know the reason why I shot this place up. This place here is a racist place.

Dispatcher: Yup, I understand that

Thornton: They treat me bad over here, and they treat all the other black employees bad over here too, so I just take it into my own hands and I handled the problem — I wish I coulda got more of the people.

Dispatcher: Yeah. Are you armed, sir? Do you have a weapon with you?

Thornton: Oh yeah, I'm armed.

Dispatcher: How many guns do you have with you?

Thornton: I got one now, there's one out, one out in the uh, the uh, factory there.

Dispatcher: Yup. OK, sir.

Thornton: I'm not gonna kill nobody else, though.

Dispatcher: Yeah, we're gonna have to have you surrender yourself somehow here, not make the situation any worse, you know what I mean?

Thornton: These cops are gonna kill me.

Dispatcher: No they're not. We're just gonna have to get you to relax

Thornton: I'm relaxed, just calm down.

Dispatcher: ... to have you, you know, turn yourself over.

Thornton: We're just talking, you're gonna play something on the news, you know I'm gonna be popular, right [inaudible] the right thing. SWAT team just rolled by in army gear. You don't know where I'm at, but, I don't know, maybe you can trace it from this phone call. But, yeah, these people here are crazy, they treat me bad from the start here, racist company. They treat me bad, I'm the only black driver they got here. They treat me bad over here, they treat me bad all the time.

Dispatcher: This is a horrible situation, I understand that...

Thornton: You don't need to calm me down, I'm already calmed down. I'm not gonna kill nobody else — I just want to tell my story so that you can play it back.

Dispatcher: You're gonna help me get you out of the building, OK?

Thornton: All right, I'm a, I get — don't worry about that, I got that taken care of, I don't need anybody to talk me into getting me out. ...

Dispatcher: Where in the building are you, Omar?

Thornton: I'm not gonna tell you that. Where they find me, that's when everything will be over.

Dispatcher: Yeah, just, you know, where are you located, are you up in the offices?

Thornton: Where they fired me, everything be all right. ... Manchester itself is a racist place.

Dispatcher: Yeah, now, um, what time did you get there today?

Thornton: Um, It was about 7 o'clock

Dispatcher: Yeah. This morning?

Thornton: Yeah, about 7 a.m., yeah, they told me to come early today.

Dispatcher: What type of weapon do you have?

Thornton: I got a Ruger SR9, 15 shot.

Dispatcher: A Ruger? SR9?

Thornton: Automatic, yeah

Dispatcher: Is it a rifle?

Thornton: No, no, it's a pistol. I like pistols too, they are my favorites.

Dispatcher: Now, uh, you're gonna make the troopers and the people come in and catch ya? You're not gonna surrender yourself?

Thornton: Well — I guess, I guess uh, maybe I'll surrender ... nah. They come and get me, have them come get me.

Dispatcher: Yeah, we wouldn't want to do it like that, Omar. You know, it's already been a bad enough scene here this morning, we want you to relax.

Thornton: I'm relaxed though, I'm done.

Dispatcher: Yeah, we don't want any more, any more, uh, you know, people to lose their life, here.

Thornton: I'm not gonna kill nobody else.

Dispatcher: OK.

Thornton: I'm not coming out, I'm not coming out, they gonna have to find me. Probably use some dogs or whatever, I don't know what you're gonna do. Anyway.

Dispatcher: How much ammunition you have with you?

Thornton: I got uh, I shot, uh oh.

Dispatcher: What was that?

Thornton: It's all right. I guess it's got me ... I have to take care of business. Tell my people I love them, and I gotta go now.

Dispatcher: Omar. I really want you to help me stop this situation. OK?

Thornton: OK.

Dispatcher: If you work with me we'll get this to stop, OK? Omar? Omar Omar? OK ... [to others] Still alive ...

> [Within minutes of making that 911 call, Omar Thornton (supposedly) kills himself, although it appears he may have been shot by a sniper]

The Aftermath

According to company officials, Thornton was caught on surveillance video stealing beer on a previous occasion. When the company offered him a choice of being fired or resigning, Thornton signed the resignation papers and was being escorted out of the building when he opened fire.

An unidentified female who claimed to be acquainted with a close friend of Thornton's allegedly wrote a statement that said, *"Thornton was set up,"* and added that the videotape used as evidence of him stealing did NOT show an actual theft taking place.

Four Critical Questions

1. If Thornton was stealing from his employer and this theft was captured on videotape, why hasn't that tape surfaced in the media? This would give more weight to the claim by company officials that Omar Thornton was fired for just cause. The media has aired controversial videos in the past: the police beating of Rodney King, and a video of a Chicago cop beating a white female bartender who refused to serve him more alcohol.

2. Does the videotape show Thornton stealing cases of beer (putting them into his personal vehicle) OR does it show him moving beer from one location to another -- a normal part of his job as a warehouse driver?

3. If company officials allowed a black employee to be tormented the way Omar Thornton and his witnesses claimed, would the same officials be capable (and motivated) to manufacture a reason to fire him?

4. If Thornton was set-up and unjustly accused and fired – after being severely mistreated on a daily basis by racist whites on his job -- does this explain the kind of RAGE that triggered a mass murder?

Unfortunately, Thornton's accusers are the only people who are capable of revealing the truth – and they're sticking to their "story." Regardless of the facts, this following axiom holds true:

AXIOM #6: "THE BLACK VICTIM = A VICTIMLESS CRIME" THEORY. A BLACK PERSON IN A CONFLICT WITH A WHITE PERSON (OR A WHITE SYSTEM) CANNOT BE THE VICTIM IN A WHITE SUPREMACY SOCIETY. THE BLACK INDIVIDUAL IS ALWAYS AT FAULT, REGARDLESS OF WHO INITIATED THE CONFLICT, OR WHAT FACTS OR EVIDENCE IS PRESENT.

Our Analysis

This is NOT intended to condemn Omar Thornton, who was clearly a victim of racism/white supremacy, OR to condone his decision to take eight lives. A tragedy like this demands that compassion for both parties be balanced with truth and logic.

However, what needs to be said in the interest of promoting justice MUST BE SAID, even if it offends or hurts feelings. The reader is free to agree or disagree with what is written here or anywhere else in this book. We have done our best to be fair, to tell the truth, and be correct in what we understand and know to be true.

Only Two Options: Submit OR Resist

There are only two options for blacks who engage in interracial relationships (have sexual intercourse) with whites WITHIN a white supremacy society:

1. **to submit to white supremacy**
2. **to resist white supremacy and self-destruct**

Omar Thornton is a classic case of the inability to submit AND resist at the same time. In other words, it is impossible to lay down with (the human face of) white supremacy at night and get up in the morning and effectively fight it, anymore than you can go UP and DOWN at the same time and NOT rip your body apart. Submitting AND resisting white supremacy at the same time WILL RIP A BLACK MIND APART.

*The following is a **FICTIONAL STORY** based on the facts that have been reported in the mainstream media and in no way is intended to defame any real human beings. **This analysis is the product of the authors' imaginations,** in our attempt to illustrate the psychological dangers of submitting AND resisting WHITE SUPREMACY.*

Imagine this:

The first emotion **Black Male A** has when he wakes up in bed next to a white female is a feeling of dread, knowing he must go to a job where he'll be subjected to the same racism from his white coworkers and bosses that he has dealt with for over three years.

On his way to his job assignment he stops in the men's room. On the bathroom wall, he sees racist graffiti on the wall that says -- *"Kill all niggers"* and storms out to find a supervisor. The white supervisor blows him off and tells him to "stop being so sensitive, that's the problem with you people."

When **Black Male A** tells his union rep about the incident, he gets the same callous response, and is told the union will look into that trivial matter when they "get the time."

For the rest of the day, **Black Male A** is in a quiet rage, as he experiences more on-the-job sabotage and racist comments from his coworkers. He is aware that his coworkers have already heard about the incident that morning because the consensus around the warehouse is he was "another nigger playing the race card."

After another long day of being mistreated, **Black Male A** returns home to a white female who does not and cannot understand what he is going through, even if she tries to sympathize. He knows she will never understand, and he dare not tell her about the growing hatred in his heart for white people.

Black Male A tosses and turns at night while his white female sleeps peacefully by his side. He will wake up, exhausted, in a few hours to face another tortuous day with racist whites who want to rob him of his ability to feed, house, and clothe himself.

When the alarm goes off, he showers, gets dressed, and kisses his white female companion goodbye before he leaves to face what is starting to feel like an army of hostile whites, who despise him because he is black.

That night **Black Male A** engages in sexual intercourse with a white female (white supremacy wearing a human face) for surely, part of her appeal – perhaps, all her appeal – to that tortured black soul lies in his secret (and child-like) belief that having a white female will make him more human to the whites who despise his black skin.

However, his white female companion cannot deliver the one thing he so badly needs: white acceptance (safety from racist whites), but he cannot bring himself to blame her, so he must blame himself for NOT measuring up.

Black Male A tries harder to be the best black man he can be, because he is not allowed to JUST BE (A MAN), but is always on trial; always being judged wherever he goes. Even when he goes into a store, he is the most likely person in America to be followed by store security.

Even wearing a business suit, he is the most likely person in America to cause a white female to hold her purse and her thighs tighter if he walks into an elevator. And when he shops at the local supermarket with his white female, there are always (white) eyes judging and condemning him.

Black Male A is still determined to be the best "black" he can be, which is why he avoids associating with other blacks socially – especially black females -- because their presence confirms his worst fears: *too much black is not a good thing around whites.*

Black Male A is exhausted, trying to be a "good black" (man) because he is not allowed to JUST BE A MAN. He is exhausted because he has given his all -- his time, love, sex, and money -- and receiving less in return.

Black Male A does not complain even when he is financially exploited or physically assaulted by his white female companion because his need to be accepted is stronger than his fear of being abused and taken advantage of.

He would never make this kind of Herculean effort for a black female – not because he dislikes black females -- but because he has nothing to prove to someone who cannot offer him the white validation he desperately needs.

With a black female, he can JUST BE (A MAN), take off his "mask," and be himself. He is NOT always on trial because of the "wrongness" of his skin color, but will always be fully human to the black female. If he is lucky enough to find a compatible black female partner, he will get in exactly where he FITS IN -- but **Black Male A** does not know that.

Instead, **Black Male A** continues the futile cycle of going to the racist white union reps and the racist white bosses to complain about his racist white coworkers then returns home to his (racist suspect) white female to complain about other racist whites. Whatever comfort he needs to soothe his mind and spirit he cannot find at work OR at home.

Because he has separated himself from his ONLY TRUE ALLY – the black female – he has NO PSYCHOLOGICAL OR PHYSICAL DEFENSES from the wrath of white supremacy.

Black Male A lacked the perspective that could ONLY come from those who have walked in his shoes: *another black person,* who could have warned him that being in a sexual relationship with a white female might antagonize his white male coworkers and cause them to retaliate against him.

Unfortunately for **Black Male A**, black friends, lovers, spouses, etc., cannot validate the white-identified black person who desperately seeks white acceptance.

His days are surely numbered as he attempts to resist white supremacy (by day) and submit to white supremacy (every night) until that day comes when his black mind splits apart at the seams -- and **Black Male A** is driven to pick up a gun and kill his tormentors -- and possibly himself.

Black Male A's attempt to submit AND resist white supremacy at the same time led to a tragic case of psychological suicide and mass murder.

A Less Fatal Example Of Submission And Resistance To White Supremacy Via Interracial Sex

On August 10, 2010, **a Black Female** called the Dr. L. talk radio show for advice on how to handle her growing resentment toward her white husband of three years who did not defend her when other whites (his friends and family) made racist comments about blacks (practicing racism) in her presence.

Unfortunately for the **Black Female Caller**, Dr. L. (a white female) seemed less than sympathetic and in fact, used the word "nigger" eleven times during the call, which she justified by saying *"black guys use that word all the time."*

She warned the **Black Female Caller** not to *"NAACP me... if you're that hypersensitive about color, and don't have a sense of humor, don't marry out of your race."*

During a CNN interview, the **Black Female Caller** later said, *"I was calling to get some help and I did not expect to hear the things that she said to me. I didn't want to turn this into a racial thing, I just wanted some advice."*

Our Analysis

There are only two psychological options for blacks who engage in interracial sex with whites WITHIN a white supremacy society:

1. **to submit to white supremacy**
2. **to resist white supremacy and self-destruct**

*The following is a **FICTIONAL STORY** based on the facts that have been reported in the mainstream media and in no way is intended to defame any real human beings. **This analysis is the product of the authors' imaginations** as we attempt to illustrate the psychological dangers of submitting AND resisting WHITE SUPREMACY.*

Imagine this:

Black Female B turned to her white husband then to another white person (a talk show host) to complain about her husband's racist white friends and relatives. **Black Female B's** SUBMISSION to white supremacy is rooted in her denial that her (white) husband could NOT be a racist if he married a black female. Despite her claim that she is happily married, it is obvious her resentment toward her white husband had been building up for some time.

The **Black Female B's** RESISTANCE to white supremacy was the act of confronting her (white) husband about his silence when his white friends and relatives practiced racism against her. After getting no support from her white spouse, she asked another white person (a talk show host) what to do about the racism other whites were practicing in her presence.

Black Female B DOES NOT UNDERSTAND (or refuses to accept)that even a white person who is married to a black (or non-white) person is STILL A RACIST if he or she is practicing racism against their non-white spouse or other non-whites.

Her husband's silence speaks volumes and may be a crime of OMISSION by remaining silent while other whites practiced racism against his black wife. It is also possible that he allowed his friends and family members to do his talking for him.

It is likely **Black Female B's** husband had practiced racism in her presence BEFORE they were married, and that he practiced racism against other blacks (and non-whites) when she was not around. If this is the case, one could imagine his thinking might go something like this:

"What's up with this naïve black female? She's in MY world, and racism/white supremacy is part of MY world. I will never take her side against (my) white people. After she is long gone, I will still be white, will always be white, and will continue to enjoy the white privileges that have been guaranteed me from birth.

In order to continue receiving those "benefits," whites must practice racism against non-whites. My white peer approval and white privileges matters more than this marriage (which my friends and family said should have never happened in the first place).

Doesn't she know she has to adapt to the ways of white people if she wants to be with a white person? White people don't have to adapt to the black world, because we have all the power. If this black female wants this marriage to last, she must adapt to my (white) world and keep her mouth shut about racism because I'm not interested in that information."

The Talk Show Host's "advice" essentially amounted to the same thing:

"You naive black female, YOU made the choice to be with a white man, so you must adapt to his (our) world, and his (our) world is based on white dominance/black submission. That's the deal and the bed you made by marrying a white man, and you must lie in it, lumps and all. Why a white man would marry someone (black) like you with all the nice, single white females around, totally disgusts me. So, if you're experiencing racism, suck it up, because I'm really not interested in that information!"

Unless **Black Female B** examines her real reasons for marrying a white male who DOES NOT DEFEND HER from whites who are practicing racism against her IN HIS PRESENCE, there's a good chance she will get involved with another white male if she ever divorces her current husband.

The Bottom Line:

1. Anyone who condones your mistreatment is NOT your friend
2. Anyone who condones your mistreatment should NEVER be your friend
3. Anyone who condones your mistreatment cannot be trusted
4. If you are sleeping with someone who allows you to be mistreated, you are sleeping with your "enemy" NOT your "ally."

Based on our two fictional stories, what do Black Male A and Black Female B Have In Common?

1. It is likely both dated whites exclusively prior to their last relationship.
2. Both possibly believed being involved with a white person would make them more acceptable to other (racist and racist suspect) whites
3. Both confided in white people about the racism they were experiencing from other whites, and neither got the support they needed
4. Neither understood that it is impossible to serve two masters at the same time: ***white supremacy AND black normalcy***
5. Engaging in sexual intercourse with whites blinded both to the hardcore truth: sexual intercourse with whites does NOT eliminate OR offer any protection against racism.

Maximum-Emergency Compensatory Justice

According to Neely Fuller, Jr.'s book -- **"The United Independent Compensatory Code/System/Concept: A Textbook/Workbook for Thought, Speech and/or Action for Victims of Racism/White Supremacy"** -- the ninth area of people activity is WAR.

The book explains the **"Maximum-Emergency Compensatory Justice,"** which is defined as:

"The willful deliberate elimination of one or more Racists (White Supremacists), through death, and, the willful and deliberate elimination of self, through death, by a victim of racism (non-white person), acting alone, acting according to a detailed plan, and acting only after he or she has judged that he or she can no longer endure the effects of Racism and/or that he or she is no longer able to effectively promote justice, except by eliminating one or more Racists, and by eliminating his or her self, as a subject to the racists."

Mr. Fuller's book in NO way promotes violence but recognizes the pressure cooker of racism can make its victims react in violent, unpredictable ways.

Why Omar Thornton Should Be A Wake-Up Call For Black America

There are thousands of **Black Male As** and **Black Female Bs** in America who have sexual intercourse with whites without understanding how sex with whites is used as a weapon to maintain white supremacy. They do not understand the psychological price they will pay when they attempt to SUBMIT and RESIST white supremacy at the same time.

The REAL issue is NOT whether blacks mistreat other blacks. Certainly, whites mistreat other whites; Hispanics mistreat other Hispanics; and Asians mistreat other Asians.

It is SEXUAL SUBJUGATION (disguised as interracial "relationships" and "marriages") when a white person is practicing racism against their black partner OR does not defend their black partner when other whites are practicing racism against him or her.

The reader is free to accept or reject our analysis (and warnings) in this book, and decide for him or herself whether it is beneficial or destructive to engage in OR avoid interracial relationships (and sexual intercourse) with whites in a white supremacy system.

There are THREE psychological options for blacks who engage in sexual intercourse with whites WITHIN a white supremacy society: (1) *submit (commit psychological suicide,* (2) *resist (and self-destruct),* or:

(3) *STOP HAVING SEX WITH WHITE PEOPLE -- until the system of white supremacy has been eliminated.*

"Perhaps I should begin with something obvious -- something so obvious that it escaped my attention for almost thirty-five years:

All black men are insane.

Furthermore, it is safe to say that there never has been a sane black man in this society. Almost any living thing would quickly go mad under the unrelenting exposure the climate created and reserved for black men in a white racist society..."

— Bob Teague, author of "Letters to a Black Boy"

CHAPTER 38

MY KIND OF SISTA
(A true story)

A few weeks ago, I was shopping with my wife at a national health foods chain when I observed a conservative-looking black male in his mid to late 20s, accompanied by an Asian female, who was spooning rice and beans into a cardboard container.

This young black male, who looked like he wouldn't be caught dead listening to a Snoop Dogg CD, seemed real uncomfortable in his brown skin. Later, as we were walking to our car, my wife said the young black male refused to look her in the eye.

Don't get it twisted, my wife, she never stares or glares at interracial couples. It ain't her style nor is it mine. She will smile and speak to anyone -- strangers, white folks, old folks, as long as they don't give her a reason to get in that butt.

The reason she refuses to stare, make comments, or roll her eyes at the sight of a black man with a white or Asian female is she hates giving the couple any reason to think she is jealous. She is fond of saying, *"I got no use for a black body with a white or an Asian brain."*

My wife's got great people instincts. The proof? She sees right through my ass most of the time. Just like EF Hutton, I always listen when she speaks. Lest you think I'm too biased, let me say that interracial dating for black folks would be NO problem for me personally, IF we didn't live in a white supremacy system where blacks and whites are NOT treated equally.

BUT

As long as the white system is waging WAR against the black community; and black children are dying in the streets; and unarmed black males are murdered-by-cop; and black unemployment is three times higher than the rest of the nation -- including illegal workers; as long as a white man with a criminal record has a better chance of landing a job than a black man with a college degree; as long as 70% of black children are being raised by single/divorced black mothers; as long as almost one million of my people are rotting in the prison-industrial-complex; as long as black folks don't produce anything, control anything, and are totally dependent on everybody else for what we need; as long as black men should make their OWN women, children, and communities OUR PRIORITY like EVERY (REAL) MAN ON THE PLANET, and as long as I know BLACK UNITY IS THE KEY TO OUR SURVIVAL; *I will always be against interracial relationships for black people.*

The MAIN REASON the UNIFIED Asian, Arab, Indian, Hispanic, and white communities have thriving BUSINESS AND ECONOMIC BASES, and SAFE and SANE communities is they have INTACT, stable families made up of the same race of men and women (for the most part). That tells me it's only common sense that black folks BETTER do the same damn thing. We don't have to reinvent the wheel, we just need a SET OF OUR OWN.

Getting back to the story...

I started checking out this young brother's body language, wondering why he was so uptight, and I started thinking, "This young brotha is real fugged-up. He knows somewhere inside his mixed-up skull that something ain't right about what he's doing, or maybe the REASON he's doing it. But he's wrong about that. He's doing exactly what he's been programmed to do, especially if he's got a black body with a white brain that can't think for itself.

And DON'T be fooled by that Asian "woman of color" bullshit.

A brother I know said he married an Asian woman because he was afraid to marry a white woman and look like a sell-out. Now, this brother admitted upfront that he wasn't in love with his wife when he married her, so "color-blind love" had nothing to do with it.

He deliberately CHOSE a non-black woman because of his own black inferiority complex. He thought marrying a non-black female she would give him more status as a dark-skinned black male -- and set him apart from other blacks.

Am I saying every black person in an interracial relationships hates themselves? No, but in my experience, MOST have serious issues with other black people and themselves. Of course, this is just my experience.

Getting back to the story...

Now, if you asked this young black male why he was so uptight being seen in public with his Asian girlfriend, he would probably blame it on other "ignorant, intolerant people."

But the fact is if HE wasn't comfortable in the role he was playing OR with the person he was with, then HE'S got the fugging problem, not the other "ignorant people." After all nobody twisted his arm, right?

But he's walking around, trapped in confusion, with that white traffic cop inside his skull, directing his thinking and actions that tell him black is inferior.

Just a dazed zebra stumbling in the midst of hungry lions...

So, he and this Asian girlfriend got into the checkout line across from us. And he still couldn't raise his eyes above his chest. And then I noticed who was standing on the other side of the cashiers: an older black lady in her sixties just staring at his ass like: *"You little mothafugger (!)"*

I had to laugh because the look on her face was FIERCE! I said (to myself), oh hell yeah, sister, you got that right. These little negroes are the same ones YOU raised from tiny babies who now think they're too good for a black woman.

The same BLACK WOMEN who birthed them, fed them, stayed up all night with them, burped them, and wiped their noisy, messy little black baby asses, or sat in the emergency room at three am praying her baby boy's temperature went down (like my Moms did with me).

She was the one who cheered him on at his performance as a bunny rabbit at the Easter Sunday church play, and years later, cheered him on from the stands at his high school games...

NOT the Asian, Hispanic, or white female.

The Black woman was the one who worked two jobs, took care of the house, cooked the food, oiled the scalps, combed and braided the hair, ironed the clothes, BOUGHT the damn clothes (if she was a single moms), and did without, just to put her black son through high school and college, paying for graduations, proms, parties, field trips, jackets, Christmas gear, and student fees; his first car, and sometimes his first condoms...

NOT the Asian, Hispanic, or white female.

I can't count HOW many black women I know *personally* who raised their shorties by themselves, which is why I love and respect black women more than any man could love his women, cause I had one of those classic Moms, and sad to say, I pity any man or woman, black or white, who didn't have a Moms like the one I had.

My Pops was a good but a hard man, who grew up back in the day when it was brutal being a black man. He didn't do a lot of kissing or hugging, but showed love by keeping a roof over our heads, food on the table, and even a few toys at Christmas, so I'm grateful to Pops for that -- but my MOMS was the one who gave us unconditional love.

Enough said about that, back to the story...

So this older black lady was looking like, *"...these little niggas know they got some fugging NERVE..."* to take all that education, money, love and support that black women invested in them to a white, Hispanic, OR Asian female who NEVER once walked in a picket line, never got spit on, never integrated a lunch counter, never got bit by police dogs, or blasted with fire hoses, or called a nigger to her face (or behind her back).

They never marched around the police station or around the block because black boys (and men) were dying in the streets. They never contributed ONE DIME or ONE DROP OF SWEAT to the liberation of black people, and never gave a damn or a dime unless there was something in it for them (like sex or alimony). And they damn sure never rode on a bus for eight hours to Jena, LA to fight for six black boys nobody knew from a hole in the ground.

And I said to myself, hell yeah, sista, hell yeah, you is ABSOLUTELY RIGHT to make that little negro squirm...with that Asian female on his arm.

I BET she was the kinda sista who would stand with her arms folded at the door and refuse to let that black son, brother, or uncle walk in HER house with an Asian or white female to eat up HER fried chicken, HER cornbread, and HER collard greens that SHE paid HER good, hard-earned money for, just because his black ass was tired of eating Campbell soup casseroles, or Hamburger Helper, or some foreign cuisine that will never take the place of his black momma's soul food.

And I bet

that tired black sister -- who had seen the Civil Rights movement up closer than most of us -- was TIRED of watching so many TIRED black sons, uncles, nephews, brothers, and cousins, bringing home anybody but a black woman.

And she was TIRED of wondering:

"Is this what we black women marched for, scrubbed white women's floors for, got spit on for, beat for, fire-hosed for, sacrificed for, and died for? To be discarded by black males like some worthless black trash that had outlived its usefulness?"

So instead of setting two more plates, and checking her hurt feelings at her OWN door, that righteous sister told that little dishonorable nigga to STEP! until his black ass CAME CORRECT and brought home somebody who LOOKED LIKE HIS BLACK MOMMA.

And you know what?

I had the feeling that's exactly the kind of sista she was...

"You and I may go to Harvard, we may go to York of England, or go to Al Ahzar in Cairo and get degrees from all of these great seats of learning. But we will never be recognized until we recognize our women."

-- "Message to the Black Man in America" by the Honorable Elijah Muhammad

For Black Folks Who Think Race Doesn't Matter

For black folks who think race doesn't matter,

The next time you complain about the lack of black unity
And the poor quality of life in the black community
Because you have no protection or immunity
From the rogue policeman's reign of cruelty
As they shoot black men like dogs in the street

Remember those words that once sounded so sweet:
Race doesn't matter

The next time you have to go to the white man for a job,
With your hat in hand,
And you can't get a $10 business loan
To open a lemonade stand

And you lose your home due to predatory loan programs
Designed by rich white men
Who don't get stopped for driving
And having black skin

Remember those words: Race doesn't matter

When a black man can't get a job even with a college degree
But a white man with a criminal record
Gets a job like he's crime-free
And we can't get no respect as a black man

And even the white female who grabs her purse
At the sight of us understands
That EVERY MAN on this planet better have a PLAN
Because it's OUR JOB to take care of our women and children
On our OWN land

Remember those words: Race doesn't matter

When you can't catch a break
And you wonder how an empty wallet
Can stop an empty stomach ache
And we look back and remember who was there
When we were little more than a tiny pooh bear

Because the next face we'll see in our mind's eye
Is a black woman with a brown face and a big smile
And in our darkest days, we'll recognize OUR OWN
And we'd better pray that our foolish ways
Have NOT turned the black woman's heart to stone

So, it's time to wise up, my black brothers or be prepared to pay
Because the day of God's reckoning ain't that far away
We better get down on our knees and humbly pray
That God will take mercy on our dishonorable ways

Because instead of protecting our black women and children
We chose to play sex games with whites and Asians
Who don't give a damn about our culture or issues
Where we're forced to take a stand

It's a black thing, baby
An Asian or white female just can't understand

All she can do is raise confused black children
With no true racial identity
Who will be as useless as Tiger Woods
When it's crunch time for black unity

So remember my words to my little ditty
A dishonorable man will be shown NO PITY.

-- Umoja

Recipe #13

Pit the Black Male Against the Black Female

"Therefore kill all that are of the male sex, even of the children."   -- Numbers 31:17-18 (King James)

****

How do you destroy a race of people?
You destroy the family.

How do you destroy the family?
You divide (and conquer) the male and female.

How do you divide (and conquer) the male and female?
You destroy the bond between them.

How do you destroy the bond between the male and female?
By destroying the self-respect of the male.

How do you destroy the self-respect of the male?
By turning him against himself.

How do you turn the male against himself?
By turning him against his woman. No fruit can be superior to the tree it came from. No plant can be superior to the soil that nurtured it.

And no man can despise the womb (or woman) that gave him life without despising himself.

Umoja

CHAPTER 39

THE BLAME GAME

The **"Blame Game"** -- the last RECIPE of **Black Gender Wars** -- is designed to make black people blame OTHER black people instead of *blaming the WHITE PEOPLE IN CHARGE (WPIC)*.

It is crucial black people understand how this game is played so we can NEUTRALIZE the intended effect: *mass confusion and conflict between the black male and black female* in the following areas:

- education
- employment
- sex
- family
- HIV/AIDS
- entertainment
- politics

THE EDUCATIONAL BLAME GAME

While black boys are discouraged from pursuing higher education, black girls are encouraged to excel. By the time both reach the adult age, the better-educated black female may develop (false) feelings of superiority and contempt for the lesser-educated black male.

The educated black female will then face a MANUFACTURED shortage of compatible black males to date and marry and will BLAME black males for not "measuring up to her standards" INSTEAD of asking herself WHY black boys are MORE likely than black girls to be placed in "special education," excluded from college preparation courses, given the drug Ritalin to curb their natural curiosity (intelligence), and penalized by disciplinary rules that make it easy to expel black boys from the educational system altogether.

The lesser-educated black male may develop (false) feelings of inferiority and will BLAME black females for having "unrealistic standards" INSTEAD of asking himself WHY so many black males have an inferior education, OR why he is focusing on the *college-degreed, six-figure-paycheck, professional black female* when SHE DOES NOT represent the majority of black females in America.

The black male and female are BLAMING each other instead of BLAMING the WHITE PEOPLE IN CHARGE (WPIC) who created a racist educational system that penalizes BOTH of them.

"The hardest hit group of workers – African-American men – were hit hardest again. Their unemployment rate is 17.3 percent, up from 16.7 percent, nearly double the 8.9 percent unemployment rate for white men. Women of both races fared better – 7.1 percent unemployment for whites, 13.2 percent unemployment for African Americans."

(Source: The St. Louis American, Sept 3, 2010)

THE EMPLOYMENT BLAME GAME

The Myth Of The Black Matriarchy: Blaming Black Females For The Unemployment Woes Of Black Males

In 1965, in the midst of the civil rights movement, when blacks were rising up and demanding equal rights, the U.S. government launched a deadly missile called *"The Negro Family: The Case for National Action" (aka "The Moynihan Report")*.

This (racist) report, commissioned by Senator Daniel Patrick Moynihan, used U.S. Labor statistics to shift the blame from a racist system onto the weary shoulders of the black female: *"...the black woman had substantial advantages over the black man educationally, financially, and in employment."*

However, in the 1960s the majority of black women worked in the lowest-paying occupations -- teaching, clerical, and domestic work -- and were paid less than white males, white females, and in some cases, less than black males. Despite these FACTS, the black female became a convenient (and safe) scapegoat for the under-employment and unemployment woes of black males.

By linking -- *"the professional and educational advancement of black women to high juvenile delinquency levels, high crime levels, poor educational levels for black males..."* -- the deceptive report ignored the main reason black females HAD to work outside the home: **the black man was barred from jobs that allowed him to be the sole provider of his family.**

The condition of poor and unemployed black males was blamed on the POWERLESS black female instead of placing the BLAME where it belonged: on the **WHITE PEOPLE IN CHARGE (WPIC),** who created the economic conditions that produced massive black poverty in the first place.

The Black Man Was Forced From The Home

When blacks fled the racist, segregated South and migrated north for a better life, they faced rampant discrimination in employment and housing. Unable to find work that paid a living wage, many blacks were forced to seek government assistance.

As more blacks became dependent on welfare, the rules were changed, forcing the black man to leave the home if the family received benefits. The black man was stripped of the *main thing* every man needed to feel like a (real) man: *the ability to protect and provide for his family as the head of his household.*

Unable to find work, some black fathers and husbands were faced with two gut-wrenching choices: (1) stay, and let their children go hungry, OR (2) leave, so their wives and children would have food and shelter.

Of course, there was a third, more humane, and moral option: allow black men the SAME opportunity to work, earn a living wage, and support their families, the same way white men were allowed to do.

"That's part of the sexual confusion. With the black females becoming more and more in positions of being the man and the woman, lots of them are becoming just that – so called bi-sexual, and black males, a lot of them are throwing up their hands and giving up and they are becoming females or want to be because it's less pressure."

– Neely Fuller, Jr., author of 'The United-Independent Compensatory Code/System/Concept A textbook/workbook for victims of racism (white supremacy)

It is important ONE FACT be firmly established in the minds of ALL black males and females:

Black males and females have NO POWER over ANYTHING that happens within the boardrooms of Corporate America -- including whether they will be hired, promoted, or fired.

That being said, only a "manageable" number of educated black females are allowed to advance ahead of the black male, who may be just as ambitious and capable, but may not be given the same educational and employment opportunities -- OR encouragement and guidance.

The majority of black males AND females in America make less than $50,000 a year BECAUSE the vast majority of lucrative educational and employment opportunities are reserved for white people.

Regardless of these FACTS, the black male and female still BLAME and fight each other over the handful of crumbs that fall from the economic table INSTEAD of blaming the *WHITE PEOPLE IN CHARGE (WPIC) who are practicing economic racism against ALL black people.*

THE SEX ROLE REVERSAL BLAME GAME

The "Strong, Independent Black (Super) Woman"

The black female has been PROGRAMMED to see herself as a strong, don't-need-no-man, independent, "super-black-woman," which is a stark contrast to the image of the feminine white female who needs (and deserves) to be rescued, protected, and financially supported by white AND black males.

During the 1970s, black women were encouraged BY white females to join the (white) woman's "liberation movement" to fight male oppression but white females seldom, if ever, talked about the **SYSTEM OF WHITE SUPREMACY** -- or how racist white females fully participated in, benefited from, AND often LED the way in the economic exploitation and degradation of black females.

While there is nothing wrong with being strong or independent, too much "independence" can be a two-edged sword for the "strong black female" because a "superwoman" is never rescued or protected: *she is always expected to save herself.*

By constantly reminding the black male of her (super) strength and super-woman abilities, she is UNDERMINING the same (black) men she will criticize for not being better, stronger men.

Perhaps, it is time for the black female to strike the phrase -- *"I'm a strong, independent black woman"* -- from her vocabulary and REPLACE it with one that AFFIRMS her femininity, feminine strength, and encourages mutual respect between the black male and the black female:

"I'm a feminine, hard-working black woman who respects AND appreciates a strong, masculine, hard-working black man."

Is The Black Man Becoming "Extinct?"

This myth is false for the following reasons:

- The Black Man is NOT A Dinosaur.

- This is NOT the Ice Age.

- A species becomes EXTINCT ONLY when Nature has selected that species for Natural Extinction and overpowers that species' ability to survive in its natural environment.

- If the Black Man is the MOST FERTILE man on the planet, it is logical to assume (Mother) Nature has NOT selected him for NATURAL EXTINCTION.

- When the Black Man is overpowered by UNNATURAL, manmade forces (like the system of white supremacy) that is NOT EXTINCTION; that is GENOCIDE.

- Only the CREATOR (Mother Nature) has the POWER to make the black male EXTINCT, not the racist white male and female.

The "Weak, Emasculated, Extinct Black Man" Image

"The only free people in America is the white male and the black female."
-- Archie, 58, restaurant cook

Surprisingly, the above sentiment is fairly common among (some) black males over the age of forty. The question is: how did the **WHITE PEOPLE IN CHARGE** manage to convince (some) black males that the powerless black female had MORE "freedom" than the privileged white female in a white supremacist society? One answer:

"The Negro Family: The Case for National Action" aka "The Moynihan Report" painted a dismal (and false) picture of the black family as a **"black matriarchy,"** a household dominated by aggressive, "emasculating" black females. In reality, most black households in the 1960s were HEADED by black males, who were largely present in the home.

Unfortunately, some black males -- in a desperate attempt to seek psychological relief from (and a safer scapegoat for) their oppression -- have bought into the MYTH (LIE) that black females are the major obstacle to their manhood INSTEAD of **BLAMING** the **WHITE PEOPLE IN CHARGE (WPIC)** who are practicing educational, economic, social, political, and psychological warfare against them.

The Black Community Has NEVER Been A Black Matriarchy

In 1925, only three percent of black families were headed by women. The marriage rate for blacks during the Great Depression was higher than the marriage rate for whites even though blacks were poorer on average than whites.

Only AFTER jobs for low income blacks were replaced by welfare, crack cocaine, high-powered weapons, the "War on Drugs," and mandatory sentencing for NON-VIOLENT DRUG OFFENSES, did black family stability take a nose-dive. With almost one million black men -- many of them FATHERS -- in prison, the black female was forced to become the head of the household.

Make no mistake. The black community is STILL a male-dominated society. It does not matter that black females head up almost 70% of black households. That is an economic and social reality (tragedy), *NOT a cultural choice.*

Like all males in a male-dominated society (like America) most males, in general, reject female leadership, and black males are NO exception. However, most women -- and black women are no exception -- actually welcome strong male leadership. In other words, most black men will not follow black women, but most black women will follow black men. The proof:

1. the preacher
2. the politician
3. the pimp

Whether it is the church, the meeting hall, or the street corner, black men usually lead; black women usually follow. With a few exceptions, black women are the foot soldiers and seldom the generals in most black organizations.

"Single Black Women, Count Your Blessings"
-- USA Today

"Single black women choosing to adopt."
-- CNN

"Single black women being urged to date outside race" -- Washington Post

"Marriage Is For White People"
– Washington Post

"Why successful black women can't find a good man." – ABC News Special

"Why Can't a Successful Black Woman Find a Man?" -- ABC Nightline

"Black Women See Fewer Black Men at the Altar" -- New York Times

BLAME-GAME THE BLACK FAMILY OUT OF EXISTENCE

Single, Childless Black Female Celebrities Are Rewarded

What do Oprah, Tyra Banks, Whoopi Goldberg, and Wendy Williams have in common? They are rich, famous, SINGLE, usually CHILDLESS, usually MANLESS, and are the BEST ROLE MODELES for young and impressionable black females that white supremacy can buy.

Not only is *"being single"* marketed as the BEST CHOICE for black females, it is being HAMMERED into the heads of hundreds of thousands of frustrated, single black females as their ONLY CHOICE.

Black Fathers Stereotyped As Deadbeat Fathers

Black males have been routinely demonized and stereotyped as the worst "deadbeat fathers" in the nation, but the most prolific "deadbeat fathers" in American history were the slave owners who over a 400-YEAR period raped and impregnated MILLIONS of African slave women and SOLD *their own children into slavery (!)* Without a doubt, the ULTIMATE DEADBEAT FATHERS.

Unfortunately, good black fathers have been rendered INVISIBLE in the American media. These missing images program the black female to see the black male as incapable of fathering his children, and programs young black males -- especially fatherless young black males -- to think being a loving, responsible father is something black men just don't (or can't) do.

Create Child Support And Divorce Laws That Penalize Black Males To Discourage Them From Marrying Black Females

The court systems make divorce and child support proceedings as disagreeable, painful, and punitive as possible to discourage black males from marrying, forming stable families, or parenting their own children. Some black males view marriage or ANY legal commitment to a black female and their black children -- including REFUSING to sign a birth certificate -- as a luxury and a lifestyle they cannot afford.

Allow Poor Black Females To Benefit From Remaining Single

After the welfare system was REVISED to force black males out of the home, the black-male-headed household (and marriage to a black male) became an obsolete concept for many poor black mothers.

What is the (white) government's message to a poor, 17-year-old black girl who can get her own apartment, food stamps, medical benefits, and a check for NOT marrying the father of her children? *that a two-parent, black-male-headed household is a luxury (and a lifestyle) she cannot afford.*

Black males and females are blaming each other INSTEAD of BLAMING the WHITE PEOPLE IN CHARGE who deliberately created the circumstances that destroyed the black family.

Some Unanswered Questions About Black Females & The HIV/AIDS Blame Game

- If black males are having sexual intercourse and breeding with large numbers of white females (and obviously having unprotected sex), why isn't the HIV rates for white females increasing?

- If 22 percent of black males married outside their race, why aren't the HIV/AIDS infection rates going up for non-black females?

- If married white senators, governors, and preachers are coming out (or being enforced out) of the "closet," why aren't the HIV rates for privileged white females rising?

Maybe we asking the WRONG questions and BLAMING the wrong people...

THE HIV/AIDS BLAME GAME

Make Black Males The Low-Down, On-The-Down-Low, HIV-Infected Killers Of Black Females

"The rate in 2006 of new infections in black women...was nearly 15 times that in white women." The article went on to say that "...some women report being infected with HIV/AIDS by boyfriends or husbands who they later found out were sleeping with men." - U.S. News and World Report (2008)

As HIV/AIDS ravaged the black community, the sexual behavior and drug addictions of the black community were put under a public microscope, effectively BLAMING black people for becoming HIV-infected.

After John King, a divorced black male, appeared on the Oprah Winfrey Show in 2004, and confessed to sleeping with men while he was married, black males became synonymous with the HIV-infected closet homosexual living the "down-low" lifestyle. In 2010, Oprah Winfrey revisited the topic, and once again, focused on black males who make up *less than 15% of the male population.*

Is The HIV/AIDS Epidemic Another "Tuskegee Experiment?"

In October 2010, the U.S. government officially apologized for a 1940s STD (Sexually Transmitted Disease) Study in Guatemala where (white) American scientists DELIBERATELY INFECTED prisoners and patients in a mental hospital with syphilis.

The SAME government researcher who led the study in Guatemala was also involved in the infamous **TUSKEGEE EXPERIMENT** where 600 black males were **DELIBERATELY INFECTED WITH SYPHILLIS** -- without their knowledge -- allowing infected black males to infect countless black females for over FORTY YEARS, so white "researchers" could study the effects of the disease on their black Victims.

In 1990 Dr. David Acer, an HIV-infected Florida dentist, was accused of infecting six of his patients with the disease. According to the Centers for Disease Control (CDC), this (supposedly) was the FIRST KNOWN instance in which a health care provider transmitted HIV to a patient by a method *other than unprotected sexual intercourse.*

Sexually transmitted "diseases" may serve a more sinister purpose: In the 1970s, South Africa developed race-specific bio-weapons to target blacks and Asians. In September 2000, the Project for a New American Century published a document that described race-specific bio-weapons as "politically useful tools." There should be NO doubt in any rational black mind what these bio-weapons are being designed to do -- *and WHO the targets will be.*

In spite of all the above, the stereotyped "down-low" black male and "sexually immoral" black female are BLAMING EACH OTHER for a highly suspicious "HIV/AIDS" epidemic they DID NOT CREATE.

"Maybe the reason for the advent of black men in Hollywood wearing dresses is if the black man can play the man roles and the woman roles, then there will be no need for THE BLACK WOMAN (the spiritually strong one).

You see the point I am trying to make is that the white man knows that once you get more than one black woman in the same room together something happens, a mysterious energy fills the room with an unexplained aura. The force of black women on a movie set will cause something and/or do something.

There are things brothers won't do in front of black women that they'll do in front of white people. But when a black woman is around, a sort of reality check happens and the black woman will ask the black man:

"Why are you doing this? Why are you resorting to such buffoonery and homosexual ways? Wake up, what are you doing?"

And, indeed, if that were to happen, the whole white man's plan would die."

— Ryan, 40, black male, government employee

THE ENTERTAINMENT BLAME GAME

"I find my mind still lingering on some of the images in most TV commercials and shows with all these black males with white and bi-racial females. I mean, I was literally out in public and would just see a black man walk past me and I would get DISGUSTED. No words, the brother didn't even look my way, but I would get angry inside. TV programming is a monster." -- Marcia, 32, health care worker.

Hollywood-Produced/Promoted "Black" Films Usually Fall Into One Of Two Categories:

1. the "good black" female triumphing over the "bad" black male: (*The Color Purple, Waiting To Exhale, I Can Do Bad All By Myself, For Colored Girls, Diary of a Mad Black Woman, Precious*)
2. the "good black" male triumphing against the odds *without* the support of ANY (good) black females (*The Blind Side, The Pursuit of Happiness, most Denzel Washington and Samuel Jackson movies*)

It appears the ONLY "black relationships" that are acceptable by white Hollywood standards MUST portray black males and females as apart OR as the enemies of each other. Black males and black females are NEVER shown in positive scenarios where they are cooperating or solving problems together, or in positive romantic/sexual interactions that do not involve a black male wearing a dress, or some other form of comedy or buffoonery.

Interracial sex, rape, and incest scenes are the *ONLY forms of "black sexuality"* that are tolerated in most Hollywood-produced films because these images PIT the black male and female against each other and provoke hostility between them both on-screen AND off-screen. These images ALSO reinforce the (white) perception that black sexuality is animalistic and savage.

Even the vast majority of TV shows and commercials usually promote the "evil, dominating, and unattractive black female" and the "weak, foolish black male" who are either arguing, disrespecting, or opposing each other.

The black male and black female BLAME each other (and black entertainers) for the degrading images of black people INSTEAD of blaming the WHITE PEOPLE IN CHARGE (WPIC) who own and control the --

-- music industry, Hollywood and TV studios, national and cable news networks, radio stations, magazines, advertisers, sponsors, FCC licenses, and Censors that create, script, approve, produce, sponsor, and broadcast the degrading images of black males and females all over the entire WORLD.

339

THE BLACK APOLOGIST (CAN'T BLAME ANYBODY) GAME

"I truly believe there are whites who are struggling with racism, and there are a lot of white people who may not be the brightest people in the world, who don't understand how racism works, just like a lot of blacks don't understand how they have been programmed."
-- Amiri S., professor of black studies

The trademark of the **"Black Apologist"** is his or her REFUSAL to BLAME white people for their racist behavior. They may insist that whites are victims of the "system," too, and are often found coming to the defense of a white person being accused of practicing racism.

The **Black Apologist** can be found among all educational or income groups; may be male or female; but is more likely to be a college-educated, black male professional who earns his living in a predominantly white setting.

They may wear Afrocentric hairstyles and dress, and change their birth names to an African name, but upon closer inspection, it is clear what they REALLY value the MOST is what white people have given them: *their degrees, diplomas, awards, titles, jobs, paychecks, material possessions, AND white sexual partners.*

The **Black Apologist** usually lives in a predominantly white area, socializes with whites, and is sexually involved with whites. They are so intimate with (and psychologically dependent on) whites, they are COMPELLED to make excuses for white people *EVEN when white people are mistreating them.*

The **Black Apologist** may be well-meaning, but his or her confusion and contradictory perspectives actually PROMOTE white supremacy instead of helping to eliminate it. This explains why **Black Apologists** are in such high demand by the **WHITE PEOPLE IN CHARGE**. ANY BLACK PERSON **who is** praised by powerful whites or white institutions should ALWAYS BE A RED FLAG to the black collective that he or she is knowingly OR unknowingly promoting white supremacy.

The Professional Black Apologist

The **"Professional Black Apologist"** is a shameless AGENT who is PAID to take the FOCUS OFF WHITE PEOPLE, and REFOCUS THE BLAME on black people. They are regular guests on so-called conservative AND progressive talk shows but are seldom allowed to host their own show on the same networks.

They are often rewarded with lucrative book deals, sponsorships, and various, nefarious, and secretive funding for organizations that seem to exist ONLY to promote deception and confusion around racial issues.

They are usually sexually involved with or married to whites, OR secretly involved with white males. They have NO empathy or loyalty to their own kind and are extremely useful tools in promoting white supremacy by BLAMING the powerless black collective instead of rightfully **BLAMING** the **WHITE PEOPLE IN CHARGE** who control everything that happens in America.

THE POLITICAL BLAME GAME

Using Showcase Blacks as Political Scapegoats

The term "**Showcase Blacks**," coined by Mr. Neely Fuller, Jr., author of The United Independent Compensatory Code/System/Concept, refers to the high-profile blacks that are constantly paraded before the public. They may be political dignitaries, pro athletes, entertainers, educators, business people, Supreme Court justices, and even US Secretaries of States.

Showcase Blacks are used to put a "black face" on unpopular government and corporate policies. Whenever a white politician or policy maker appears before the cameras, **Showcase Blacks** are ALWAYS standing in the background to give the impression that blacks are conspiring with corrupt white officials to deceive and defraud the public. In reality, these black bobbing heads have no power to agree or disagree with anything.

Showcase Blacks are also used to redirect citizens' anger FROM white policy makers TO a black spokesman or woman. For example, a black female is "promoted" to the president of a utility company shortly before gas prices are hiked.

In the Jena Six case, six black boys were charged with felonies for a high school fight. The Louisiana District Attorney's office assigned a black attorney to handle the case -- and to take the blame and absorb the wrath of the black collective to protect his white bosses from charges of racism.

Pitting One Showcase Black Against Another

It is common for two **Showcase Blacks**, usually males, to appear on a network or cable news show, and have a heated debate over a government or social policy that neither one has any control over. In fact, there are only four reasons ANY black person is given a mike and national exposure/air-time:

1. *to argue with another black person*
2. *to degrade or ridicule another black person (who may or may not be present) or black people in general.*
3. *to praise a white person (who may or may not be present)*
4. *to promote white supremacy or black inferiority (practice deception)*

All the above takes the FOCUS off the WHITE PEOPLE IN CHARGE, who are actually causing whatever PROBLEM the two black (powerless) people are arguing about. The black people are simply pawns in the BLAME GAME by taking ALL the attention off what the **WHITE PEOPLE IN CHARGE ARE DOING** and putting ALL the focus on what black people are SAYING.

Showcase Blacks may not understand (or accept) how they are being used, and ultimately BLAMED for something they have NO control over, but their very public performances will make it appear that black -- NOT white people -- are the real problem.

THE ULTIMATE BLAME GAME

Showcase Blacks Increase White Resentment

The popularity of a **Showcase Black** among the white collective does NOT increase acceptance of blacks in general, anymore than Michael Jordan and Michael Jackson's popularity with their white fans caused a reduction of racism.

In reality, **Showcase Blacks** in high-profile positions and occupations actually increase envy and resentment among whites, NOT acceptance, by creating the (false) illusion that blacks have more opportunities than whites.

TV specials about Black America create even more resentment because they create the (false) perception that blacks are getting MORE attention (help) than whites when, in reality, NEITHER group is getting the help they need -- which is *why these shows were created.*

Showcase Blacks (who have no real power) are the perfect scapegoats (and lightning rods) for white fear, frustration, and rage. Since **Showcase Blacks** are rarely accessible to the public, this resentment and anger is often directed at everyday blacks in the form of increased racism, discrimination, and violence.

Like an irate customer who is overcharged by the phone company, his only recourse is to talk or vent to *a customer service rep* (employee) who has no real power to change the corporate policy -- but is PAID to take the abuse AND the blame for that policy.

The **Showcase Black's** high-profile position is designed to redirect the rage of the increasing oppressed and impoverished white population to that Showcase Black or Blacks -- and by default to the black population INSTEAD of BLAMING the **WHITE PEOPLE IN CHARGE (WPIC).**

Scapegoating blacks sets the stage for MORE racism; MORE violence against blacks; MORE unemployment, and MORE incarceration of blacks, and *may eventually lead to the mass genocide of black people within America's borders.*

If this sounds like an unbelievable scenario, one only need remember that a very similar scenario occurred in Germany during the 1930s:

> *"You see if we go back to Nazi Germany and Joseph Gerbels, who understood if we keep putting out negative images of semites and the Jewish religion, we can train the population to say: 'Look, they're animals, they're not human. And so the sooner we get rid of them, the better."* -- Dr. Frances Cress Welsing, author of "The Isis Papers," speaking on the future of black people in America, during an appearance on Tony Brown's Journal.

The **Ultimate Blame Game** makes the degraded black female (an HIV-infected whore, welfare parasite, and monster mother), AND the degraded black male (an HIV-speading, closet homosexual, rapist, criminal, buffoon) **the black scapegoats** for the economic crimes of the **WHITE PEOPLE IN CHARGE (WPIC)** who control everything that happens in America.

STOP BLAMING BLACK PEOPLE

To all my friends, family, and associates

For the last two years I have been a harsh critic of our first black president. In doing so, I have downplayed the obvious: if he is NOT in charge (as I have stated many times), why am I focusing so much attention and resentment in his direction INSTEAD of focusing all my attention on the **WHITE PEOPLE IN CHARGE (the WPIC)?**

That being said, while I dislike the role all Showcase Blacks play in the unseemly scheme of things, and the blind allegiance some black people have for a black man with a fancy title, I am going to avoid targeting black people for ridicule and will FOCUS 99.9995% of my attention on the real problem: **THE WHITE PEOPLE IN CHARGE (the WPIC).**

I would strongly suggest all non-white people do the same and stop fighting, fussing, cussing, arguing with, gossiping about, snitching on, degrading, mistreating, and killing other black and non-white people. All the problems -- including the dysfunctional behaviors and mental illnesses of so many black people -- are caused by the CREATORS and the MAINTAINERS of the white supremacy system: the **WHITE PEOPLE IN CHARGE (the WPIC).**

I sincerely apologize for my earlier confusion, and for doing what I have been programmed to do all my life: *blame black people for what the WHITE PEOPLE IN CHARGE are doing to black people and to all the non-white people on the planet.*

Telling the Truth is not about Hate

I do not HATE anyone, including white people
I am cordial and courteous to all people, including white people
I do not deliberately step on the toes of white people as I pass them by
I do not spit on white children as they walk to an "integrated" school
I have never made a white child cry by calling them an ugly name
I have never dragged a white person by the neck behind a pick-up truck
I have never sodomized a white male with a plunger handle or a screwdriver while wearing a policeman's uniform
I have never shot an unarmed white person 41 or 50 times
I have never let a terrified white child sit on a roof for four days after a hurricane
My conscience and record are clear
But there is one thing I hate: racism, injustice, and BLAMING black people...

For what the white people in charge are doing.

CHAPTER 40

THE BALLOON AND THE BASKET

She was a beautiful mahogany-brown Balloon who loved soaring high in the blue skies. Attached to the Balloon was a handsome, sturdy brown Basket who provided stability and kept the Balloon from getting too close to the sun. The strong brown tethers (cords) that had held them together for the last thousand years had endured a thousand terrible storms.

One day, the Balloon and the Basket passed over a traveling circus where hundreds of shiny red, blue, green, and purple balloons floated on long, silky strings above the striped tents. The Basket was awestruck. They were the most beautiful balloons he had ever seen -- mainly because they weren't *brown*. It didn't matter that they were too small and puny to lift a basket his size; he was still impressed.

The winds picked up and carried the Balloon and the Basket away from the circus. Heartbroken, the Basket watched as the brightly colored balloons shrank in the distance.

The Basket blamed the Balloon for being too big to steer against such a strong wind. If only he could be free of the Balloon, his life would be perfect! When the Balloon heard the Basket grumbling below, she decided *she* was tired of being controlled by the Basket. If only she could be free of the Basket, her life would be complete!

Below them, the huge, jagged white rocks and swirling waters beckoned to the Balloon and the Baskhet. "Come on, take a swim," the waters coaxed the pair. "We promise we won't let you drown."

The Balloon and the Basket paid the deceptive waters no mind. They had survived more than a thousand years together by avoiding the dangers of the jagged white rocks and raging waters.

Tragically, their dependence on each other was now the main thing driving them apart. They had been a team for so long that they took each other for granted. Secretly, each believed he or she would be better off apart, and each made plans for their escape.

The next afternoon, the westerly winds blew the Balloon and the Basket toward the circus tents and the brightly colored balloons. This time, the Basket came prepared. He took a long sharp stick from the bottom of his basket and started poking holes in the Balloon until he heard sharp hisses of air.

The Basket was so intent on being free; he didn't notice that the Balloon was sawing away at the strong brown tethers that held them together with a saw she'd hidden away.

With each poke of the Basket's stick, they descended another 50 feet. Now, they were only 200 feet above the jagged white rocks and swirling waters. The Balloon frantically sawed faster and faster.

When the last tether was completely severed, the sturdy brown Basket went into a free fall, tumbling over and over toward the jagged white rocks. When the Basket realized his fatal mistake, he called out for the Balloon to save him but she was too busy plugging up the holes he'd made.

With a loud crash and a terrifying scream, the Basket hit the jagged white rocks and broke into a thousand pieces. The swirling waters pulled what was left of the once sturdy brown Basket beneath the rolling white foam. The Balloon shouted with joy! She was finally free! Without the weight of the Basket and his controlling ways, she was soaring higher than ever before!

Then the Balloon noticed her smooth, slick surface was melting. She was too close to the sun! With a cry of dismay, she tried to descend to a safer altitude but the torn brown tethers were of no use in steering.

Frightened, and in agony, the Balloon cried out for her beloved brown Basket! Like the Basket, she realized her fatal mistake too late. The Basket had allowed her to soar, but he had also kept her safe.

When the Balloon bounced off the sun, she exploded into a thousand shiny-brown pieces! What was once a magnificent brown Balloon floated down to the jagged white rocks and was consumed by the swirling white waters.

Then something happened that had never happened in the history of time. The swirling waters rose until they completely covered the jagged white rocks, and for the first time in a thousand years, the raging waters were calm and peaceful.

Without the Basket, the Balloon could not steer clear of the dangerous sun. Without the Balloon, the Basket could not rise above the dangerous white rocks. Together they made a formidable team. Apart, they were doomed.

THE END OF ALL STORIES

"The lion cannot survive alone;
without the lioness, he will perish."

-- Umoja

The Bottom Line

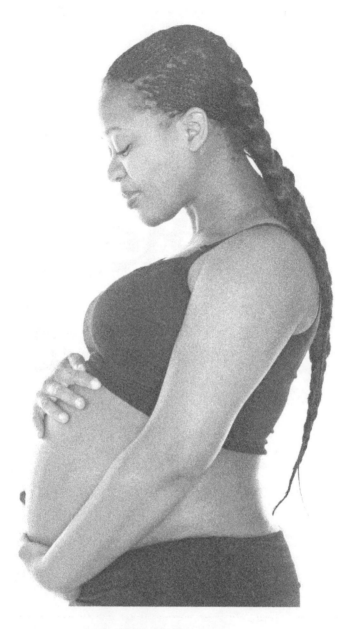

BLACK LOVE =
The Black Male + The Black Female + The Black Womb
= White Genetic Extinction

CHAPTER 41

THE BOTTOM LINE:
WHITE GENETIC SURVIVAL

Obviously, the reader is free to accept OR reject any of the ideas or theories presented in this book. However, ONE UNIVERSAL TRUTH is undeniable: *whites are experiencing a global infertility crisis.*

The Evidence

- Host John Gibson, during the May 11, 2008 segment of his program, "My Word" on Fox News' The Big Story, advised his (white) viewers to *"...do your duty. Make more babies."* He went on to report that nearly half of all children under the age of five in the U.S. are minorities.

- Russian President Vladimir Putin was so concerned about the declining population of Russia, he paid couples to have babies. Russia will lose close to 45 million – 1/3 of its population -- over the next 50 years. (2008).

- *'Global White Population to Plummet to Single Digit—Black Population to Double. As a percentage of world inhabitants the white population will plummet to a single digit (9.76%) by 2060... the big gainer in the population derby will be blacks or sub-Sahara Africans...will expand almost 133% to 2.7 billion by 2060 (25.38% of the world's population). Of the seven population groups studied, only whites are projected to sustain an absolute decline in numbers."* (2008 report by the National Policy Institute).

- *"By the middle of this century, if present fertility patterns continue, 60 percent of the Italian people will have no personal experience of a brother, a sister, an aunt, an uncle, or a cousin; Germany will lose the equivalent of the population of the former East Germany; and Spain's population will decline by almost one-quarter. Europe is depopulating itself at a rate unseen since the Black Death of the fourteenth century. When an entire continent, healthier, wealthier, and more secure than ever before, fails to create the human future in the most elemental sense -- by creating the next generation -- something very serious is afoot."* -- (SOURCE: *'Is Europe Dying? Notes on a Crisis of Civilizational Morale'* by George Weigel, History News Network, Aug 05)

The LOGICAL Conclusion

As long as **black fertility** is seen as the enemy of **white genetic survival, any form of black love between the black male and black female** will always be under attack by the white supremacy system.

Wombs For Rent

Women in Africa and India living in poverty are "renting" their wombs to wealthy white couples when the white wife has no uterus, an under-developed uterus, or medical conditions, and is unable to carry a baby to term.

The couples provide the sperm and eggs. The eggs are fertilized in a TEST TUBE. The embryo is then transferred into the uterus of the surrogate "mother.

The non-white female -- who is often a mother herself -- must abandon her OWN children to live in a "surrogacy center" until the baby is born, usually under conditions that the non-white females could not afford for their OWN children. Some object to this practice, labeling it the "colonization of the womb" by whites.

Others justify it. "You guys have no idea what it is like to want a child so badly and not be able to have it," wrote one white female in response.

The surrogate mothers do it for survival. Vohra is one of those women. "My husband and I only earn 50 rupees ($1.20) a day. My husband and I want to give our children a future and this is the only way to do it."

The Cress Theory Of Color Confrontation

Dr. Frances Cress Welsing, a famous African-American psychiatrist and the author of *'The Isis Papers: The Keys to the Colors'* (1991), states that White Supremacy is practiced by the global "white" minority on the conscious and unconscious level to ensure their genetic survival by any means necessary.

Dr. Welsing contends that because of their "numerical inadequacy" and "color inferiority," white people may have defensively developed "an uncontrollable sense of hostility and aggression" towards people of color, which has led to "confrontations" between the races throughout history.

Repressing their own feelings of inadequacy, whites *"set about evolving a social, political, and economic structure to give blacks and other 'non-whites' the appearance of being inferior."*

Whether the reader accepts or rejects Dr. Welsing's theories, it is undeniable that whites are in the "numerical minority" on the planet. It is also undeniable that whites are experiencing a fertility crisis, AND a negative population growth rate (there are more deaths than births).

Countries That Made The Negative Population Growth List:

Ukraine	Hungary	Germany
Russia	Romania	Czech Republic
Slovakia	Italy	Greece
Japan	Poland	Austria
Lithuania	Croatia	

Women of Color Are the Most Fertile

The fertility rate (the total number of children the average woman is likely to have) ranges from seven or more children per woman in developing countries in Africa to around one child per woman in Eastern Europe. Certainly, the number of white females who choose to abort, remain childless, or have fewer children, contributes to the low white birth rate.

However, the skyrocketing demand for fertility drugs, fertility clinics, sperm banks, sperm donors, artificial insemination, in-vitro-fertilization, test tube babies, U.S. and overseas adoption mills tells a different story: **the rate of infertility among whites is increasing.**

Do All Races Practice Skin Color Supremacy?

Mr. Neely Fuller, Jr., in his 1969 Textbook for Victims of White Supremacy, described racism as a "universal operating system of white supremacy rule and domination in which the majority of the world's white people participate."

Mr. Fuller suggested that economic forms of government such as capitalism and communism were created to perpetuate white domination and that the white "race" is really an "organization" dedicated to maintaining control over the world. In addition, he argued that people of color have never imposed "colored" supremacy on anyone.

Some might argue that Mr. Fuller is incorrect, and that white supremacy is simply human nature, because it is natural to discriminate against people who look different. They might also add that slavery existed all over the world long before Europeans enslaved Africans 400 years ago.

Certainly, it is true that human beings of all races have enslaved other human beings throughout history, but this usually happened after the victors won a war or a conflict. The victors NEVER justified this enslavement with a system of SKIN COLOR SUPREMACY. If one looks at the overwhelming historical evidence, it appears Mr. Fuller's argument may be correct.

Countless battles have been fought between warring tribes throughout human history, but those tribes never justified these wars with a system of SKIN COLOR SUPREMACY. Nowhere on earth does a system of SKIN COLOR SUPREMACY exist EXCEPT among white people (Europeans).

If it was normal (human nature) for ALL races to kill and oppress other races based on skin color differences alone, there would be a HISTORY (and evidence) of such skin-color-based conflicts and systems. For example:

- Brown people would have developed a system of brown-skin supremacy
- Red people would have developed a system of red-skin supremacy
- Black people would have developed a system of black-skin supremacy
- Yellow people would have developed a system of yellow-skin supremacy

America -- as we know it -- would be a very different nation, as would most of the world, because Native Americans, Africans, and the first (black) Australians would have **murdered or enslaved the first European arrivals on sight, instead of helping them survive in the new world.**

Black Is Genetically Dominant/ White Is Genetically Recessive

NOTE: The authors do not pretend to have any scientific expertise. As is true in this entire book, the reader is free to accept or reject any theories or explanations presented here. The following is based on our own research and logically drawn conclusions:

According To The Genetic Phase Of Biology, Black Is Genetically Dominant, And White Is Genetically Recessive.

Ancient fossil discoveries in the late 1970s by Louis Leakey, a British/Kenyan archaeologist and anthropologist, and his expedition, concluded that the first man and woman originated in Africa.

If Mr. Leakey is correct that all human life began in Africa, it is logical to assume the African man and African woman are genetically capable of making all the colors of humanity, which includes black, red, yellow, brown, and white.

Genetically AND logically speaking, "brown" is just another shade of black; "red" is another shade of black; "yellow" is another shade of black; and "white" is another shade of black.

However, **politically** speaking, "white" is NOT a shade of black because white is a "non-color." How do we know this is true? White supremacy classifies ALL non-whites as "people of color," which means **white cannot be a color.**

Is There A Link Between Melanin And Fertility?

If the FERTILITY RATE per woman in developing countries in Africa ranges from seven or more children, and the fertility rate in Europe is one child per woman, we might draw some logical (but not necessarily scientific) conclusions:

1. Africans have more melanin than Europeans because dark skin has more melanin than light skin.
2. Africans have one of the highest fertility (birth) rates in the world.
3. Africans are genetically dominant (can produce all the skin colors, including black).
4. Therefore, Africans are in the LEAST danger of becoming genetically extinct -- except by artificial, man-made means (genocide).
5. Europeans have less melanin than Africans because light skin has less melanin.
6. Europeans have the lowest fertility (birth) rate in the world.
7. Europeans are genetically recessive (can only produce one color, which according to white supremacy is a non-color: white).
8. Therefore, Europeans are in the MOST danger of becoming genetically extinct (by natural selection).

Therefore, it is logical to assume there might be a connection between skin color, melanin, and fertility.

TRUTH IN CINEMA

"Children of Men" (2006). Plot: A science fiction film set in the year 2027. After two decades of global human infertility, in the midst of societal collapse, a miracle occurs. A young woman is pregnant; the first pregnancy on earth in 18 years. A government agent agrees to transport her to a safe sanctuary where scientists can study the birth of her child and hopefully save humanity from extinction. **The pregnant female is a young African woman.**

Contrary to white supremacy propaganda, dark skin is NOT a sign of genetic inferiority. In fact, "dark" usually represents the stronger (original) version while "light" usually (but not always) represents a weaker, diluted, or artificial version that lacks something that is found in the original.

"If you want bread with no nutritional value, you ask for white bread. All the good that was in it has been bleached out of it, and will constipate you. If you want pure flour, you ask for dark flour, whole-wheat flour. If you want pure sugar, you want dark sugar." -- Malcolm X

If the African man and woman possess the MOST MELANIN, it could mean Africans, genetically and biologically speaking, are *the most powerful people on the planet,* and the *greatest genetic threat to white survival.*

This would explain why dark-skinned black males are more likely to be unemployed, arrested, incarcerated, assaulted, or murdered by police than light-skinned and non-black men -- AND explains why the darkest-skinned black woman is the most degraded and demonized woman on the planet.

Are Black Females The Enemies Of White Genetic Survival?

Involuntary and Coerced Sterilization of Black Females

According to government documents, forced sterilization in the U.S. occurred from 1897 to the early 1980s. For example, the first sterilization law of 1929 in North Carolina, targeted the *"mentally ill, the retarded, and the epileptic"* to protect impaired (defective) people from parenthood.

Women were targeted for sterilization for being "promiscuous, lazy, unfit, or sexually uncontrollable" individuals. Since black women were assumed to be all the above, they made up 64% of all the women who were sterilized by 1964.

Charity Hospital in New Orleans, Louisiana became the only hospital to serve poor blacks from the 1960s to the 1980s. Unbeknownst to its poor black patients, this was the site of mass involuntary sterilization programs by the U.S. government.

Some black women reported that they were pressured to have a c-section (a caesarean) instead of a vaginal birth, only to later discover they had been "butchered" by a doctor who tied their tubes without their consent, rendering them infertile. *It is logical to assume that the secret sterilizations of black females are STILL happening today.*

Black Males: Enemies Or Allies of White Supremacy?

If blacks are genetically the most dominant, and whites are genetically the most recessive, blacks have the most (genetic) potential to make whites genetically extinct. Therefore, it is logical to assume blacks (and Africans) will be the **MAIN TARGETS** of global genocide.

This black genetic potential has fueled the FALSE belief and fear that the black male who breeds with the white female (and produces non-white offspring) is the biggest threat to white genetic survival.

In reality, it is just the opposite. The majority of these black male/white female relationships will not last, even if they have children together.

The Children Born Of Black Male/White Female Unions:

1. are more likely to be raised by single white mothers;
2. may have a closer, more sympathetic bond with the white side of their family, in particular, the white females;
3. likely to be white-identified;
4. more likely to breed with whites (or other non-whites with white parent)
5. more likely to produce offspring who will merge **undetected** with the white population.

The future generations of these black male/white female unions will produce whites who will be more fertile (due to the more melanated black male), resulting in an INCREASE in overall white fertility, which will possibly extend the life of **White Supremacy** and **Black Oppression.**

Therefore, the black male who breeds with the white female represents:

The single biggest threat to black liberation and are the biggest non-white allies of racism/white supremacy.

The Basic Instinct Of Every Species Is Genetic Survival

What does the smallest microorganism have in common with the most sophisticated human animal? **The instinctual drive to reproduce and perpetuate its own species.** Therefore, non-whites must ask themselves a critical question:

What is the most logical (and desperate) response of any species that fears extinction -- and has the sophisticated brainpower to address their inadequate numbers?

In the 1970s, South Africa developed race-specific bio-weapons to target blacks and Asians.

In September 2000, the Project for a New American Century published a document in which Dick Cheney described race-specific bio-weapons as "politically useful tools". (SOURCE: Alex Jones' "End Game" DVD, www. infowars.com)

It is up to the readers to decide the truth for themselves.

"A third fear involves a slightly different scenario -- a world in which non-white people might someday gain the kind of power over whites that whites have long monopolized...

And then what? Many whites fear that the result won't be a system that is more just, but a system in which white people become the minority and could be treated as whites have long treated non-whites.

This is perhaps the deepest fear that lives in the heart of whiteness. It is not really a fear of non-white people. It's a fear of the depravity that lives in our own hearts: Are non-white people capable of doing to us the barbaric things we have done to them?"

Robert Jensen, "The Fears of White People"(white professor, University of Texas)

CHAPTER 42

WHY WHITE SUPREMACY
WILL NEVER END VOLUNTARILY

Why would whites collectively --- who depend on a system that guarantees MORE privileges for people classified as "white" -- voluntarily END that system? This is a logical question all blacks should ask themselves:

Any group of people who CREATES an immoral and unethical system cannot be trusted to dismantle that system. Any group that BENEFITS UNFAIRLY from a system they CREATED knows it is NOT in their best interests to reveal the TRUTH about that SYSTEM to the group that is being PENALIZED.

It is crucial that non-whites understand that the system of white supremacy will NEVER be dismantled by those who created it; who depend upon it; and who benefit from it. No amount of begging, crying, pleading, marching, protesting, threatening, boycotting, tantrum-throwing, assimilating, integrating, self-hating, interracial dating, breeding, or marrying will eliminate racism/white supremacy.

13 Reasons White Supremacy Will Never End Voluntarily

Reason #1: "Whiteness" Is The Foundation Of White Supremacy

White supremacy could not exist without "whiteness." The only reason "whiteness" exists is to practice white supremacy. Racism could not exist without "race." The only reason "race" exists is to practice racism.

As explained in Chapter 19 (page 129) -- there is only one race: *the white race.* The "white race" is the ONLY so-called race that is able to practice racism. The only reason racism and white supremacy exist is to mistreat people based on color, who are classified as "non-white;" and who are falsely identified as the "black, brown, red, or yellow races." Therefore, "race" is a FALSE concept used to JUSTIFY mistreating people based on color (practicing race-ism).

Some "Whites" Are "Whiter" Than Other Whites

Even whites make a distinction between the "original settlers" -- the white Anglo-Saxon Protestants (WASPS) and the European (non-white) tribes that immigrated to America during the 1800s. For example, when the Irish immigrated to the U.S., they were NOT seen as white, and were given jobs considered too dangerous for slaves since black slaves were considered valuable property.

Noel Ignatiev, in his book, 'How The Irish Became White,' explains how the Irish were allowed to "become white" if they agreed to endorse and practice racism against blacks. The dark-complected Italian immigrants also faced rampant discrimination because of their lower caste (non-white) European status.

That being said, "whiteness" is NOT a fixed identity but can be "adjusted" on an *as-needed basis*. This is indisputable PROOF that "whiteness" is a **manmade concept; a code of behavior; and a political IDENTITY** that serves the NEEDS of the most powerful and privileged whites.

It is also proof that the white supremacy system can guarantee white privileges and benefits for all the people classified as white ONLY AT THE EXPENSE of those who are classified as non-whites.

If "whiteness" is a manufactured identity, then white superiority does NOT and CANNOT EXIST, and is based on LIES and DECEPTION, when it comes to "white superiority" in history, civilizations, inventions, ancient origins, histori- cal artifacts, music, art, science, medicine, cuisine, technology, and literature.

Reason #2: To Maintain The System Of White Supremacy, White Wealth, And White Privilege

When someone benefits from a system, they are understandably reluctant to change that system. For example, Coworker A makes 20% more than Co- worker B even though their jobs are identical. Eventually, Coworker B becomes suspicious and asks Coworker A about his salary. Coworker A avoids the ques- tion and denies he is treated any differently than any other employee.

He also hides the fact that he is related by marriage to the personnel man- ager. Coworker A knows it is to his advantage to avoid direct answers to Co- worker B's questions. Otherwise, Coworker B might take some action (like filing a lawsuit) that causes Coworker A to lose his "privileges."

Most people -- including Coworker A -- cling to the (often false) belief that they are honest and ethical people EVEN when they are benefiting from the mistreatment of others. This "belief" requires MASS SELF-DECEPTION on the part of those who benefit, and MASS DECEPTION towards those who are being mistreated. In a system of white supremacy, it is necessary to:

- convince non-whites they are NOT being mistreated
- convince non-whites they are disadvantaged because they are inferior
- convince whites they have earned advantages because they are superior
- convince whites that they are being mistreated by non-whites
- convince whites that non-whites deserve to be mistreated
- convince whites to keep silent even when racism is happening in front of them

Reason #3: Peer Pressure

Whites are subject to a great deal of peer pressure to be racist from racist whites, or at the least, to not interfere in the business of those who practice racism.

It is EXTREMELY RARE for any white person to do more than give lip service to eliminating racism because to do so would require him or her to give up the privileges and entitlements reserved for whites. It would also mean facing reprisals (and punishments) for breaking the "white code."

Reason #4: False White Innocence

In 1992, Jane Elliott, a white former schoolteacher turned anti-racist activist, appeared on the Oprah Winfrey show and conducted the following experiment without the knowledge of the studio audience:

Before the audience was seated in the studio, they were divided into two groups: the blue-eyed people and the brown-eyed people. The show's producers immediately escorted the brown-eyed people to their seats and offered them donuts and coffee in clear view of the blue-eyed people who were treated rudely and forced to stand for two hours. By the time the blue-eyed audience members were seated in the studio, they were furious.

Mrs. Elliott poured gasoline on the fire by saying their unruly behavior was proof that blue-eyed people were less intelligent and more violent than brown-eyed people.

Even after Mrs. Elliott revealed that the entire audience had been part of a social experiment on racism, most of the blue-eyed audience members continued to rant and rave about the way they had been treated. Mrs. Elliott calmly reminded them that being mistreated for two hours was nothing compared to dealing with racism on a daily basis.

"White people do not live in the same reality that people of color do," Mrs. Elliott explained. "We think that because we have all these freedoms, everybody else has them, too. That isn't the way it is."

For the first time in their lives, the blue-eyed audience members got a taste of real-life racism, and discovered that being mistreated for having the wrong eye (or skin) color was an infuriating and demoralizing experience. Regardless, most of the whites in the audience fiercely resisted Mrs. Elliott's message because to understand it would mean losing their imaginary (white) "innocence" about the cruelty and realities of racism.

It is logical to assume the white people who fought Mrs. Elliott's lesson the hardest, **were most likely the most guilty of practicing racism.**

Mrs. Elliott's REAL CRIME wasn't playing a trick on the blue-eyed people in the audience; it was breaking the unofficial, unspoken rule for whites in a white supremacy system: **never, ever admit or reveal PUBLICLY as a white person that white privilege exists.**

Reason #5: Guilt (AKA The Fear Of Being Exposed)

When non-whites bring up the subject of racism, many whites feel it is a personal indictment (attack) against them. Even when non-whites criticize the government, some whites become angry and defensive because they see these (white) government officials as extensions of themselves.

A week after Katrina devastated New Orleans in 2004, John W., a white employee, asked his black coworker, Joe S., if the government was lax in its rescue efforts because most of the people were black. When Joe said absolutely, Tom became defensive. *"Oh, so now you hate all white people?"*

This illogical, almost hysterical, response could mean John secretly agreed with his black coworker but still felt the need to justify the (white) government's actions. In addition, many white males identify with the powerful white males who run Corporate America and the US government in a desperate attempt to distance themselves from the (inferior) female and non-white masses.

This explains why so many poor and working-class white males cling to a Republican Party that has done nothing for poor and working-class white males.

The blatant racism of Katrina and the fear of guilt-by-association fueled John's reaction. Otherwise, there would have been no reason for him to take his black coworker, Joe's, criticism of the government so personally.

Non-whites should not take any comfort in white guilt. Guilt is non-productive for the victims of white supremacy because it rarely results in a change in the behavior of those who benefit from injustice. In fact, too much guilt actually has the opposite effect by creating resentment and a tendency to justify one's behavior rather than correct it.

Reason #6: Indifference

A white woman who identified herself as a "white supremacist" was asked the following question by her black interviewer: *"What do you think white people would do if the US government did to blacks what the German government did to the Jews?"*
"Nothing," she said.
"You don't think whites would say or do anything about it?"
"No, because it wouldn't be happening to us."

While this seems like a chilling response, it is an honest one. This is why it is crucial for non-whites to educate ourselves about the system of white supremacy, and to focus on CHANGING OUR BEHAVIOR, not wasting energy trying to change the behavior of those who practice AND benefit from racism.

Reason #7: The Unwillingness To Allow The Non-White Victims To Determine The Punishment For The Crimes Of Racism

The Victimizers should NEVER be allowed to dictate what their punishments or penalties will be; just like a prosecutor would not ask an armed robber how much prison time, if any, he should serve. Only the VICTIMS have the right to determine their damages, and what it will COST to make them whole again.

When the Victimizers are allowed to be their OWN judge and jury, the outcome is predictable: ***the victims never get the justice they deserve.***

Reason #8: White Supremacy Is The Biggest Mental Illness (And Addiction) On The Planet

Racism/white supremacy is an economic, political, and social system; a behavioral necessity (genetic survival); and a psychological addiction (a mental illness).

As long as racism/white supremacy benefits those who practice it, they will continue doing it. The more it is practiced, the more psychologically addictive it becomes. It is important that the Victims of racism UNDERSTAND that those who practice racism, ENJOY PRACTICING RACISM. If this were not the case, racism/white supremacy would not be the most dominant system on the planet.

Reason #9: Non-Whites Are Enablers Of White Supremacy

For white supremacy to function, the non-white majority on the planet must be convinced that they are so inferior to whites, and DESERVE to be exploited, mistreated, and murdered.

For example, there are five people in a room who are over six feet tall. A sixth person, who is five feet tall, enters the room, and announces that short people are superior to taller people. The shortest person in the room has never met the other five people, but is basing her superiority on their physical differences: their height.

The ONLY way the shortest person in the room can "prove" she is superior to the tallest people in the room, is to convince them that short is better than tall. However, if the tallest people in the room refuse to accept that definition of superiority, that superiority is NONEXISTENT.

In other words, for one person to be superior to another person, SOMEONE MUST AGREE TO BE INFERIOR. It doesn't matter what the "superior" person says, does, wears, owns, creates, or is able to do, UNLESS she can convince the other five people in that room to AGREE to be inferior, she cannot be SUPERIOR - except in her OWN mind. Following the logic:

- If non-whites did not COOPERATE with white supremacy, it could not exist.
- If non-whites did not betray, degrade, or mistreat other non-whites, white supremacy would not exist.
- If non-whites did NOT teach their children that white is superior by their words and deeds, white supremacy would not exist.
- If non-whites did NOT place whites on a pedestal economically, socially, intellectually, sexually, or romantically, white supremacy would not exist.
- If non-whites did NOT believe they were inferior AND agree to be inferior, white supremacy could not exist.

...because there is no way TEN PERCENT of the world's population could physically overpower the other NINETY PERCENT without their cooperation.

Reason #10: To Prevent Revenge/Retribution/AND Reparations For The Crimes Committed By Whites Against Non-Whites

When one group (the Victimizers) commits massive crimes against another group (the Victims), the Victimizers only have three choices:

1. To make amends to the Victims (massive reparations, giving up their unearned privileges, and dismantling their system of injustice)
2. To neutralize the Victims (keep them in an inferior position)
3. To exterminate the Victims outright (genocide)

If the Victimizers are NOT willing to make amends (lose their privileges, power, and wealth), and if it is NOT in their immediate best interest to exterminate their Victims, they must find a way to CONTROL them.

This is the ONLY way to guarantee the Victimizers' safety, prosperity, and superior position over their Victims. The Victimizers cannot allow their Victims to become whole, to unite with one another, or to gain ANY knowledge OR any advantage that will make them equal to (or greater than) their Victimizers -- because the TABLES MIGHT BE TURNED AGAINST THEM.

Reason #11: White Genetic Survival

"One of the greatest dangers the white world faces is our decreasing numbers. If we do not take drastic measures to reduce the non-white populations, we will face certain extermination or enslavement." -- a quote on the declining white birth rates (name withheld by request).

Reason #12: A Lack of Shame (Contrition)

On January 17, 2011, the Oprah Winfrey Show took *'A 25-Year Look Back on Race in the USA.'* There were numerous scenes where whites apologized to blacks for previous wrongs.

The whites in the audience were moved; the blacks were moved; even Oprah was moved. One older black male guest hoped that by watching the show, more (white) people will be moved, *"to stand up for what's right."*

Certainly, some blacks assume these seemingly heartfelt "apologies" will SHAME whites into dismantling the system of white supremacy. However, this (false) belief flies in the face of a 500-year reality.

Certainly, whites who practice racism KNOW they are harming non-whites, and whites who remain silent while other whites practice racism KNOW they are BENEFITING from mistreating non-whites.

It is time to GET REAL about our situation and FACE FACTS: No amount of TV shows, or Oprah "feel-good" moments will stop those who benefit from white supremacy from practicing it -- and SHAME has nothing to do with it. It has EVERYTHING to do with white genetic survival -- *by any means necessary.*

There Are Basically Two Types Of 'Shame:'

- **Inward Shame** -- is CONTRITION -- and often occurs in someone's most private moments when they are sincerely ashamed for something they have thought, said, or done *because they knew it was wrong.*

  Real "shame" does not require an audience, and is a highly motivating factor in CHANGING one's behavior, or making amends for previous wrongdoings.

- **Outward Shame** -- is the EMBARASSMENT at being publicly exposed or caught in the act of doing something other people disapprove of -- even if that person does not believe their behavior was incorrect (is not sorry).

  This type of "shame" does NOT CHANGE behavior, but actually increases the odds of deception. The person's true motivation is NOT shame, it is the fear of being exposed, ridiculed, opposed, or punished by their peers or their superiors. Their victims' feelings or pain has NO importance to them; only their own feelings are considered.

  For example, after Hurricane Katrina and the grossly cruel, inhumane, unjust, and RACIST mistreatment of blacks was exposed to the entire WORLD, white America was outwardly "ashamed" (embarrassed) at being publicly EXPOSED as RACISTS.

  This led to a very public and very well-advertised outpouring of help from the white collective -- even while those same whites were still practicing racism against blacks (and other non-whites).

  However, within days of the storm, black Katrina survivors were once again demonized and blamed by the US government, the white media, and the white collective for being abandoned and grossly mistreated by the own government.

  Embarrassment and the fear of EXPOSURE are the ONLY kinds of "shame" the Racist White Male and Racist White Female are capable of feeling when it comes to mistreating blacks (or other non-whites).

Reason #13: White Supremacists Love Their Work

The ONLY way white supremacy could have existed for as long as it has existed (over 500 years) *is the WHITE PEOPLE IN CHARGE and their white foot soldiers really enjoy their work and have NO INTENTION of stopping what they are doing: practicing racism.*

White genetic survival -- by any means necessary.

THE

CURE:

A
Black
Love
Revolution

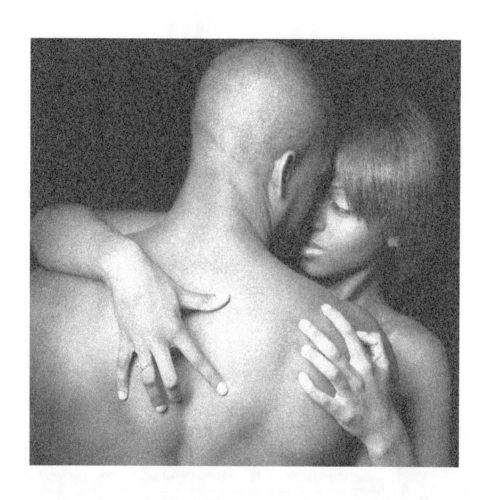

"The Revolution Will Not Be Televised." -- Gil Scott-Heron

CHAPTER 43

BLACK LOVE IS A
REVOLUTIONARY ACT

What is a Black Love Revolution?

A Black Love Revolution is a TRANSFORMATION of black minds, bodies, and spirits. It is a FUNDAMENTAL change in the way we THINK, SPEAK, and ACT towards one another. **Black Love** is cherishing our ancestors by acknowledging their pain and vowing to NEVER let our history repeat itself.

Black Love is having EMPATHY for those who are still suffering in a nation whose riches were built on our sweat, blood, and tears. **Black Love** is UNITY, standing together, protecting one another, and recognizing we are IN THIS TOGETHER. *Black love is belonging to each other again.*

Black Love is a RETURN to the kind of LOVE we once had for one another before we were robbed of the KNOWLEDGE OF SELF.

A **Black Love Revolution** is the love between a Black Man and his Black Woman; between a parent and a child; a sister and a brother; a neighbor or co-worker; an acquaintance or a stranger; *and a deep, abiding love for SELF.*

Is Black Love Taboo (In A White Supremacy Society)?

Absolutely. If the authors have accomplished NOTHING ELSE with this book, we hope we have proven beyond a doubt that there are powerful forces that are determined to destroy the bond between the black male and black female. *Why is Black Love taboo?* The answer is simple:

Black Love = Black Procreation = Black Population Increase = Black Unification = THE END OF WHITE SUPREMACY.

Which leads to another critical question:

Who Will Control The World's Most Valuable Resources? The Original Owners OR the Plunderers and Invaders?

Africa is the world's second largest continent after Asia. Africa has 70% of the world's cobalt, 90% of it's platinum, 40% of its gold, 98% of it's chromium, 70% of it's tantalite, 64% of manganese, one-third of it's uranium, 70% of the world's coltan (most mobile phones contain coltan), 30% of the world's diamond reserves, the world's largest exporter of bauxite, the largest undiscovered oil reserves in the world *and the birthplace of the MOST FERTILE SOIL AND THE MOST FERTILE PEOPLE ON THE PLANET.*

Our Enemies Know The Truth

"When you invade a place for its resources, you wipe out the indigenous population." -- movie, 'Battle: Los Angeles' (2011)

In the 2009 movie "2012," planet earth experiences a series of catastrophic, natural disasters that threaten to wipe out humanity, sparking a massive, secret project to build giant arks that will be able to withstand the coming floods.

The only people who can afford a ticket on the arks are wealthy whites. At the last minute, a small number of non-whites and poor whites are allowed on board. Where are the arks - filled with the last survivors on earth -- headed? ***The only place on earth where survival is possible: AFRICA.***

This movie left one critical question unanswered:

If the MAJORITY of survivors are wealthy whites, what are their plans for the African people who already inhabit (and OWN) the only continent left standing? The answer is OBVIOUS.

There Is No Mystery, The Signs Are Everywhere

Yet our enemies have managed to deceive us with their lies and false promises of racial equality while the mass destruction (genocide) of the African Man and Woman -- the ORIGINAL OWNERS of the most valuable land and resources on earth -- is being planned even as these words are being written. ***Our enemies know whoever controls Africa's wealth, controls the ENTIRE WORLD.***

The Most Powerful Act
A Black Male and Black Female Can Commit
Is To Love One Another

And we can start by...

Forgiving each other

What If Tomorrow Came And White People Had No Power Over Black People?

What if we woke up tomorrow and the world was a place where whites had no power over black people?

What if we lived in a world where black people generated our own power, pumped our own water, grew our own food, built and ran our own schools, manufactured our own products, policed our own communities, controlled our own elections, owned and managed our own corporations, land, resources, cities, towns, states, and nation?

What would happen if black people didn't need anything from white people because we could supply whatever we needed for ourselves?

Would blacks beg whites to validate and include us? Would black males put white females on a pedestal? Would black females give white males more respect than black males?

Would ANY black person EVER look in the mirror and think -- "I'm ugly because I don't look more white"?

If this world came into existence TOMORROW, would we change the way we think, feel, and act toward whites, toward other black people, and toward ourselves?

If the answers to all the above is "YES!" this should be a wake-up call to every black man and woman on the planet to:

CHANGE WHAT WE THINK, SAY, AND DO -- TODAY.

Epilogue:

A (still) Perfect Marriage

CHAPTER 44

A (STILL) PERFECT MARRIAGE (WITH A HAPPIER ENDING)

The "Perfect Couple"

They met in college through mutual friends. The moment he saw her, he knew she would be his wife. After twenty years of marriage, and three children, they still laugh at each other's jokes and cuddle like teenagers in darkened movie theaters.

They laugh, too, whenever their friends and family call them "the perfect couple," because no marriage was perfect. Secretly, they are proud to wear the label because their union had survived the marital storms that sank much weaker vessels.

As a daily reminder, an engraved plaque hangs on the wall above their bed: *"What God has joined together, let no man put asunder."*

The Unthinkable Happens

On a cold, moonlit night in their quiet suburban neighborhood, a shadowy figure slips in through the partially open kitchen window. The peacefully sleeping couple is startled awake by a flashlight shining in their faces.

The armed intruder -- a powerfully built man in a white Halloween mask -- orders the couple to strip naked, growling obscenities as the wife reluctantly complies.

There is the harsh rash of a zipper as the gunman loosens his pants. The husband and wife exchange a look of dread, but there is a resolve in their faces; in their eyes, that remains unspoken.

As the gunman moves toward the wife, she slaps her right hand over her heart and collapses to the floor in a dead faint. The armed intruder is caught off guard, since this wasn't part of his script. The husband lunges at the gunman. The two men are locked in a death grip, one trying to hold on to his gun; the other fiercely determined to take it.

The wife jumps to her feet, grabs a pair of scissors from the dresser and drives the tempered steel deep into the gunman's back. Shrieking with pain and rage, the intruder drops his weapon. The gun slides across the hardwood floor. Both men dive for it. The husband reaches it first but is tackled by the gunman, who is younger and more muscular.

The wife – a can of mace in hand – aims the spray right into the eye holes of the mask. The gunman screams. Stumbling, bleeding, and half-blinded, he rips the white mask off. The husband scrambles to his feet, aims, and pulls the trigger.

The sound is deafening, rattling the window panes, and filling the room and their nostrils with the acrid smell of gunpowder. The intruder is sprawled on the floor, eyes wide open. The entrance wound is a round hole the size of a dime in the center of his forehead.

Shaking, the wife dials 9-11, her eyes rising from the dead man on their bedroom floor to her husband, who is walking toward her. Their eyes meet, and to her surprise, he is smiling. It is a grim smile, but one filled with satisfaction for *a job well done.*

He did what every man would do – should do -- under the circumstances: protect his wife, his woman, his children, and his home. That's why they had discussed – had even rehearsed – what they would do if a stranger ever violated their home.

By the time the wife hangs up the phone, she's smiling, too, a brittle one edged with pride. Her husband had done what every woman expects her man to do under the circumstances: protect his wife, his woman, his children, and his home.

And she had done what every husband expects his wife, his woman, to do: to have this back and to risk her own life and safety – if necessary -- to back him up. While they waited for the police to arrive, they stood by the bed, hands clasped together, staring at the plaque above their bed. Their God had never abandoned them in their time of need; and he would not abandon them now.

No Regrets

It was a terrible thing that happened on that terrible night, but they made a silent pact that they would not cry, moan, or wring their hands with regret. There would be no false sadness or hollow statements about the "tragic death of another human being."

Because the intruder wasn't human, not in either of their eyes. He was a wild, vicious animal that had to be PUT DOWN. A VICTIMIZER, a RAPIST, and a THIEF OF PEACE, who would have viciously murdered a man whose only crime was protecting his wife and children.

They were relieved -- and ecstatic -- that the armed intruder in the white face mask was dead. Had they left him alive, even if he had been caught, convicted, and sent to prison, they would have to look over their shoulders for the rest of their lives, knowing revenge was always a possibility once his sentence was served. Who knows how many innocent victims had been spared by taking one depraved life?

This was not a time for tears or sadness; they had great reason to rejoice. They still had the perfect marriage.

Try To Imagine A Time...

When no VICTIMIZER, RAPIST, or THIEF OF PEACE would be able to beat, torture, strip naked, fondle, rape, or murder our daughters, sons, mothers, fathers, wives, or husbands in front of our eyes because we will GIVE OUR LIVES TO STOP THAT FROM EVER HAPPENING AGAIN.

And if you can't imagine that, try imagining this:

YOU will NEVER stand naked on any slave auction block, or prison intake line, and you will never put yourself OR your loved one OR your neighbor OR your neighbor's children in harm's way again because you are them and they are you, because we WILL BELONG TO EACH OTHER AGAIN; a DNA-connected community of African souls that reaches from continent to continent and all around the world.

To stop BLACK GENDER WARS, we must STAND TOGETHER, AND SHOUT in a TWO-BILLION-STRONG African voice:

"Never Again!!!"

"I freed thousands
of slaves. I could
have freed thousands
more, if they had
known they were
slaves."

Harriet Tubman
(1820-1913)

Black LOVE

Counter Warfare

"The art of war teaches us to rely not on the likelihood of the enemy's not coming, but on our own readiness to receive him; not on the chance of his not attacking, but rather on the face that we have made our position unassailable."

-- Sun Tzu,
'The Art of War' (544-496 BC)

CHAPTER 45

BLACK LOVE COUNTER WARFARE SOLUTIONS & SUGGESTIONS

What Is Counter-Warfare?

Counter-Warfare is a strategy of non-violent resistance to the system of racism/white supremacy, the most SOPHISTICATED MIND GAME ever designed. In self-defense, non-whites must develop an equally powerful counter-intelligence to neutralize the "mind games" by:

CHANGING THE WAY WE THINK (EDUCATION).
CHANGING OUR BEHAVIOR (CONSTRUCTIVE ACTIONS)

13 Counter Warfare Strategies

1. Recognize We Are At War
2. Admit We Have A Problem: Mentacide
3. Become Knowledgeable About the System Of White Supremacy
4. STOP Keeping White People's Secrets
5. STOP Obeying the "White Traffic Cop" Inside Your Head
6. The Theory of Non-Participation
7. Minimize Conflict (stop name calling & fighting)
8. Maintain A Psychological Distance From White People
9. Become Comfortable With Being Uncomfortable
10. Show Black Love Freely, Openly, and Publicly
11. Adopt The Mantra of Black Unity
12. 33 Rules of Disengagement
13. Become a Leader of One

The **Counter-Warfare Strategies** put the focus where it belongs: on what black people CAN and MUST do, NOT on what white people might OR should do. We did not get in this terrible condition overnight, and we will NOT solve our problems overnight. We cannot afford to waste any more time talking about what white people should do for us -- and find a way to do for SELF.

If we need better schools for our children, we must POOL our resources and CREATE better schools. If we need more jobs, we must POOL our resources and CREATE our own jobs.

We cannot afford to wait one second longer for "someone else" to end racism. *We have already waited 500 YEARS.* It is time to STOP begging, marching, and protesting. It is time to STOP expecting the white elite to eliminate the white supremacy system that was designed for their sole benefit. *All we will get is what we have always gotten: the false appearance of real change.*

The Real Revolution Takes Place Between Our Ears

As we watch the civil rights clock spinning backwards, it should be clear that despite all our "progress," black people still control nothing in America, including the ability to rescue one black person off a roof after Hurricane Katrina.

Once we become empowered (illuminated) with knowledge of self, and knowledge of how the system of racism/white supremacy works, we will attract other empowered individuals who seek real change – not the kind of "change" that is seen on television under the banner of a "National Convention."

We must stop deluding ourselves that such FALSE displays offer any real change. THEY DO NOT. They are simply updated dog-and-pony shows to pacify, deceive, and exploit the masses. We know from history that black leaders who TRULY advocate real change are NEVER rewarded, promoted, or given airtime by the same powerful elites who created the system of injustice.

Real change is not glamorous or pleasant. It has nothing to do with being popular, articulate, or presenting an attractive image. It does not happen while we sit in front of a television set, or walk into a voting booth and push a button. Real change is hard, dirty, and dangerous work.

Fortunately, none of the suggestions in this book are hard, dirty, or dangerous. They do not require money, special skills, talents, bravery, or bloodshed. In fact, most suggestions involve NOT doing something that wastes our precious time and money, or that harms us individually or collectively.

These recommendations (as well as the contents of this book) are a FRAME-WORK that the reader can adapt as he or she sees fit, and decide what is beneficial, constructive, and useful, and what is not. No one, including the authors of this book, represent the voice (or voices) of authority.

STRATEGY #1: RECOGNIZE WE ARE AT WAR

A Quick Summary Of Black America's Worsening Dilemma

Black labor has become obsolete in America. In many inner cities, the menial, low-skilled and low-paying jobs that poor blacks used to do -- and are still willing to do -- are farmed out for maximum profit to illegal (slave) labor. Automation (machines) and computers have eliminated the rest.

In spite of record unemployment for blacks, (estimated at over 35% in 2010), America is still importing unskilled AND skilled non-white labor from Latin America and India. The picture for educated, professional blacks in corporate America is just as dismal. Glass ceilings have turned to concrete. Unions, good jobs, benefits, and guaranteed pensions are becoming relics of the past.

As a result, the hard-won gains from civil rights and affirmative action over the last 40 years are being systematically wiped out. After two terms of the Bush Administration efforts, affirmative action is little more than a controversial and fraudulent memory that clearly ignored the FACT that the biggest beneficiaries of affirmative action were AND still are white females.

Black farmers have yet to receive compensation for stolen farmland and government discrimination. Blacks are losing land and houses at a record pace in dozens of predominantly black cities where gentrification (land grabs), subprime mortgages, reverse-redlining (targeting black areas for fraudulent home loans), foreclosures, and property tax and eminent-domain schemes designed to force blacks out of major cities – and out of their homes and communities.

In predominantly black schools all across the country, black children are mis-educated and under-educated by design, while many black schools are closing their doors for good. Black boys are being "tracked" into "special education classes" or "non-college prep" classes or expelled for minor offenses to DELIBERATELY destroy their intellectual potential and self-confidence.

The unrelenting onslaught of white Hollywood via the buffoonery comedies, sitcoms, and "reality shows" is polluting the minds and morals of black youth. White decision-makers and their black puppets deliberately pair the black male with anyone but a black female in movies, TV shows, TV commercials, and rap videos to divide and conquer (and demoralize) the black male and female.

Over one million black men and black women rot in penal institutions, many for non-violent drug "crimes," while white drug users of crack, powdered cocaine, prescription drugs, and meth get "intervention," drug treatment, fines, or a slap on the wrist for their "illness." To add more injuries to the massive injuries inflicted on Black America by America's "criminal" justice system, prison authorities callously turn a "blind eye" to the epidemic of inmates AND guards raping other inmates.

Rampant homosexuality flourishes in prisons where black males in their sexual prime are forced to live in cages with other sexually frustrated males. It is NO accident that black ex-felons infected with HIV, AIDS, & Hepatitis C are deliberately released back into the black community without education, job skills or medical treatment for their contagious diseases.

It is UNDENIABLE that the white supremacy system and their white foot-soldiers are waging a VICIOUS WAR against black people on four levels: educational, economic, psychological, and reproductive.

It is also increasingly clear that (white) America has no patience or sympathy for poor (or "uppity" blacks), and is rapidly and quietly building more prisons while it closes black schools in preparation for...what?

$104 Million Dollar Juvenile Detention Center To Be Built East Baltimore – while city is closing predominantly black schools (SOURCE: Our Weekly, Nov 11, 2010, http://ourweekly.com/los-angeles/104-million-juvenile-detention-facility-be-built)

What is White America's plan for black youth?

THE ANSWER SHOULD BE OBVIOUS.

STRATEGY #2: ADMIT WE HAVE BEEN DAMAGED BY 500 YEARS OF OPPRESSION AND ARE STILL SUFFERING FROM "MENTACIDE"

To be a white-identified black is MENTACIDE – the destruction of what should be a black-centered, self-respecting, and self-loving mindset. The late Dr. Bobby Wright, who popularized the term "mentacide," defined it as: *"the deliberate and systematic destruction of a group's mind with the ultimate objective being the complete extermination of the group."*

Scholar and author Dr. Mwalimu K. Bomani Baruti offers this explanation: *"When you willingly think and act out of someone else's interpretation of reality to their benefit and against your survival. It is a state of subtle insanity, which has come to characterize (more and more) Africans globally."*

It is UNDENIABLE that the black community is having an moral and spiritual crisis that no amount of money or material things can heal. We have allowed our black "heroes" and role models to be chosen (by the white media) on the basis of fame and money -- NOT on the content of their characters.

We have gone from a people who would risk life and limb fighting for the rights of ALL BLACK PEOPLE to a people who are disconnected from the pain and suffering of our OWN kind.

We claim to be "black and proud" yet seldom pass up the opportunity to condemn and stereotype each other for the entire world to see. We ridicule our beautiful African features while denying that we secretly hate the man or woman in the mirror.

We teach our children -- by example -- to dislike and disrespect themselves and then look on in puzzled frustration as our black children increasingly choose the road to self-destruction and despair.

If we are doing well economically, we blame those who have not been so lucky, even if we KNOW the system of white supremacy will ONLY allow a small minority of blacks to "achieve" the American Dream.

If we want to heal our BLACK NATION, we must put aside our (false) EGOS and BELIEFS and ADMIT WE ARE SICK. Like any crack addict, blacks in America must kick our addiction to WHITE SUPREMACY CRACK and ADMIT we have been programmed to see other black people AND ourselves THROUGH CONDEMNING WHITE EYES. It is time to TELL OURSELVES THE TRUTH.

Let TRUTH Become Our Drug Of Choice

STRATEGY #3: BECOME KNOWLEDGEABLE ABOUT THE SYSTEM OF WHITE SUPREMACY AND OUR TRUE STATUS IN IT

"If you do not understand White Supremacy (Racism), what it is, and how it works, everything else that you understand, will only confuse you."
-- Neely Fuller, Jr. (1971)

Until we understand WHAT white supremacy is and HOW it functions, we will NOT understand what is happening to non-white people all over the planet. We can't create solutions until we understand the problems, the same way we can't build a house without building a foundation. What we will wind up with is a shaky, unsafe building that will topple when the first storm hits.

In the RESOURCES section (page 401) there is a list of books, CDs, DVDs, and websites that will increase your understanding of white supremacy so you will recognize HOW and WHEN it is being practiced.

STRATEGY #4: STOP KEEPING WHITE PEOPLE'S SECRETS

Tell your children the TRUTH about racism/white supremacy

Jewish parents know how important it is to teach their children about the Jewish Holocaust so their children will KNOW they must be vigilant against their enemies. One reason so many black parents shy away from teaching our children about racism or slavery *is we do not know enough about our history to teach anyone else. (Strategy #3).*

Once black parents understand how the system of white supremacy works, they will understand how important it is to make their children aware of WHAT is happening -- and WHY it is happening to black people all over the world.

We must STOP pretending and lying to ourselves that we should let our children "make up their own minds about race," and prepare them for the psychological attacks they will face both inside (the television/movies) AND outside the home (the white supremacy system).

If we do NOT prepare them, we should be prepared for our children to be psychologically devastated when the TRUTH hits them square between their eyes. It is a CRIME to let another generation of black children come out into a racist society without PREPARING them for what WE KNOW they will face in the white world.

ELIMINATE phrases like "good hair," pretty (light) skin color, pretty (light) eyes, and bad (nappy) hair from your vocabulary. Do NOT allow anyone to degrade black people in front of your children and explain WHY you object to it.

Encourage your children to question everything they see and hear, give them TRUTHFUL answers, and let them express their opinions. Let them know there are NO STUPID QUESTIONS, but you may not know all the answers.

Black children are born with *an abundance of intelligence* until the media, educational system, racist whites, and unconscious black adults kill their confidence, self-esteem, and intellectual potential.

Replace television watching and video games (that do all the THINKING for them) with books, games, and toys at teach them to THINK ANALYTI-CALLY and use their creative and motor skills, like building blocks, puzzles, and chemistry sets. If we want our children to be able to compete intellectually with children from every part of the world, the time to prepare them is RIGHT NOW.

STRATEGY #5: STOP OBEYING THE WHITE TRAFFIC COP IN YOUR HEAD

Since slavery, blacks have been programmed to act against our own self-interests, survival, and humanity for the benefits of whites. THINK FIRST before speaking to, acting against, or harming another black person.

Understand that ANYTHING that harms another black person HELPS the system of white supremacy maintain its power -- which is why blacks are rewarded for hurting and betraying each other.

Ask yourself, "whose eyes am I using when I judge other black people?" Remember -- when we condemn black people for BEING BLACK, we are CONDEMNING OURSELVES -- and our CHILDREN.

Before you SPEAK or ACT, ASK yourself: do my actions make me part of the solution or part of the problem? Will my speech OR actions make this world a better, safer place for my children and grandchildren -- or will my words and actions make things worse?

STRATEGY #6: THE THEORY OF NON-VIOLENT/NON-PARTICIPATION

NON-PARTICIPATION is the most powerful weapon we possess. We have the freedom to NOT PARTICIPATE in those things that demean or short-change black people. This includes NOT spending our hard-earned dollars where they are not respected.

For example, in 2007, at the biggest fashion events in New York City, Paris, and Italy, top American and European designers, like Jil Sander, Burberry, Bottega Veneta, Roberto Cavalli, and Prada had no black runway models.

"I am virtually never allowed to photograph black models for the magazines, fashion houses, cosmetic brands, perfume companies, and advertising clients I work for. Whenever I ask to use a black model I am given excuses such as, '...black models do not reflect the brands values.'"
-- Fashion photographer, Nick Knight.

Despite the lack of black representation on the runways, in high-fashion advertising, and behind the scenes of the fashion industry, blacks have plenty of representation at the cash registers when we collectively spend billions on designer clothing, accessories, shoes, and apparel.

Utilizing the POWER of NON-PARTICIPATION, we would STOP begging (or demanding) to be included, and STOP BUYING WHERE WE CAN'T WORK. No dialogue would be necessary. Our CONSTRUCTIVE ACTIONS would speak for themselves. A constructive (and self-respecting) response to the racism in the fashion industry would be:

"They don't have to hire blacks for their fashion shows. They have the right to hire (or not hire) whoever they see fit. They can do their thing, and we'll do our thing. Just understand this "thing" cuts both ways. We don't have to include them in our shows OR spend our money with them, either."

The black collective would then spend our fashion dollars with our black designers and turn their wonderful creations into OUR fashion status symbols. To take a page out of the white economic book, non-black designers could participate ONLY *if they hire blacks and advertise in black-owned media.*

We would REFUSE to PARTICIPATE or SUPPORT ANY people, places, and things that do not respect our dollars, and START CIRCULATING those precious dollars in our own communities.

STRATEGY #7: MINIMIZE CONFLICT

MINIMIZE conflict at home, at work, in public, and at all places. Avoid unnecessary contact with people who seek conflict with you. The powers-that-be use conflict to divide and conquer the black male and female.

According to the *"United Independent Compensatory Code/System/Concept"* by Neely Fuller, Jr., there are **Ten Basic Stops** that help to eliminate Racism and produce Justice for all Victims of Racism:

1. Stop Snitching (to get ahead of someone else)
2. Stop Name-Calling (describe what a person does or says rather than calling them a name. For example, instead of calling a person a "liar," repeat what they said and say that what was said was "not true."
3. Stop "Cursing" (because it is insulting and demeaning, and promotes conflict, hostility, and violence).
4. Stop Gossiping (saying something ABOUT a person that we would not be willing to say directly to that person with others listening).
5. Stop Being Discourteous (showing a lack of consideration or acting or speaking in such a way that shows little to no regard for how others will be affected).
6. Stop Stealing (because it promotes injustice and places a greater value on "things" than on people or justice).
7. Stop Robbing (using the threat of bodily harm to take something from another person that does not belong to you promotes injustice).
8. Stop Fighting (if people cannot talk in a way that minimizes conflict, they should avoid contact with each other. No contact, no conflict).
9. Stop Killing (except in direct defense of self, others, and/or major property, it is best to avoid killing or maiming another person).
10. Stop Squabbling Among Yourselves And Asking Racists (White Supremacists) To Settle Your Problems (because racists often create situations where blacks are encouraged to squabble among themselves. Racists do not approve of black people solving heir own problems among ourselves without the so-called "help" of the WHITE PEOPLE IN CHARGE who created the problems in the first place because that does not promote White Supremacy.

Minimize Conflict. No contact; no conflict.

STRATEGY #8: MAINTAIN A PSYCHOLOGICAL DISTANCE FROM WHITE PEOPLE

During times of WAR, the military trains its soldiers to see the opposing army as less than human – NOT for sport or entertainment - but to maintain a psychological distance (a toughness) so the soldier will be able to kill another human being even when killing goes against his or her conscience or morality.

EXAMPLE:

During and after slavery, black women performed domestic and maternal duties for their white slave-owner OR white employer. Black women nursed white babies at their breast, raised the white children, cooked the white family's food; cleaned the white family's home, and were often (told) they were "just like one of the family."

But at the end of the day OR if that black female stepped over the invisible line separating black from white, she was quickly, and often severely reminded that she was still a "nigger." The white family SAID the black female was "just like family," YET they STILL MAINTAINED A PSYCHOLOGICAL DISTANCE from her (as a black person) so they would be able to:

- practice racism even if their actions are immoral, unjust, or cruel
- MAINTAIN the system of white supremacy and white privilege

It is MANDATORY to maintain a PSYCHOLOGICAL DISTANCE from your enemies during times of WAR, or you will have NO EMOTIONAL OR PSYCHOLOGICAL DEFENSES against them.

A Black Man's Constructive, Self-Respecting "Conduct Code" For White Females (Maintaining A Psychological Distance)

"My interactions with White females have totally changed. I try my best to not to treat a White female as a female without being discourteous or non-constructive.

- *I avoid unnecessary contact with them.*
- *I avoid unnecessary communication with them.*
- *I avoid 'reckless eyeballing' or even noticing a White female visually.*
- *I refrain from complimenting a White female in anyway unless it is for a constructive purpose especially in the area of sex.*

Anything that benignly 'defeminizes' White females in relation to me so that I am not manipulated with sex, or promises of sex, or hopes of sex and sexual play. They get the idea it seems. Unfortunately, I may have hurt some White females' feelings in the process of adapting this personal code but that's business.

It's as though they realize that I am doing things that no one at the job is doing in relation to them, and its as though that its not decent to show no sexual interest in White females.

Females seek validation from males and vice versa. It reminds a person of their gender roles and gender expectation in people relations, and it's essential to a person's sanity. Remove that validation and it will affect that person especially females. When a man ignores a woman's femininity its like taking way their 'rights' or 'powers' as a woman, which means they can't function as a female and they may doubt their femininity.

One of the reasons for this behavior is to create and maintain self-respect. Another reason for this is to reduce the chance that I can be seduced by a White female in order to be manipulated or fooled for their gain and my loss.

Another reason is to insure that you are taken seriously and not for granted to also insure that you are in the most advantageous position possible. Another reason is that I think that a White female will have more respect for a man that does not objectify them especially if he is Black, considering all of the stereotypes.

Another reason is most White females are less likely to ask you 'why do you not treat me like a lady', consequently they will be puzzled that a male especially a Black male is de-feminizing them if they even guess that's occurring.

This means that the Black male has the power in that situation because the White female will always thirst for an answer to why you treat her like she has a penis instead of a vagina and two breasts. All of this equals to power and actually empowers Black females when they are made aware of what you are doing they love it, which means I love it.

On the other hand, I have greatly improved my relations with non-white females by focusing all my masculine energy on them and trying to over validate them and I have gotten some very, very good results.

None of this is easy its requires a lot of work and discipline but this is War. It is also not easy for because I'm an art student, and at School their lots of White females. And no matter what I am a male and as far as the laws of attraction go anything is possible that's why this requires training and discipline. Think of my suggestion as one way to counter this bleaching down process."-- Black Mergatroid (2010)

For those who think Black Mergatroid's response is unreasonable, let's look at the "Conduct Code" that has been used by white males for over 500 years.

The White Male's Conduct Code For Non-White Females (To Maintain White Supremacy)

"My interactions with non-white females have changed little in the last 500 years. I avoid unnecessary contact with them if I cannot be in a dominant position or unless it involves sexual intercourse. I avoid unnecessary communication with non-white females except in the course of conducting business (making a profit) or promoting white interests (white supremacy).

I avoid 'reckless eyeballing' or even noticing a non-white female visually, especially when other whites are around. I refrain from complimenting non-white females in public, although I may do it privately (when other whites are not around), and expressly for the purpose of having sexual intercourse.

Anything that 'de-feminizes' non-white females in relation to me is done so I do not diminish white supremacy/superiority by being manipulated with sex, promises of sex, or hopes of sex and sexual play with non-white females.

Non-white females get the idea it seems, that in the white man's eyes, they will NEVER be equal to the white female. I may have hurt some non-white females feelings in the process but that's (the) business (of white supremacy).

They do NOT realize I do these things because I am part of a (white) organization that is dedicated to maintaining white supremacy, which means white males should NOT show any sexual interest in non-white females in the presence of other whites; especially in the presence of white females.

Females seek validation from males and vice versa. It reminds a person of their gender roles and gender expectation in people relations, and it's essential to a person's self-esteem. Remove that validation and it will affect that person, especially females.

When a man ignores a woman's femininity its like taking way their 'rights' or 'powers' as a woman which means they can't function as a female and they may doubt their femininity because it's important that non-white females believe they are inferior to white females.

Another reason is to reduce the chance that I can be emotionally seduced by a non-white female and be manipulated or fooled, which means a loss for me as a white man, the white race, and the system of white supremacy.

Another reason is to insure that whites are taken seriously and to insure the most advantageous position possible for whites. Another reason is white females have more respect or consideration for a white man who does NOT treat non-white females as their equals.

Another reason is most non-white females will not DARE ask a white man, 'why do you not treat me like a lady', because they do not understand that's my INTENTION: to de-feminize and dehumanize them so I will not be too compassionate toward them.

By doing so, the white male maintains the most power in that situation since the non-white female will always accept her inferior status when you treat her like she has a penis instead of a vagina and two breasts.

All of this equals to power and actually empowers white females when they are made aware of what we (white males) are doing; they love it which means I love it. By doing so, I have greatly improved my relations with white females by focusing all my masculine energy on them and trying to over validate them and I have gotten some very, very good results.

None of this is easy its requires a lot of work and discipline but this is War. It is also not easy because I'm an art student, and there are many, many beautiful and sexually desirable black and non-white females in my city who I would love to paint (nude) -- and do a lot more. And no matter what I am a male and as far as the laws of attraction go anything is possible that's why this requires training and discipline.

There are a minority of white males who sex and marry non-whites, but this still maintains the system of white supremacy because they usually get the pick of the black and non-white litter, which neutralizes these females and stops them from reproducing with non-white males. Think of my suggestion as one way to counter the browning of White America and the destruction of white supremacy.

***

Maintaining a PSYCHOLOGICAL DISTANCE from white people has NOTHING to do hating white people. It is a WAR-TIME STRATEGY that whites have used successfully against non-whites for hundreds of years -- **and it has been extremely successful.**

STRATEGY #9: BLACK PEOPLE MUST BECOME COMFORTABLE WITH BEING UNCOMFORTABLE

"We must become comfortable with being uncomfortable." – Gus Renegade, host of the C.O.W.S. radio (www.contextofwhitesupremacy.com).

The suggestions in this chapter will make some readers uncomfortable. The idea of using psychological counter-warfare against whites makes some blacks literally sweat under the collar.

However, if we are not extremely "uncomfortable" with racism, police brutality, murder-by-cop of unarmed black men and women, inferior black schools, unjust incarcerations, and economic, housing, and employment discrimination -- *nothing should make us uncomfortable.*

STRATEGY #10: SHOW 'BLACK LOVE' OPENLY AND PUBLICLY

Black Men and Women, black husbands and wives, black mothers and fathers, black sons and daughters, black sisters and brothers, black parents and children should show AFFECTION OPENLY and PUBLICLY.

It is especially important for parents to show love for each other OPENLY AND PUBLICLY in front of their children, so your children will KNOW it is NORMAL and DESIRABLE for black men and women to LIKE, LOVE, and SEXUALLY DESIRE EACH OTHER.

It is ONLY in the Western culture (and mind) that normal sexual and affection between black males and black females is considered WRONG (dirty), -- while black homosexuality is openly encouraged AND rewarded.

Showing LOVE should not be restricted to family members or romantic or sexual partners. LOVE should not be restricted to blood relations. LOVE is showing KINDNESS AND COURTESY OPENLY AND PUBLICLY to all black people -- even strangers -- so our black children will LEARN it is **NORMAL and DESIRABLE** for Black Men and Black Women to RESPECT and CARE ABOUT EACH OTHER.

Of course, we courtesy should be extended to all people but our MAIN FOCUS should be on repairing the bonds between the black male, female, and child that were destroyed during slavery and 500 years of racist oppression. Do NOT be discouraged if a "sick" person does not respond to your "kind treatment." *Push on AND keep planting the seeds of UNITY.*

We MUST love each other like our children's lives depend on it -- because they DO.

STRATEGY #11: ADOPT THE 'MANTRA OF BLACK UNITY' AND MAKE THIS OUR NEW BLACK NATIONAL ANTHEM

When you attack one of us, you attack ALL of us.

When you attack Black Men, you attack ME, (a Black Woman) because I came from a Black Man. When you attack Black Women, you attack ME, (a Black Man) because I came from a Black Woman.

When you degrade, stereotype, or harm ONE OF US, you harm ME because mistreating ONE is the same as mistreating ALL OF US.

STRATEGY #12: THE 33 RULES OF DISENGAGEMENT

Stop Showing Off, Bragging, And Talking Too Much

1. STOP styling, profiling, bragging, and boasting about who you are, what you look like, or what you have. It matters more WHO you are when no one is looking.
2. STOP showing off or trying to impress white people. *They don't care.*
3. ALL opposition to racism should be constructive and promote justice and correction; not avenge racial wrongs. If the offending parties refuse to stop practicing racism, replace dialogue with constructive self-help strategies.

Sex & Relationships

4. STOP HAVING SEX WITH STRANGERS, acquaintances, and people we are not committed to. Sex is SPIRITUAL as well as PHYSICAL. Every time we have sex with another person, we absorb the spiritual nature (good or bad) of our sexual partner, and this becomes part of OUR spiritual nature.
5. STOP HAVING UNPROTECTED SEX outside of marriage. This will limit the spread of venereal diseases, manmade viruses, the number of unplanned pregnancies, and at-risk, neglected children.
6. STOP HAVING SEX FOR MONEY and material things. You do not have to stand on a street corner to be a PROSTITUTE. If you are selling your precious body for a promotion, favors, money, or things, *you are PROSTITUTING yourself.* This is true for males and females.
7. STOP MAKING BABIES if you are not in a committed marriage with a committed partner. We must break the generational curse of the dysfunctional black family and at-risk black children.
8. STOP HAVING CHILDREN YOU ARE NOT WILLING OR ABLE TO RAISE, love, nurture, provide for, and protect. This will break the generational curse of the dysfunctional black family and at-risk black children.
9. STOP HAVING BABIES to hang on to a man or a woman. If they don't want you, why do you want them? *Above ALL else -- respect yourself.*

Stop Worshipping Money And Material Things

10. STOP CHOOSING ROLE MODELS for our children because they are rich. Stop looking to strangers to be "role models" and become your own children's role models. Children need role models at eye-level: parents, adults, teachers, police officers, firefighters, and the businesspeople in their communities.
11. STOP TEACHING OUR CHILDREN TO LOOK OUTSIDE THEMSELVES and teach them to VALUE what is already inside. If we help build them their self-respect and self-esteem from the gifts GOD gave them, our children won't need black role models, superstars, showcase blacks, false prophets, political pimps, Holy White Grails, OR white validation.

Self-Respect/Self-Reliance

12. STOP DEMANDING RESPECT from other people. You do not have a social contract with everyone you meet. The only person who is obligated to respect you is YOU. Unless someone's behavior harms you (other than hurting your feelings), the most POWERFUL RESPONSE is to put them on IGNORE. Worry MORE about respecting yourself.

13. WE DO NOT CONTROL ANYTHING in a white supremacy system but OURSELVES. We cannot out-police the police; outspend the super-rich; out-fight the military; or out-televise the networks, BUT we do have control over the most important possession we own: OURSELVES. We can refuse to participate in anything that degrade, demean, and destroys black people.

14. STOP DOING THOSE THINGS THAT REQUIRE FREE WILL and work against our individual and collective interests. For example, no one can make us buy, listen to, or watch a CD, movie, or DVD that degrades black people.

15. STOP PRAISING BLACK PEOPLE because they are bi-racial or their skin color, hair, skin, and eyes makes them look more white than black. What does that say about YOU (and your self-esteem) if you look more "black?"

16. STOP SUPPORTING BLACK ENTERTAINERS, artists, politicians, poets, filmmakers, scholars, and activists who degrade black people by promoting negative stereotypes.

17. STOP DISRESPECTING BLACK PEOPLE. No one can make us disrespect black people or call black people foul names. No one can make us turn against our mothers and fathers, wives and husbands, sons and daughters, or neighbors. No one can make us replace love with hate. No one can make us place a white woman or white man on a sexual pedestal, or knock a black man or black woman off one.

18. STOP PARTICIPATING IN ACTIVITIES THAT DESTROY THE BLACK COMMUNITY. For example, if we stopped using drugs, the drug dealers would be forced to find another profession. If we refused to buy stolen merchandise, the burglars, robbers, and thieves would be forced to find a legitimate source of income instead of victimizing their communities and filling up the nation's prisons. If we refused to buy or watch degrading movies, TV shows, and music videos, *they would stop making them*.

19. STOP EXPECTING WHITE PEOPLE TO SOLVE OUR PROBLEMS. It is OUR responsibility to solve our own problems because we have the most to lose if we don't.

20. BECOME YOUR OWN AUTHORITY on the things that affect your life and family. We must become our own authority (educate ourselves) so we cannot be deceived OR intimidated by those who practice racism.

21. STOP WORKING AGAINST THE INTERESTS OF BLACK PEOPLE. In other words, the system of white supremacy requires our COOPERATION and PARTICIPATION in harming other black people.

Save The Children & The Black Family

22. TAKE CONTROL OF THE EDUCATION OF OUR BLACK CHILDREN so their intellectual potential will not be destroyed by the anti-black educational system. We must start our own independent school systems so we can empower our children with the TRUTH, instead of allowing them to be poisoned by LIES -- and an inadequate education.

23. STOP LETTING THE RADIO, TELEVISION, VIDEO, AND DVDS RAISE YOUR CHILDREN. Spend more FAMILY TIME talking, at the bookstore, the playground, and the library.

24. TURN OFF THE TELEVISION AND STEREOS (once in a while) and read a book (like this one) in front of your children. Our children imitate what they see us do -- NOT what we tell them to do.

25. TEACH OUR CHILDREN TO LOVE THE WRITTEN WORD. If our children are taught to love the written word, they will always be in the LEARNING MODE. Blacks adults must educate themselves by reading books (like this one), and encourage the massive intellectual power of our children.

26. TEACH YOUR CHILDREN TO LOVE THE WRITTEN WORD. The reason slaves were punished for reading is the slave-owners knew READING led to THINKING. The same thing is true today. The average black public school deliberately makes LEARNING boring, humiliating, and painful. If our children hate to read (or learn), they will be forced to rely on their enemies for information -- and everything else they need.

27. DO NOT CONDUCT ILLEGAL AND DISHONEST ACTIVITIES IN FRONT OF YOUR CHILDREN or accept the reality that your children will not respect you even while they IMITATE you.

28. STOP FUSSING AND FIGHTING WITH YOUR CHILDREN'S MOTHER OR FATHER. Our children must take priority over our own selfish ego interests. We made the decision to have them (or didn't make the right decision to NOT have them). Our children did not ask to be born. We must NOT make them pay for our foolishness.

29. ADOPT THE 80% RULE FOR BUILDING STRONG MARRIAGES AND FAMILIES. Each partner giving 50-50 means BOTH are half-ass, half-stepping. If each partner gives 80%, there will always be a SURPLUS (160% total effort) of love, care, empathy, support, and CONSTRUCTIVE ACTIONS. If your partner is willing to give only 50% or less, it may be time to get a new partner. If this applies to you, it may be time for serious self-analysis or to consider the OPTION of being alone).

Politics

30. HOLD ALL BLACK POLITICIANS TO THE HIGHEST POSSIBLE STANDARDS. Demand to know WHAT they are going to do for us, not what they think we should be doing for ourselves BEFORE they get our votes. Demand that all black politicians treat black voters with the same respect they give non-black voters.

31. UNDERSTAND THAT A POLITICIAN IS A POLITICIAN IS A POLITICIAN. A POLITICIAN IS NOT A PREACHER. We do not need them to preach at us, we need to know what they are GOING TO DO FOR US IF WE VOTE THEM INTO OFFICE. If, after ONE term, they cannot prove they are working in the black collective's best interests -- VOTE THEM OUT OF OFFICE.

32. BLACK CIVIL RIGHTS ORGANIZATIONS THAT ARE FUNDED BY OUTSIDERS (non-blacks) should be automatically suspect. Everyone has an agenda. Until we know what their agenda is, they should not be trusted.

33. DO NOT TRUST the "Showcase Blacks" who are used to wow and amaze us. Their "success" has NOTHING to do with progress for the black masses. Black progress can only be measured by what happens to the black masses, not to a few handpicked blacks. Even the cruelest master must throw his starving dog an occasional bone to keep it loyal AND to keep the dog from attacking its tormentor. (Yes, we are the starving dogs, not the masters).

STRATEGY #13: BECOME A "LEADER OF ONE"

1. **BECOME A LEADER OF ONE**. Once the INDIVIDUAL is empowered, they do not depend on other people to do the right thing.

2. The empowered individual raises EMPOWERED CHILDREN. This also ensures that a "movement" does not rest on the shoulders of one man or one woman. An empowered individual is spiritually CONTAGIOUS – if their actions are just, constructive, and righteous. The empowered individual can spread the gospel in a way a so-called national leader cannot.

3. The empowered individual leads by example; the national leaders CANNOT because most have already been purchased, bribed, or threatened into cooperating with our enemies. They are the wily foxes in sheep's clothing and the false prophets who will lead the (black) sheep to slaughter.

4. Most civil rights organizations are like sprinters. They start off running at full speed and are out of steam – and ideas -- before the end of the race for justice. The empowered individual is a marathon runner; in the race for the duration. The empowered individual is a LEADER OF ONE and does not get frustrated as easily as those whose power comes from a group, because he (or she) is NOT totally dependent on what a GROUP does OR does not do, and is not disabled because a so-called "leader" is disabled.

5. By choosing NOT to participate in those things that demean or degrade black people, we increase our PERSONAL POWER and SELF-RESPECT.

6. You cannot control anyone but yourself. By making more self-respecting decisions, you will influence others around you – even those that try to make you look or feel foolish.

7. BECOMING A LEADER OF ONE means you are making a powerful change from low to HIGH SELF-RESPECT. This may frighten and intimidate those who are still locked into self-disrespecting behavior. Do not let them discourage you. Before you know it, they will be singing your praises.

8. If you have children, teach by example. When your children hear you say you refuse to do X or Y because it is disrespectful or harmful to black people – *they are listening to you.* We must plant the right seeds in our children if we want to grow flower gardens instead of weeds.

9. **STUDY THE SYSTEM OF RACISM/WHITE SUPREMACY** so you will understand how it works. You cannot defeat racism if you do not understand how racism/white supremacy works.

10. STOP ASKING (BEGGING) for inclusion into a club (the White Supremacy system) that does NOT want you as a member. If you become a "token member," you become part of the problem, NOT the solution.

11. POOL OUR SKILLS, RESOURCES, MONEY, AND TALENT to benefit and enrich the black collective instead of making other communities stronger and richer with our dollars.

12. STOP TRUSTING SHOWCASE BLACKS simply because they are black. Being a black "first" does not mean they will work on our behalf. Pay MORE attention to what they DO (or don't do) and LESS on what they say.

13. STOP HATING ON OTHER BLACK PEOPLE. When we pull someone UP, we pull ourselves UP. Encourage the CONSTRUCTIVE efforts and ambitions of other black people because those efforts help the entire black collective.

The Power Of Universal Karma = The Universal Boomerang

The **Universal Boomerang** is the most powerful force in the world. It is GOD-FORCE. Karmic. Universal. What good we put out into the universe will be returned to us. If we are just and morally correct, what our enemies put out into the universe against us will be turned *against* them.

We Will Attract The Kind Of Justice We Deserve

We must not make the mistake of imitating those who abuse their power. Once the black collective regains our sanity and self-respect, only then should we seek unity with the non-black masses to fight for a more peaceful, and God-loving planet ruled by *Universal Man, Universal Woman, and the Law of Universal Justice.*

Each ONE, teach ONE
Do what YOU can, where you can
Become your own LEADER OF ONE
Pass this book along

Resources

Recommended Reading / Viewing

BOOKS

Trojan Horse: Death Of A Dark Nation by Anon

The Isis Papers by Dr. Frances Cress Welsing

The United-Independent Compensatory Code/System/Concept: A textbook/workbook for victims of racism (white supremacy) by Neely Fuller, Jr.

The United-Independent Compensatory Code/System/Concept: A Compensator Counter-Racist Codified Word Guide by Neely Fuller, Jr.

Enemies: The Clash of Races by Haki R. Madhubuti

Asafo: A Warrior's Guide to Manhood by Mwalimu K. Bomani Baruti

Homosexuality and the Effeminization of Afrikan Males by Mwalimu K. Bomani Baruti

Mentacide by Mwalimu K. Bomani Baruti

The New Jim Crow: Mass Incarceration in the Age of Colorblindness by Michelle Alexander

Brainwashed: Challenging the Myth of Black Inferiority by Tom Burrell

The African Origin of Civilization: Myth Or Reality by Cheikh Anta Diop

The Destruction of Black Civilization by Chancellor Williams

How Capitalism Underdeveloped Black America by Manning Marable

The Conspiracy to Destroy Black Boys by Jawanza Kunjufu

What They Never Told you in History Class by Indus Khamit-Kush

Africans at the Crossroads: African World Revolution by John Henrik Clarke

The Spook who sat by the Door by Sam Greenlee (a novel)

The Golden Age of the Moor by Ivan Van Sertima

Your History J.A. Rogers by J.A. Rogers

The Secret Books of Egyptian Gnostics by Jean Doresse

Message to the Blackman in America by Elijah Muhhamad

Return to Glory: The Powerful Stirring of the Black Race
by Joel A. Freeman, PhD, and Don B. Griffin

Black Man of the Nile and His Family by Yosef Ben-Jochannan

No Disrespect by Sister Souljah
Midnight: A Gangster Love Story by Sister Souljah

Recommended Internet Radio & TV Shows

Gus T. Renegade and Justice
(C.O.W.S. at www.contextofwhitesupremacy.com)

Edward Williams - Counter-Racism Television Network
(www.counter-racism.com/c-r_tv/)

Recommended Websites

- www.trojanhorse1.com
- www.counter-racism.com
- www.racism-notes.blogspot.com (Gus Renegade)
- www.justdojusticetoday.blogspot.com
- http://nonwhitealliance.wordpress.com
- www.drafrika.com (Dr. Africa)
- www.waronthehorizon.com
- www.ebonynewschannel.blogspot.com
- www.cree7.wordpress.com
- www.thecode.net
- www.mindcontrolblackassassins.wordpress.com
- www.facebook.com/umarthepsychologist
- www.finalcall.com
- www.blackagendareport.com

Black-Owned Bookstores:

- www.azizibooks.com
- www.TWPBooks.com
- www.counter-racism.com
- www.akobenhouse.com
- www.houseofnubian.com
- www.houseofkonsciousness.com
- www.freemaninstitute.com
- www.afriware.net

AUDIO CDS

Racism & Counter Racism by Dr. Frances Cress Welsing

Maximum Development of Black Male Children by Dr. Frances C. Welsing

The Psychopathic Racial Personality by Dr. Bobby E. Wright, PhD

(above available at: www.houseofnubian.com)

No Sex Between White and Non-White People by Neely Fuller, Jr.
Racism and Counter Racism by Neely Fuller, Jr.

Racism and Counter Racism by Neely Fuller, Jr.

(available: www.counter-racism.com)

Return to Glory: The Powerful Stirring of the Black Race
by Joel A. Freeman, PhD, and Don B. Griffin

(available at www.freemaninstitute.com)

DVDS

Dr. Frances Cress Welsing on Phil Donahue Show

Dr. Frances Cress Welsing Debates Dr. William Shockley & The Analysis of The Bell Curve

The Isis Papers by Dr. Frances Cress Welsing

Racism and Mental Health by Dr. Frances Cress Welsing

Worship of the African Woman as Creator by Dr. Yosef Ben Jochannan

(above DVDs available at: www.houseofnubian.com)

A White Man's Journey Into Black History
by Joel A. Freeman, PhD

(available at www.freemaninstitute.com)

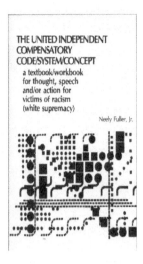

The United-Independent Compensatory Code/System/Concept: A textbook/workbook for thought, speech, and/or action, for victims of *racism (white supremacy).

In this book, Mr. Fuller outlines steps that victims of racism can take to decode the language and actions of white supremacy and not to further fall victim to it by their own response. Mr. Fuller has analyzed what black people can do in every part of their lives and behaviors, to counter the system, to use codification to logically counter white supremacy's code.

To order a copy, contact: Neely Fuller, Jr., 905 6th Street, S.W., #212-B, Washington, DC 20024 OR call (202) 484 -5461

Dr. Francis Cress Welsing's pivotal 1991 book, **"The Isis Papers: The Keys to the Colors,"** presents a bold psychoanalysis of the system of racism/White supremacy. Dr. Welsing postulated that White supremacy exists as a behavioral reaction to the genetic recessive state of the White race. Dr. Welsing continues to practice psychiatry in the Washington, D.C. area.

The global system Welsing refers to as the cornerstone of the white supremacy power base consists of "patterns" that are found in nine areas of human activity: economics, education, entertainment, labor, law, politics, religion, sex and war.

As a (Black) behavioral scientist and psychiatrist, Welsing choose a path that complemented her training because by studying and publishing her findings relative to the mind and behavior of oppressed people worldwide, she has provided a mirror that reflects the devastating effects of racism (white supremacy). And whether or not it (white supremacy) is cloaked in another skin color, the results are just as insidious.

To order a copy, check the list of black-owned books on page 423

Index

CPSIA information can be obtained
at www.ICGtesting.com
Printed in the USA
BVHW030238040119
536873BV00034B/51/P